GUINNESS WORLD RECORDS 2017

GUINNESS WORLD RECORDS

GAMER'S EDITION

British Library Cataloguing-in-Publication Data: a catalogue record for this book is available from the British Library.

UK ISBN:
978-1-910561-39-3

US ISBN:
10: 1-910561-40-1
13: 978-1-910561-40-9

Canada:
978-1-897553-50-3

Check the official website at
www.guinnessworld records.com/gamers
for more record-breaking gamers.

OFFICIALLY AMAZING

THE JIM PATTISON GROUP

GAMER'S EDITION 2017

Senior Managing Editor
Stephen Fall

Editor
Stephen Daultrey

Layout Editors
Tom Beckerlegge,

Project Editors
Ben Hollingum,
Adam Millward

Game Consultant
Stace Harman

Talent Researchers
Jenny Langridge,
Victoria Tweedy

Head of Pictures & Design
Michael Whitty

Deputy Picture Editor
Fran Morales

Picture Researchers
Wilf Matos

Design
Paul Wylie-Deacon,
Richard Page and
Matthew Bell at
55design.co.uk

Artworker
Billy Waqar

VP Publishing
Jenny Heller

Editor-in-Chief
Craig Glenday

Director of Procurement

Publishing Manager
Jane Boatfield

Production Assistant
Thomas McCurdy

Production Consultants
Roger Hawkins,
Dennis Thon

Printing & Binding
MOHN Media Mohndruck
GmbH, Gütersloh, Germany

Cover Development
Sue Michniewicz

Ryan Dix, James Ellerker,
Paul Michael Hughes,
Kamil Krawczak, Ranald
Mackechnie, Kevin Scott
Ramos, Ryan Schude

Index
Marie Lorimer

Proofreading
Matthew White

GUINNESS WORLD RECORDS

CORPORATE OFFICE
Global President:
Alistair Richards

PROFESSIONAL SERVICES
Chief Financial Officer:
Alison Ozanne
Financial Controller:
Andrew Wood
Accounts Receivable Manager:
Lisa Gibbs
Assistant Accountant:
Jess Blake
Accounts Payable Assistant:
Victoria Aweh
Finance Managers: Shabana Zaffar,
Daniel Ralph
Trading Analysis Manager:
Elizabeth Bishop
Head of Legal & Business Affairs:
Raymond Marshall
Legal & Business Affairs Manager:
Terence Tsang
**Legal & Business Affairs
Executive:** Xiangyun Rablen
Head of HR: Farrella Ryan-Coker
HR Assistant: Mehreen Saeed
Office Manager: Jackie Angus
Director of IT: Rob Howe
IT Development Manager:
James Edwards
Developer: Cenk Selim
Junior Developer: Lewis Ayers
Desktop Administrator:
Ainul Ahmed / Alpha Serrant-Defoe
SVP Records: Marco Frigatti
Head of Category Management:
Jacqui Sherlock / Shantha Chinniah
Information & Research Manager:
Carim Valerio
Records Managers: Adam Brown,
Corrinne Burns, Sam Golin,
Victoria Tweedy, Tripp Yeoman
Records Consultants: Sam Mason,
Tom Ibison

GLOBAL BRAND STRATEGY
SVP Global Brand Strategy:
Samantha Fay

GLOBAL PRODUCT MARKETING
VP Global Product Marketing:
Katie Forde
**Director of Global TV Content
& Sales:** Rob Molloy

Senior TV Distribution Manager:
Paul Glynn
Senior TV Content Executive:
Jonathan Whitton
**Digital Product Marketing
Manager:** Veronica Irons
Online Editor: Kevin Lynch
Social Media Manager:
Dan Thorne
Digital Video Producer:
Matt Musson
Online Writer: Rachel Swatman
**Brand & Consumer Product
Marketing Manager:** Lucy Acfield
Designer: Rebecca Buchanan Smith
Junior Designer: Edward Dillon
Product Marketing Assistant:
Victor Fenes

EMEA & APAC
SVP EMEA APAC: Nadine Causey
VP Creative: Paul O'Neill
**Attractions Development
Manager:** Louise Toms
PR Director: Jakki Lewis
Senior PR Manager: Doug Male
Senior Publicist: Madalyn Bielfeld
B2B PR Manager: Melanie DeFries /
Juliet Dawson
UK & International Press Officer:
Amber-Georgina Gill
Head of Marketing:
Justine Tommey
B2B Marketing Manager:
Mawa Rodriguez
B2C Marketing Manager:
Christelle Betrong
Content Marketing Executive:
Imelda Ngouala
Head of Publishing Sales:
John Pilley
Sales & Distribution Manager:
Richard Stenning
Licensing Manager, Publishing:
Emma Davies
**Head of Commercial Accounts &
Licensing:** Sam Prosser
Commercial Account Managers:
Lucie Pessereau, Jessica Rae,
Inga Rasmussen, Sadie Smith
Commercial Account Executive:
Fay Edwards
Commercial Representative, India:
Nikhil Shukla

Country Manager, MENA:
Talal Omar
Head of RMT, MENA:
Samer Khallouf
B2B Marketing Manager, MENA:
Leila Issa
**Commercial Account Manager,
MENA:** Khalid Yassine
**Head of Records Management,
Europe & APAC:** Ben Backhouse
Records Managers: Mark McKinley,
Christopher Lynch, Matilda Hagne,
Antonio Gracia, Daniel Kidane
Customer Service Managers:
Louise McLaren / Janet Craffey
Senior Project Manager:
Alan Pixsley
Project Managers: Paul Wiggins,
Paulina Sapinska
Official Adjudicators:
Ahmed Gamal Gabr, Anna Orford,
Glenn Pollard, Jack Brockbank,
Kimberley Dennis, Lena Kuhlmann,
Lorenzo Veltri, Lucia Sinigagliesi,
Pete Fairbairn, Pravin Patel,
Rishi Nath, Seyda Subasi Gemici,
Sofia Greenacre, Solvej Malouf,
Swapnil Dangarikar

AMERICAS
SVP Americas: Peter Harper
VP Marketing & Commercial Sales:
Keith Green
Director of Latin America:
Carlos Martinez
Head of RMT – North America:
Kimberly Partrick
Senior Account Managers:
Nicole Pando, Ralph Hannah
Head of Client Services:
Amanda Mochan
Account Managers: Alex Angert,
Lindsay Doran, Lisa Tobia,
Giovanni Bruna
Project Manager: Casey DeSantis
PR Manager: Kristen Ott
PR Coordinator: Sofia Rocher
B2B Marketing Executive:
Tavia Levy
Publishing Sales Manager:
Lisa Corrado
Records Managers:
Michael Furnari, Hannah Ortman,
Kaitlin Holl, Raquel Assis,
Sarah Casson
HR & Office Manager: Kellie Ferrick

Official Adjudicators:
Christina Flounders Conlon,
Evelyn Carrera, Jimmy Coggins,
Michael Empric

JAPAN
VP Japan: Erika Ogawa
Office Manager: Fumiko Kitagawa
Director of RMT: Kaoru Ishikawa
Project Manager: Aya McMillan
Records Managers: Mariko Koike,
Yoko Furuya
Designer: Momoko Cunneen
**Senior PR & Sales Promotion
Manager:** Kazami Kamioka
PR Manager: Sawako Wasada
**Digital & Publishing Content
Manager:** Takafumi Suzuki
**Commercial Sales & Marketing
Director:** Vihag Kulshrestha
Senior Marketing Executive:
Asumi Funatsu
Account Manager:
Takuro Maruyama
Senior Account Executive:
Daisuke Katayama
**Account Executive & Event
Co-ordinator:** Minami Ito
Official Adjudicators:
Justin Patterson, Mai McMillan,
Rei Iwashita, Gulnaz Ukassova

GREATER CHINA
President: Rowan Simons
Commercial Director:
Blythe Fitzwiliam
Senior Account Manager:
Catherine Gao, Lessi Li
Account Manager: Chloe Liu
Digital Business Manager:
Jacky Yuan
Head of RMT: Charles Wharton
Records Manager: Alicia Zhao
Records Consultant: Lisa Hoffman
External Relations Manager:
Dong Cheng
**Records Manager / Project
Co-ordinator:** Fay Jiang
HR & Office Manager: Tina Shi
Office Assistant: Kate Wang
Head of Marketing: Wendy Wang
B2B Marketing Manager: Iris Hou
Marketing Executive: Tracy Cui
Content Director: Angela Wu
Official Adjudicators: Brittany
Dunn, Joanne Brent, John Garland

Guinness World Records Limited uses both metric and imperial measurements. The sole exceptions are for some scientific data where metric measurements only are universally accepted, and for some sports data. Where a specific date is given, the exchange rate is calculated according to the currency values that were in operation at the time. Where only a year date is given, the exchange rate is calculated from 31 December of that year. "One billion" is taken to mean one thousand million.

Appropriate advice should always be taken when attempting to break or set records. Participants undertake records entirely at their own risk. Guinness World Records Limited has complete discretion over whether or not to include any particular record attempts in any of its publications. Being a Guinness World Records record holder does not guarantee you a place in any Guinness World Records publication.

FOREWORD

Hello readers, Ali-A here!

It's a huge honour to introduce the special 10-year-anniversary edition of the *GWR Gamer's Edition*. Wow, 10 years! Record-breaking in games has grown and grown over the last decade, especially with the advent of streaming platforms, and it's been fantastic to have GWR's authoritative voice to attach prestige to videogame feats.

This year's *Gamer's Edition* is packed with so many incredible records. From the most watched broadcasters (cough cough) and the most played online game, to the youngest millionaire eSports champion and the biggest collections. There's also the fastest blindfolded completion of a *Pokémon* game. Like, seriously?!? Blindfolded?!? Now that's impressive...

There's a whole chapter dedicated to *Star Wars* games, too, which is an amazing franchise that has been bringing us epic adventures for well over 30 years – from the early arcade hits of the 1980s, to modern classics such as *Star Wars: Knights of the Old Republic* and 2015's *Star Wars Battlefront*.

And what about eSports, huh? That's just exploded into this gigantic "thing", with thousands of tournaments popping up across the globe and millions of fans watching superstar players dazzle with their unearthly skills. So this year's *Gamer's* introduces its first ever chapter dedicated to the world of pro gaming. Expect to see some very big names indeed.

Speaking personally, I am very proud to hold several GWR titles. Two are for my YouTube channels... and one is for building a very tall staircase in *Minecraft*! So I thank everyone for their support with winning those. GWR has created lots of thrilling world-record titles for gamers, whether they're skill-based challenges in *Rocket League* and *FIFA*, or endurance-testing marathons in *Halo* and *Mario Kart*. Long may it continue!

So where next? With VR taking off and the mainstream coverage of eSports expanding, gaming just keeps on getting more exciting. The games are getting better, the technology is becoming more powerful, and the tournaments are getting bigger.

Here's to another 10 years of *Gamer's* and lots of brilliant record-breaking.

Ali-A

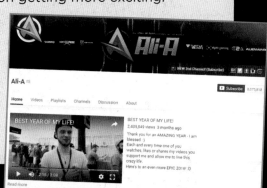

CONTENTS

We're celebrating the 10th edition of the *Gamer's Edition* with some truly out-of-this-world games and records. Take a look at our in-depth features, plus a *Star Wars* section so packed with facts that it could make even a Wookiee grin.

BE A RECORD-BREAKER

Whether you're a speed-runner or a marathon gamer, a pioneering developer or a collector of gaming memorabilia, Guinness World Records wants to hear from you!

MAKE AN APPLICATION

The first stop for any would-be record-breaker should always be **www.guinnessworldrecords.com**. Hit "Set a record" to find out how the process works and how to register an account. Email us to let us know which record you'd like to attempt.

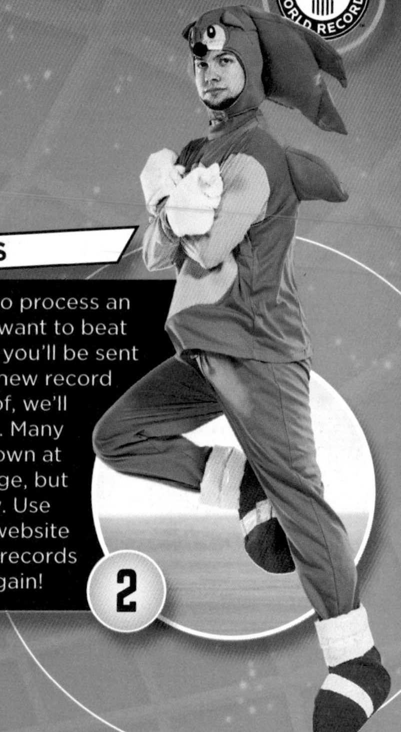

1

READ THE RULES

It takes six weeks to process an application. If you want to beat an existing record, you'll be sent guidelines. If it's a new record we like the sound of, we'll compile rules for it. Many ideas are turned down at the application stage, but we will explain why. Use this book and the website to see the kinds of records we like, then try again!

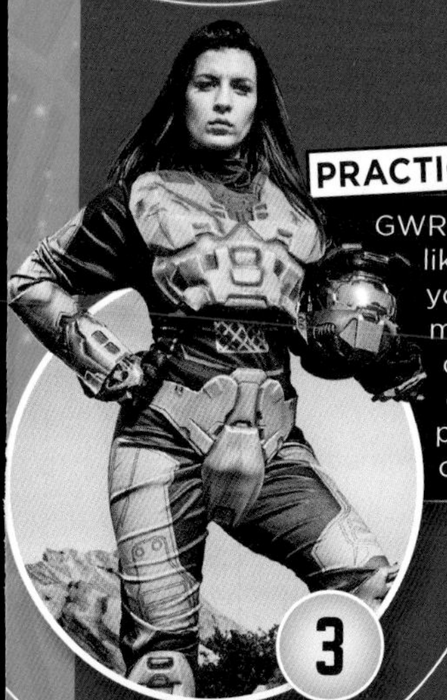

2

PRACTICE MAKES PERFECT

GWR record attempts are just like a sports competition – you need to train hard to make sure you're in peak condition to take them on. The more hours you practise, the greater your chances of success will be.

3

MAKE YOUR ATTEMPT

Once you're certain you can't score another point or shave another second off your speed-run, you're ready to take on the record. Make sure you have everything in place to meet the guidelines – you will need a good-quality video recorder, witnesses and anything else we've specified you require for a valid claim.

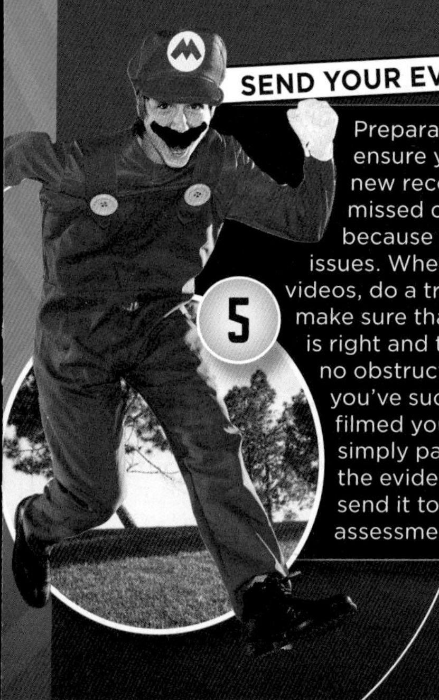

4

SEND YOUR EVIDENCE

Preparation can ensure your potential new record isn't missed or rejected because of technical issues. When filming videos, do a trial run to make sure that the lighting is right and that there are no obstructions. After you've successfully filmed your attempt, simply package up the evidence and send it to GWR for assessment. Easy!

5

6

FRAME YOUR CERTIFICATE!

You did it! Successful record-breakers will be sent an official certificate to show off to their friends. If you're very lucky, you may even be one of the fortunate few to make it on to these pages next year. And if you've missed out, there's no need to despair – you can always try again. There's no limit to the number of attempts you can make.

INTRODUCTION

Guinness World Records Gamer's Edition 2017 is the ultimate videogame guide. Our 10th annual edition is packed with hundreds of new and updated records from all your favourite titles, plus incredible stories, high scores and feature reports from across all aspects of gaming.

"OMGitsfirefoxx" – **most popular female broadcaster on Twitch** (pp.152–53)

"PangaeaPanga" – **most difficult level created in** *Super Mario Maker* (pp.70–71)

Let the games begin!
Welcome to *Gamer's Edition 2017*! We're celebrating our 10th anniversary by packing these pages with as many records as possible. Our expert consultants have hunted high and low for the biggest-selling and best-rated, the quickest and the quirkiest, the best and (occasionally) the worst.

We look at titles from across the gaming spectrum, from the blood-splattered *Bloodborne* to the high-energy *Just Dance*.

Get the lowdown on today's critically acclaimed classics, such as the award-laden *Rocket League* and *The Witcher 3: Wild Hunt*. Cult titles from *AaAaAA!!!* to *Zen Pinball*, and blockbusters from *Mario* to *Minecraft*, are all here. And on p.202, you'll find the games you'll be playing and loving this time next year.

And that's just the start. At the heart of our book is a 16-page *Star Wars* special, celebrating the **most prolific videogame franchise based on a film licence** (pp.106–21). We also take a look at the star-studded world of eSports, meeting "Suma1L", the youngest gamer to earn $1 million in eSports winnings (p.22).

And there are exclusive Q&A interviews with industry legends such as Chris Roberts, director of the hotly awaited, crowdfunded space sim *Star Citizen* (p.124).

Shoot to thrill
We've photographed a selection of the most spectacular record-breakers to reveal the personalities behind the achievements. German speed-runner "Kynos" wielded a giant Buster Sword as *Final Fantasy*'s Cloud Strife (pp.136–37). *Dark Souls* conqueror Benjamin "bearzly" Gwin took on the game in his unique way, with a suit of armour and a *Rock Band* keyboard (pp.142–43). Alex "PangaeaPanga" Tan, creator of diabolically difficult levels on *Super Mario Maker*, donned his hard hat and tool belt as Nintendo's iconic plumber (pp.70–71), while four

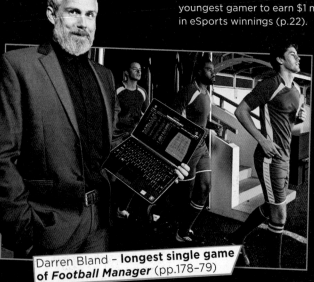

Darren Bland – **longest single game of** *Football Manager* (pp.178–79)

"bearzly" – **most alternative control methods used to complete** *Dark Souls* (pp.142–43)

"DanTDM" – **most views for a dedicated** *Minecraft* **video channel** (pp.66-69)

The **longest videogame marathon on** *Mario Kart* team (pp.86-87)

Australian marathon gamers lined up on a *Mario Kart* grid (pp.86-87).

We took Darren Bland, player of the longest *Football Manager* game, to a football club to put him in a real dugout (pp.178-79). Daniel "DanTDM" Middleton of YouTube's record-breaking "TheDiamondMinecart" channel tried his own cart (pp.66-69), although sadly our budget didn't stretch to real diamonds!

Sonja "OMGitsfirefoxx" Reid kept an eye out for radscorpions while cosplaying *Fallout 4* (pp.152-53), and lightning-fast "Leon Ip" was the new kid on the block with *LEGO® Dimensions* (pp.34-35).

Information overload
Our fantastic features take you to the heart of the gaming industry. Major players such as eSports site GosuGamers (pp.32-33) and

digital-data gatherers SuperData (pp.84-85) share their wisdom, while on pp.60-61 we profile the gamers who are so good that they can play blindfolded.

We're not the only ones with an anniversary in 2017 – it's also 25 years since the first *Mario Kart*. Check out Awesome Anniversaries (pp.134-35) to see who else is blowing out candles.

Galactic gaming
If you still want more, our friends at the videogame adjudicators Twin Galaxies have provided us with a host of new records, from old-school arcades and Atari titles to the latest eighth-gen consoles (pp.192-201). Follow our guide to being a record-breaker (p.5) and perhaps you can join them in *Gamer's Edition 2018*. Here's to another 10 years of fantastic gaming records!

"Kynos" – **fastest completion of** *Final Fantasy VII* (pp.136-37)

"Leon Ip" – **fastest time to build the Batmobile in** *LEGO® Dimensions* (pp.34-35)

YEAR IN GAMING

MAY–NOV 2015

In late May 2015, an eBayer listed a fridge loaded with some 300 *Jurassic Park* SNES cartridges. The surreal bundle was priced at $1,500 (£1,081) and was sold to a "best offer".

On 7 Jun, Sir Christopher Lee (UK, b. 1922) died aged 93. The movie icon was the **oldest videogame voice actor**, lending his austere tones to *LEGO® The Hobbit* in 2014. He was aged 91 years 316 days on the game's release.

Gamescom set a new record for **largest games convention** when 345,000 people from 96 countries attended its 2015 event held in Cologne, Germany, on 5–9 Aug.

On 26 Aug, YouTube launched its dedicated gaming platform, YouTube Gaming, to rival Twitch. Ryan Wyatt of YouTube said: "Gaming is so big now... It's astonishing."

Some 20,000 people crammed into San Francisco's Moscone West, USA, for the inaugural TwitchCon on 25–26 Sep, an event hailed by organizers as "unbelievable" and "epic".

engadget confirmed the validity of the cancelled "Nintendo PlayStation" console when it showed an early prototype powered-up. The once-fabled console was mooted in 1988.

In Nov 2015, the Pokémon franchise added a gym – in Osaka, Japan – to its network of extracurricular establishments.

JUN 2015

Giant cow defies *Witcher III* cheaters

When PC players of *The Witcher III* discovered an infinite money exploit, achieved by repeatedly killing respawned cows, developer CD Projekt created the "Bovine Defense Force Initiative" to protect its bovine population. Courtesy of patch 1.05, any player using the cheat would be attacked by a beast resembling a giant cow. It was called a Chort.

JUN 2015

Final Fantasy VII breaks internet

It was the game that had been in huge demand for the past 15 years. So when Sony and Square Enix took to the stage at E3 to announce a remake of the 1997 classic *Final Fantasy VII*, initially for PS4, the online response was so fevered that gaming sites reported that the internet had crashed. One *FF* enthusiast even pieced together four hours of video showing fans' reactions (see pp.148–49).

JUN 2015

Epic Pokémon inking quest

US tattoo artist Alicia Thomas embarked on a mission to tattoo every one of the 151 original Pokémon on her clientele, having reminisced about the series with one of her friends. "We made a joke that, 'Oh, you should tattoo all of them', and then we looked at each other and said, 'No, this should actually be a thing'," she told *Vice* magazine. When the story made the gaming news, Alicia had already tattooed around 130 different Pokémon on 130 different people.

AUG 2015

VR genius is the "meme" man

Oculus Rift inventor Palmer Luckey (USA) went viral after he appeared on the cover of *TIME*, striking an airborne pose in his company's virtual-reality (VR) headset. Photoshoppers immediately went to work dropping Luckey's image into alternative settings, including scenes from such films as *Titanic* and *The Grinch*. It made for one of the year's most memorable internet memes.

Madden movie is explosive... and strange

EA went to town and back with the promotion of *Madden NFL 16*. Ahead of the game's late-summer launch, the publisher made a short action-film parody that starred Hollywood actors Dave Franco and Christopher Mintz-Plasse as muscle-bound action heroes. A *Tyrannosaurus rex* (above) also featured. *Eurogamer* described it as the "strangest trailer imaginable".

SEP 2015

YouTube legends shine in London

London's inaugural Legends of Gaming event saw seven YouTubers battling it out in a day-long tournament. Syndicate and DanTDM (both UK, above, with *Gamer's* editor Stephen Daultrey) set a record in *Rocket League*, while a *Minecraft* record was smashed three times during the day.

OCT 2015

More animated *Resident Evil* scares in the pipeline

It already has the **most live-action film adaptations based on a game**. Now Capcom's *Resident Evil* is being treated to a third feature-length animation too. Currently slated for 2017, the film will star *RE 2* heroes Claire Redfield and Leon Kennedy, plus *Zero*'s Rebecca Chambers. Fittingly, the sixth film from the live-action series was also due for release in 2017.

NOV 2015

Donkey Kong man loses lawsuit, not head

Former *Donkey Kong* champ Billy Mitchell lost a lawsuit against the Cartoon Network – because the judge ruled that he doesn't have an exploding head! Mitchell had accused the channel of stealing his persona for a fictional gamer in its animated series *Regular Show*. However, the judge observed that the alleged likeness was a "cartoonishly evil" floating head that explodes after losing his title.

SATORU IWATA: 1959–2015

On 11 Jul 2015, Nintendo president and CEO Satoru Iwata of Japan passed away after a battle with cancer. One of the most respected individuals in the world of gaming, Iwata began as a programmer at HAL Laboratory, and in 2000 joined Nintendo, where he became president two years later. Iwata's tenure oversaw the launch of the DS and the Wii, the latter of which revolutionized games as a result of its motion-control system.

"The man was incredible: humble, funny and a true leader," tweeted *Nintendo Force* upon the news of his passing. "He was a gamer, a developer and a champion for our medium," said The Game Awards' Geoff Keighley.

YEAR IN GAMING

DEC 2015–APR 2016

In Dec 2015, a Siberian gamer announced that he was suing *Fallout 4* developer Bethesda for damages of R500k ($7,214; £4,799). He claimed he had played the game non-stop for three weeks, costing him both his job and his marriage.

...to the release of *Street Fighter V*, on 15 Feb 2016 Daigo "The Beast" Umehara went up against rapper Lupe Fiasco in an exhibition match... and lost! Daigo might have famously won the **most viewed competitive videogame match** (p.78), but this time it was Lupe who triumphed 3–2.

In Mar 2016, it was reported that Nintendo had invested around ¥40 billion ($352 million; £247 million) in an expansion to the Universal Studios theme park in Osaka, Japan.

The first Oculus Rift VR headset was shipped on 24 Mar 2016. Hygiene-conscious gamers could also buy sanitary face masks to wear beneath their headsets. Developed in Japan, packs of 100 masks were retailing at ¥2,980 ($26; £18).

In Apr 2016, Nintendo revealed that its NX console would be released in Mar 2017. The new *Legend of Zelda* game was also confirmed as a launch title.

A couple in Tunisia won a live cow after achieving a high score on the bovine-themed *Bagra*. The gamers were sent their prize in Apr 2016. Apparently, a second cow was also up for grabs!

DEC 2015

Minecraft maestro

The inaugural *Minecraft* National Championship ended with "SuperKraft11" seeing off competition from 1,000 rival gamers to bag the top prize. Not bad considering that SuperKraft11, aka Julien Wiltshire (USA), was just 10 years old. His team, Seven Arrows Elementary Team, had played a six-week season of *Minecraft* action in 40 cities across the USA.

JAN 2016

Terry's *Zelda* triumph

After five years of playing, blind engineering student Terry Garrett (USA) completed *The Legend of Zelda: Ocarina of Time* – the **most critically acclaimed videogame** (see p.37). To achieve this feat, he used an emulator that enabled save states and speakers to provide sound cues. On 2 Jan 2016, Terry uploaded his defeat of final boss Ganon to his YouTube channel.

JAN 2016

Blizzard coverage

On 4 Jan 2016, Activision Blizzard confirmed it was snapping up US eSports organizer Major League Gaming for a reported $46 million (£31 million). The deal would hand the publisher control of the streaming platform MLG.tv and its prestigious tournaments. Activision Blizzard's Mike Sepso told *Wired* that their ultimate goal was to "build the ESPN of eSports".

FEB 2016

Gamer joins wolf gang

Even real-life soccer teams are catching the pro gaming bug. German side VfL Wolfsburg signed gamer David Bytheway (UK) to its newly formed *FIFA* eSports team. Twenty-two-year-old David had represented England at the *FIFA* Interactive World Cup. A similar move was made by English Premier League club West Ham United, who signed UK gamer Sean "Dragonn" Allen in May.

MAR 2016

Stag party causes *GTA* mayhem

As if life in San Andreas wasn't hard enough, its citizens were confronted with a new and unexpected threat: an unstoppable teleporting deer. Programmed by artist Brent Watanabe (USA), the antlered anarchist roamed a modded *Grand Theft Auto V*, creating enough havoc to earn itself a four-star wanted rating. The antics of the AI-controlled deer were streamed live on a 24-hr Twitch channel, "San Andreas Deer Cam".

MAR 2016

Cover curse KO?

Heard the one about the "Madden curse", where American football stars are struck with bad luck after appearing on the cover of a *Madden* game? Sports fans are now speculating whether the same issue might affect EA's *UFC* franchise. After being unveiled as the face of *UFC 2*, the formidable Ronda Rousey lost her next fight, in Nov 2015 (above). And in Mar 2016, cover co-star Conor McGregor suffered the same fate!

APR 2016

Showtime for Mario!

When the rebooted London Games Festival took place in London, UK, one of its highlights was a performance of *Mario! A Super Musical* by the Ninfriendos Theatre Company. The colourful comedy told the tale of Bowser kidnapping Mario, leaving it to Princess Peach and Luigi to come to the rescue. The show had previously sold out at the UK's GameCity Festival in Oct 2015.

APR 2016

eGames on the road to Rio

Dreams of a videogames Olympics moved a step closer to reality with the advent of a two-day "pop-up" tournament, to be staged during the Rio Olympics in Brazil in Aug 2016. The competition was to be run by the new International eGames Committee (IEGC), with backing from the British government. Gamers from Canada, Brazil and the UK were among the first to confirm their places.

LEGENDS OF GAMING

The meteoric rise of YouTube and Twitch has created a new breed of celebrity: the games broadcaster. Launched in Jun 2014, the "Legends of Gaming" YouTube channel unites some of the platform's most watched stars as they battle it out across a summer-long gaming tournament, before eventually competing in a live final. The showdown for the 2016 season takes place on 10-11... ...son, UK. Here we meet four Legends who have made mega-waves with their captivating gaming channels, and who are serious contenders to be crowned the overall "Legend" of 2016. Remember, there can be only one...

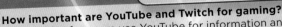

Tom Greenwood-Mears,
Legends of Gaming Live

Ashley Mariee
Channel launch:
6 Aug 2012
Subscribers:
676,106
Total video views: 46,813,144

How important are YouTube and Twitch for gaming?
About 95% of gamers use YouTube for information and entertainment. Gaming is so prominent that YouTube created the YouTube Gaming sub-platform, with its own streaming service. Twitch is seeing a huge rise in audiences with the proliferation of eSports viewers. As eSports becomes a worldwide affair, so Twitch audiences grow – 475.5 million hours of eSports were consumed on Twitch in Jul–Dec 2015. Another notable trend is mobile gaming. That's resulted in a huge rise in audiences on YouTube, while Twitch has announced that users can now livestream Android games from their PCs.

What content does your channel specialize in?
It's largely based on *Minecraft* and I mainly post mini-games and modded servers. I'm super-active with my subscribers and I think that helps me to be unique.

Which video are you most proud of?
I released a *Minecraft* parody video called ""Surviving It" – A Minecraft Parody of Krewella – Killin it" [pictured below]. It has reached over 4 million views!

Any tips for budding YouTubers?
Stay active and be persistent. When you first start, growth will be slow. Don't be put off by that.

What's the first game that you ever played?
Pokémon Sapphire on the GBA.

And your all-time favourite?
Prince of Persia: The Forgotten Sands! I could easily play through that again and again just because it was super-fun and entertaining.

Ali-A
Channel launch: 13 Sep 2006
Subscribers: 8,068,100
Total video views: 1,940,923,448

Why did you launch a YouTube channel?
I wanted to share cool gaming highlights with my mates at school – it was as innocent as that. I never dreamt that it'd lead to making gaming videos as a full-time job!

Which video are you most proud of?
Probably my 2015 montage video. After writing down all the clips I wanted to use I realized just how much stuff I'd crammed into the year! The edit took several days but it was worth it.

What games have you enjoyed recently?
I'm always playing *Black Ops III* – I'll never get bored of *Call of Duty*! I've also been playing *The Culling* on PC [left]. It's basically like *The Hunger Games* and it's super-competitive. I'd recommend it to everyone.

Any tips for new YouTubers and budding broadcasters?
Enjoy making videos! To this day, I still love making them and if I ever lost that I'd be doing something wrong. Don't expect to get 1 million subscribers overnight, either – it took me a year to get my first 100 – but stick at it and it could turn into something big.

MasterOv
Channel launch:
30 Sep 2013
Subscribers:
1,623,426
Total video views:
499,677,604

The inaugural Legends of Gaming final took place in London, UK, on 10 Sep 2015. GWR featured prominently, with visitors attempting to smash a Guinness World Records title in *Minecraft* (above) and "Legends" vying for GWR titles onstage in *Rocket League*.

Stars at the event included the pace-setting Syndicate (right) – the **most followed broadcaster on Twitch**, with 2,440,130 followers as of 4 May 2016. Also present was the mighty Ali-A (below right, receiving GWR certificates for his *Call of Duty* channel – see p.158).

Excitingly, GWR returns for the 2016 event. This time gamers can attempt GWR titles in both videogames and physical challenges, with the chance of featuring in *Gamer's Edition 2018*!

Describe your channel...
It's for people of all ages to enjoy. I play whatever games the viewers want to see, such as *Slither.io* [below] and *Hungry Shark World*. I'm no pro at the games, but it's more about having a laugh. Think of me as more of an "online best mate".

Which video are you most proud of?
It's got to be my (at the time) world record *Agar.io* score video. It was only achievable because the "OV ARMY" took over a lobby live on the stream and eliminated bigger clans. Playing with the viewers is the best!

Any tips for budding broadcasters?
Just be yourself and do what you love. The UK YouTube community as a whole is the strongest, best and friendliest by far. You rarely hear anything negative from our side of the pond.

Spencer FC
Channel launch: 4 Mar 2013
Subscribers: 1,388,363
Total video views:
295,570,467

Describe your channel...
It's a place where I express my love for soccer, whether it's playing videogames, going to matches, interviewing soccer stars or playing the sport for real. Gaming is a huge part of soccer now, and through games like *FIFA* and *Football Manager* I try to create engaging soccer stories that my audience can be part of.

Which video are you most proud of?
I staged a big match at the UK's Wembley Stadium called the Wembley Cup [right] where myself and 23 other YouTubers battled it out in an epic real-life soccer match. It's my most watched video to date.

What's your favourite all-time videogame?
Football Manager. It's not a game for those with short attention spans, but it is for soccer geeks like

me. Personally, I've invested months of my life into playing *FM* and I'm still hooked now.

What are you looking forward to most in gaming?
The rise of eSports is fascinating, particularly with *FIFA* because it's one of the world's most popular titles but it hasn't really reached the levels of other games such as *Dota 2* yet. When it does, and when the mainstream soccer world recognizes eSports, the potential for growth is amazing.

AWARDS ROUND-UP

AUDIO ACHIEVEMENT:
Everybody's Gone to the Rapture

BEST SPORTS/RACING GAME:
Rocket League

7 Apr 2016, London, UK

Award	Game
Best Game	Fallout 4
Persistent Game	Prison Architect
Story	Life is Strange
Fellowship	John Carmack
Multiplayer	Rocket League
Family	Rocket League
Sport	Rocket League
British Game	Batman: Arkham Knight
Game Design	Bloodborne
Performer	Merle Dandridge (Kate Collins), Everybody's Gone to the Rapture
Audio Achievement	Everybody's Gone to the Rapture
Music	Everybody's Gone to the Rapture
Mobile & Handheld	Her Story
Debut Game	Her Story
Game Innovation	Her Story
Artistic Achievement	Ori and the Blind Forest
AMD eSports Audience Award	Smite
BAFTA Ones to Watch Award	Sundown
Original Property	Until Dawn

3 Dec 2015, Los Angeles, USA

Award	Game
Best Family Game	Super Mario Maker
Best Fighting Game	Mortal Kombat X
Best Multiplayer Game	Splatoon
Best Shooter	Splatoon
Best Mobile/Handheld Game	Lara Croft GO
Most Anticipated Game	No Man's Sky
Trending Gamer	Greg Miller
Best Narrative	Her Story
Best Performance	Viva Seifert (Hannah Smith), Her Story
eSports Team of the Year	OpTic Gaming
eSports Player of the Year	Kenny "kennyS" Schrub (Counter-Strike: Global Offensive/Team EnVyUs)
eSports Game of the Year	Counter-Strike: Global Offensive
Best Indie Game	Rocket League
Best Sports/Racing Game	Rocket League
Developer of the Year	CD Projekt RED (The Witcher 3: Wild Hunt)
Game of the Year	The Witcher 3: Wild Hunt
Best Role-Playing Game	The Witcher 3: Wild Hunt
Games for Impact	Life is Strange
Best Fan Creation	Portal Stories: Mel
Best Art Direction	Ori and the Blind Forest
Best Action/Adventure Game	Metal Gear Solid V
Best Score/Soundtrack	Metal Gear Solid V

16 Mar 2016, San Francisco, USA

Award	Game
Lifetime Achievement	Todd Howard
Pioneer	Markus "Notch" Persson
Ambassador	Tracy Fullerton
Audience	Life is Strange
Game of the Year	The Witcher 3: Wild Hunt
Best Technology	The Witcher 3: Wild Hunt
Innovation	Her Story
Best Handheld/Mobile Game	Her Story
Best Narrative	Her Story
Best Audio	Crypt of the NecroDancer
Best Debut	Ori and the Blind Forest
Best Visual Arts	Ori and the Blind Forest
Best Design	Rocket League

BEST HANDHELD/MOBILE GAME:
Her Story

EXCELLENCE IN NARRATIVE:
The Witcher 3: Wild Hunt

19 Mar 2016, Austin, USA

Award	Game
Game of the Year	The Witcher 3: Wild Hunt
Excellence in Technical Achievement	The Witcher 3: Wild Hunt
Excellence in Narrative	The Witcher 3: Wild Hunt
Mobile Game of the Year	Her Story
Tabletop Game of the Year	Pandemic Legacy
Excellence in Gameplay	Metal Gear Solid V
Excellence in Art	Bloodborne
Excellence in Design	Bloodborne
Most Enduring Character	Lara Croft (Rise of the Tomb Raider)
Excellence in Animation	Rise of the Tomb Raider
Excellence in Visual Achievement	The Order: 1886
Excellence in SFX	Star Wars Battlefront
Excellence in Musical Score	Ori and the Blind Forest
Excellence in Multiplayer	Rocket League
Excellence in Convergence	Batman: Arkham Knight
Most Valuable eSports Team	Evil Geniuses
Most Entertaining Online Personality	Greg Miller, Kinda Funny
Most Promising New Intellectual Property	Splatoon
Most Fulfilling Crowdfunded Game	Undertale
Matthew Crump Cultural Innovation	Undertale
Gamer's Voice: Single Player	SUPERHOT
Gamer's Voice: Multiplayer	Gang Beasts

BEST XBOX GAME:
Ori and the Blind Forest

30 Oct 2015, London, UK

Award	Game
Best Original Game	Bloodborne
Best PlayStation Game	Bloodborne
Best Storytelling	The Witcher 3: Wild Hunt
Best Visual Design	The Witcher 3: Wild Hunt
Ultimate Game of the Year	The Witcher 3: Wild Hunt
Best Gaming Moment	Bloody Baron quest, The Witcher 3: Wild Hunt
Best Audio	Ori and the Blind Forest
Best Xbox Game	Ori and the Blind Forest
Best Multiplayer	Grand Theft Auto Online
Playfire Most Played	Grand Theft Auto V
Best PC Game	Grand Theft Auto V
Best Indie Game	Kerbal Space Program
Gaming Personality	"PewDiePie"
eSports Icon	Anders Blume, Counter-Strike: Global Offensive
Most Wanted Game	Fallout 4
Best Family Game	Splatoon

OUTSTANDING ACHIEVEMENT IN GAME DIRECTION: *Fallout 4*

18 Feb 2016, Las Vegas, USA

Award	Game
Game of the Year	Fallout 4
Outstanding Achievement in Game Direction	Fallout 4
Role-Playing/Massively Multiplayer Game of the Year	Fallout 4
Adventure Game of the Year	Metal Gear Solid V
Action Game of the Year	Star Wars Battlefront
Outstanding Achievement in Sound Design	Star Wars Battlefront
Mobile Game of the Year	Fallout Shelter
DICE Sprite Award	Rocket League
Sports Game of the Year	Rocket League
Outstanding Achievement in Online Gameplay	Rocket League
Outstanding Achievement in Animation	Ori and the Blind Forest
Outstanding Achievement in Art Direction	Ori and the Blind Forest
Outstanding Achievement in Original Music Composition	Ori and the Blind Forest
Outstanding Achievement in Character	Rise of the Tomb Raider
Outstanding Achievement in Story	The Witcher 3: Wild Hunt
Outstanding Technical Achievement	The Witcher 3: Wild Hunt
Outstanding Achievement in Game Design	The Witcher 3: Wild Hunt
Family Game of the Year	Super Mario Maker
Fighting Game of the Year	Mortal Kombat X
Racing Game of the Year	Forza Motorsport 6
Strategy/Simulation Game of the Year	Heroes of the Storm
Handheld Game of the Year	Helldivers

HARDWARE ROUND-UP

Although the future may seem "virtual" with VR all the rage, there is still plenty of time for "normal-screen" gaming. Or even tiny-screen gaming for that matter...

Initially given away with the official Raspberry Pi magazine, *The MagPi*, in Nov 2015, the Raspberry Pi Zero is a fully working computer the size of a credit card. The initial magazine run of 10,000 copies sold out in days – but, as of 23 Mar 2016, the Zero was available for an appropriately modest £4 ($5), not counting the adaptor kit that you'll probably need too.

Smach down but not out?

With a 5-in 1080p touchscreen display, 128 GB storage, 8 GB RAM and AMD APU, the portable Steam machine Smach Z was shaping up to be something special. However, despite raising €160,984 of its €900,000 target on Kickstarter, the project was shelved Dec 2015. The makers have indicated the will set a less ambitious goal, build a mo advanced prototype and try again...

Small is beautiful

In 2009, Canadian engineer Mark Slevinsky (below) built the **smallest playable arcade machine**, which measured just 124 x 52 x 60 mm (4.88 x 2.05 x 2.36 in). However, in 2015, a project appeared on Kickstarter claiming to be even smaller: Tiny Arcade by Ken Burns (USA). Made from acrylic or wood, the fully playable cabinet (above) purportedly measures just 75 x 40 x 32 mm (2.95 x 1.57 x 1.26 in). It features an analogue joystick and more than 20 "retro-type" games. By the end of its campaign, it had raised triple its funding target.

PS4 sales heaven

Sony hopes that the PS4 – the **biggest-selling eighth-generation console**, with sales of 39.81 million units as of 21 Apr 2016 – will go on to become the biggest-selling console overall, and there's good reason to be optimistic. In Nov 2015, the manufacturer revealed that the PS4, launched in Nov 2013, had sold 30.2 million units in its first two years of release. This compares favourably with the PS2, the current **biggest-selling console** (157.68 million units sold), which shifted 26.68 million units in its first two years on sale.

Famicom super save!

There used to be a time when saving games relied on battery-powered cartridges. In Sep 2015, a Japanese gamer known as "Wanikun" tweeted that he had left his Super Famicom switched on for 20 years so that he didn't lose his save data in the 1994 game *Umihara Kawase*. He ended up retaining power for an estimated 180,000 hr – far longer than the life of a cartridge battery!

A virtual future...

When it comes to hardware, 2016 was the year of virtual reality. Kickstarted by Oculus Rift (see below), this revolutionary tech throws gamers *inside* the action, with series such as *EVE Online*, *Gran Turismo* and *Minecraft* already announced with VR support. SuperData predicts that 70 million VR headsets will be sold by the end of 2017, making for a market worth an estimated $8.8 bn. Here are just a few of the options available.

HTC Vive

Developed in partnership between HTC and Valve, the PC peripheral uses "room-scale" technology to transform rooms into sprawling 3D spaces. Wall-mounted lasers map your location, which enables impressive freedom of movement. However, you'll need decent space to truly reap its benefits.

Microsoft HoloLens

Microsoft's kit mixes virtual reality tech with augmented reality. By doing so it projects interactive, high-definition holograms into a user's real-world surroundings. It can be used for bringing digital projects to life, as well as for playing a new breed of games.

PlayStation VR

Known as "Project Morpheus" in its dev period, the VR is slated for release in Oct 2016. For use with the PS4, it inevitably has a raft of major supported games in the works. However, Sony is also keen to realize its potential for social experiences and with non-gaming applications.

Oculus Rift

Samsung Gear VR

A collaboration with Rift-meisters Oculus, the Gear VR hit the streets in Nov 2015. It connects to recent versions of the Galaxy smartphone via micro-USB, and uses a custom inertial measurement unit (IMU). Samsung claim it "brings reality to the virtual".

Most expensive VR acquisition

When Facebook bought Oculus VR – makers of the Oculus Rift headset (main image) – on 25 Mar 2014, the price tag was serious. Zuckerberg and co paid $400 million (£242 million) in cash, plus 23.1 million Facebook shares worth $1.5 billion (£909 million). The Rift, which began as a Kickstarter indie, works with Android and PC. It was released in Mar 2016, complemented by some of the 40 or so games developed for it.

ESPORTS

With million-dollar prizes up for grabs, competitive gaming has evolved into a lucrative spectator sport. For the elite players, it is a demanding and all-consuming profession.

MAXNOM

Youngest gamer to earn $1 million in eSports winnings

In 2014, "Suma1L" aka Syed Sumail Hassan (b. 13 Feb 1999), moved from Pakistan to Illinois, USA, to pursue a career in professional gaming. His decision paid off in style when, aged just 16 years 176 days, he won The International 2015 *Dota 2* championships as part of the legendary US eSports team Evil Geniuses. In doing so, Suma1L netted himself $1,326,022 (£855,426). As of 16 Feb 2016, his total career earnings stood at $1,753,171 (£1,210,050).

EVOLUTION OF ESPORTS

Let the pro games commence!

Competitive gaming has come a long way since *Tennis for Two* was served to the public 58 years ago. Mega sponsorship deals, online streaming services and dedicated eSports associations mean that the top tournaments can now offer huge sums of prize money. Meanwhile, hundreds of thousands of fans tune in to watch thrilling contests in games such as *League of Legends* and *S*

1958
William "Willy" Higinbotham's (USA) *Tennis for Two* – the **first videogame** – introduces the concept of competitive videogaming to the public.

1972
The **first videogame tournament** sees around 24 players compete in the Intergalactic *Spacewar!* Olympics at Stanford University's Artificial Intelligence Laboratory.

1980
More than 10,000 gamers compete in the *Space Invaders* Championship, hosted by Atari at locations across the USA. Eventual champ Bill (now Rebecca) Heineman (USA) wins an enviable *Asteroids* cocktail machine.

2000
The Korea e-Sports Association (KeSPA) is founded to oversee South Korea's drive for pro gaming. Competitions in *Warcraft III* and *StarCraft* are widely broadcast across 24-hr cable channels.

1998
Daigo "The Beast" Umehara (JPN, left) defeats Alex Valle (USA) in the *Street Fighter Alpha 3* International Finals. It kick-starts a 15-year period of dominance for the gamer.

2002
Major South Korean companies, including Samsung and SK Telecom, begin sponsoring pro *StarCraft* teams. This injects big money into competitive gaming and shapes the lucrative sport as we know it today.

2005
"Lil Poison", aka Victor De Leon III (USA, b. 6 May 1998, right), becomes the **youngest signed pro gamer** when he signs an exclusive deal with America's Major League Gaming (MLG), aged just six.

2005
Swedish *Counter-Strike* clan Ninjas in Pyjamas become the **first gaming team to be represented by a sports agent**.

2015
League of Legends gets its **first pro female player** when Maria "Remilia" Creveling (USA) qualifies for the Championship Series in Aug.

2016
In Jan 2016, Activision Blizzard announces it has purchased Major League Gaming for $46 m (£31 m).

2015
ESL introduces randomized drugs testing at its *Counter-Strike: GO* tournament ESL One Cologne. Organizers say testing will become the norm.

2015
Nintendo's World Championships returns after a 25-year absence. John Numbers (USA, above right) wins, showing "impulsive mastery" in *Super Mario Maker*.

1981

America's Walter Day founds Twin Galaxies – the **first videogames adjudicator** – in Ottumwa, Iowa, USA. Months later, its Twin Galaxies National Scoreboard opens.

VIDEO HALL OF FAME

1983

Twin Galaxies hosts its first nationwide Video Game Masters Tournament. High scores are submitted to GWR twice a year, up until 1986.

1990

The final of the first Nintendo World Championships is held in Los Angeles, California, USA. Winners receive a $10,000 (£6,100) US savings bond, a Geo Metro Convertible, a rear-projection TV and a *Mario* trophy.

1996

Tom Cannon (USA) hosts a 40-man *Street Fighter* competition in Sunnyvale, California, USA. Six years later his event becomes the mighty fighting videogame tournament Evolution Championship Series (EVO).

1996

The inaugural QuakeCon event is held in Texas, USA. To date, it's the **longest-running pro eSports tournament organizer**.

2008

Nine separate eSports associations found the International e-Sports Federation (IeSF), determined to see pro gaming recognized as a legitimate sport.

2006

The **oldest competitive gamer**, Doris Self (USA), passes away, aged 81. Doris had been a competitive *Q*bert* player since setting a record on the game on 1 Jul 1984.

2010

Eleven *StarCraft* players are given lifetime bans for deliberately throwing matches – the **first eSports match-fixing scandal**. A South Korean footballer and an alleged gangster are also implicated in the well-publicized fallout.

2014

A sell-out 40,000 fans cram into the Seoul World Cup Stadium in South Korea to watch the *League of Legends* World Championship final. To date, it's the **largest live attendance for an eSports tournament**.

2014

Annual *Dota 2* tournament The International smashes the $10-m (£7,359,547) prize-pot barrier – that's a bigger pool than the one at Super Bowl 2014!

2011

Online video service Twitch launches, enabling millions of fans to watch eSports tournaments through live streams.

MOBA ROUND-UP

MOBAs (Multiplayer Online Battle Arenas) are the dominant force in pro gaming. Fast-paced matches typically involve two teams vying to destroy each other's strongholds.

Longest win streak in *Dota 2*

Swedish team Alliance (left) won 25 *Dota 2* matches without defeat, according to *GosuGamers*. *Dota 2* (Valve) evolved from a *Warcraft III* mod, which was first created in 2003. It's now a huge draw in eSports, typically pitching two teams of five against each other in strategic battles laced with magic.

Highest-earning eSports gamer

As of 14 Mar 2016, Peter "ppd" Dager (USA, right) had earned $2,155,025 (£1,497,930) from competing in *Dota 2* and *Heroes of Newerth* (Frostburn, 2010) matches. The bulk of his fortune was won in *Dota 2* as part of a conquering Evil Geniuses team. Pundits have hailed him as one of the most "influential strategists" in *Dota 2*.

Largest prize pool for a debut eSports world championship

Hosted on 9–11 Jan 2015 in Atlanta, Georgia, USA, the first Smite World Championship offered a prize pool of $2,612,260 (£1,722,520). Eight teams competed in the finals, with the five-man US team Cognitive Prime (inset) taking top honours. *Smite* is a mythological-themed MOBA that was released in 2014.

Q&A with *Dota 2* star Sumail "SumaiL" Hassan (PAK, right)

At 16 years 176 days, you became the youngest gamer to earn $1 million in eSports. How does it feel?
Winning the *Dota 2* world championships in 2015 [The International] was all that mattered. I proved that I am the best. The money was a bonus – I got to buy my family a house!

When did you start gaming?
The first game I played was the RTS *Age of Empires*, when I was around seven years old. I have only played three computer games in my life: that, *Dota 2* and *Counter-Strike*.

How much training do you have to do in *Dota 2*?
Every player in my team Evil Geniuses plays for about 10 hr a day. It really depends on how much you want to improve. If you want to become the best you just keep playing. I played for about 322 hr last month.

What does training involve?
We mostly play public games against random players. And we train as a team once a day. This is so that we're not just a bunch of skilled individuals who have no idea what to do when we play together in tournaments.

Do you get nervous or excited playing in front of audiences?
Neither. I would say that I am an emotionless guy...

---

10 YEARS OF GAMER'S

Dota 2 is a team game, so securing the kill oneself isn't necessary – the most assists in a *Dota 2* match is 68, achieved by Ivan "ArtStyle" Antonov (UKR) on 20 Mar 2015.

60
Number of pro *Dota 2* teams active as of Mar 2016. This included eight in North America, 14 in China and 12 in western Europe.

In Jan 2016, the Garnes Vidaregåande secondary school in Norway announced that eSports would become part of its core curriculum from Aug 2016. The course involves 5 hr of study per week.

FACT!

42
Percentage of *Dota 2* gamers who are aged 15–19, according to a survey conducted by the eSports group Team Razer.

Highest-earning *Smite* player

The eSports stars Andrew "Andinster" Woodward, John "BaRRaCCuDDa" Salter and Brett "MLCst3alth" Felley (all USA) had each scooped a total of $305,839 (£212,585) from various tournaments and competitions featuring the MOBA *Smite* (Hi-Rez Studios, 2014), as of 14 Mar 2016.

PUBLISHED ON VALVE'S OFFICIAL YOUTUBE CHANNEL, THE DOCUMENTARY *FREE TO PLAY* OFFERS AN INSIGHT INTO *DOTA 2* PRO GAMING. IT FOLLOWS THREE GAMERS COMPETING IN THE FIRST *DOTA 2* INTERNATIONAL IN 2011.

Highest-earning *Heroes of Newerth* player

German gamer Maurice "KheZu" Gutmann is the most successful player of *Heroes of Newerth* according to e-Sportsearnings. As of 14 Mar 2016, his prowess in this beast-infested MOBA had won him $48,141 (£33,462).

Most kills in a *Dota 2* match

Based on stats from datdota, a rampant Ilya "Illidan" Pivtsaev (RUS) racked up 44 kills in a single *Dota 2* match on 10 Dec 2014. He was playing as the Anti-Mage hero and was competing at StarSeries XI Europe for Virtus.pro 2.

Highest-earning *Dota 2* **player**
As of 14 Mar 2016, Saahil "UNiVeRsE" Arora (USA) had earned $2,148,114 (£1,493,120) in prize money from playing *Dota 2* on the pro circuit. The 26-year-old supremo is pictured below left, after he pocketed more than $1.3 m (£838,639) as part of the Evil Geniuses team that won The International 2015 in Seattle, USA.

DOTA 2

Largest eSports prize pool for a single tournament

Hosted on 3–8 Aug, the fifth annual *Dota 2* championship, The International 2015, offered a prize pool of $18,429,613 (£11,836,998). This princely sum was partly raised through the sale of the MOBA's latest virtual compendium, which included in-game challenges, rewards and treasures. Evil Geniuses (USA, pictured) beat Chinese surprise package CDEC in the final. In doing so, they became millionaires overnight, taking home $6,634,661 (£4,280,070) – the **largest eSports prize won by a team**.

MOBA ROUND-UP

In the eSports battle arena, *League of Legends* and *Dota 2* are two powerful forces, but *Heroes of the Storm* is one new contender in town, keen to win over the baying masses...

IN SEP 2015, MAYOR OF TAIPEI, KO WEN-JE, WAS INTERVIEWED IN A STATE BROADCAST DRESSED AS *LEAGUE OF LEGENDS* CHAMPION SURGEON SHEN. THE MAYOR WAS SUPPORTING HIS COUNTRY'S TEAMS AT THE LOL WORLD CHAMPIONSHIP.

Longest win streak in *Heroes of the Storm*

On 26 Apr 2015, the eSports unit Tempo Storm HotS (above) beat rivals Shot and the Bullets: Reloaded (both USA) to kick-start a 34-match winning streak in pro *Heroes of the Storm* contests. According to *GosuGamers*, the run spanned nine tournaments and lasted just over two months. The deadly quintet were finally upended in the arena by Cloud9 (USA).

10 YEARS OF GAMER'S

In *League of Legends*, players killed minions for gold. On 1 Jul 2014, "xPeke" (ESP) made the **fastest 300 minion kills in a pro match**, achieved in 21 min 52 sec during the EU LCS Summer Split.

4,949

Euros wagered by a *League of Legends* fan on 8 Oct 2015 – the most money wagered on a single eSports bet at Betway.

Largest audience for an eSports tournament

Running for four weeks in October, Riot Games' 2015 *League of Legends* World Championship attracted 334 million unique viewers – that's more than the entire population of the USA. The prestigious tournament was broadcast live via online and TV channels across the world. The UK's BBC honed in on the action, too, airing eSports for the first time in its history.

On 31 May 2015, *League of Legends* pro Seon "Space" Ho-San sparked controversy when he stopped a pro match for 45 min in order to use the toilet. Rules state that matches can only be paused for injury or illness.

FACT!

Longest pro *League of Legends* match

A titanic tussle between the USA teams compLexity and Team Curse lasted 1 hr 20 min 37 sec on 12 Jul 2014. The match was part of the North American League Championship Summer Series and saw compLexity's Robert "ROBERTxLEE" Lee emerge from the virtual carnage triumphant. The US gamer chalked up a ferocious 719 minion kills in the process – the **most minion kills in a pro *League of Legends* match**.

Highest-earning *Heroes of the Storm* player

As of 15 Mar 2016, Chinese eSporter Sun "xiaOt" Li Wei had won $70,261 (£48,942) from competing in *Heroes of the Storm*. "xiaOt" previously tasted moderate success competitively playing two other Blizzard titles – *Warcraft III* and *StarCraft II*.

Highest-earning *Bloodline Champions* player

As of 15 Mar 2016, Sweden's Viktor "ViktorY" Corneliusson had earned $4,500 (£3,134) playing Funcom's multiplayer action game, according to e-Sportsearnings.

Largest audience for an eSports match

A total of 36 million fans saw South Korea's SKTelecom T1 (above) defeat fellow countrymen KOO Tigers in the final of the 2015 *League of Legends* World Championship. The match was staged at the Mercedes-Benz Arena in Berlin, Germany, on 31 Oct 2015 and was streamed officially on Twitch, YouTube and Azubu.

Highest-earning *League of Legends* gamer

As of 14 Mar 2016, Lee "Faker" Sang Hyeok (KOR, below) had pocketed more prize money than any other *League of Legends* pro. The hotshot gamer earned $489,762 (£340,427) from competing in 27 tournaments. Amazingly, more than half of those winnings were amassed by the time he was 17 years old.

Most chosen hero in *Heroes of the Storm*
Based on data tracked by GosuGamers, the master spellcaster
Jaina Proudmoore (inset) had been selected in 2,497 competitive
matches as of 17 Mar 2016. However, the hero with the **highest hero
win rate** in *Heroes of the Storm,* based on a minimum of 200 matches,
is Anub'arak the traitor king. He tasted victory in 54% of his pro bouts.
Both heroes originally hail from the *Warcraft* universe.

Most eSports tournaments for a game before launch

When Blizzard announced that it was
developing a new MOBA called *Heroes of
the Storm* (originally dubbed *Blizzard DOTA*),
experts predicted it would become a major name
in eSports. That claim was well evidenced by the
game's competitive popularity while it was still in beta.
Between 16 Sep 2014 and its full release on 2 Jun 2015,
HotS had been contested in at least 40 tournaments.
Pictured in the main image is a scene from Blizzard's
first Heroes of the Dorm event on 28 Mar–26 Apr 2015.

STARCRAFT

Publisher: Blizzard Ent.
Developer: Blizzard Ent.
Genre: Strategy
Debut: 1998
Main games: 2
Expansions: 4

Most watched *StarCraft II* match

The grand final of the Intel Extreme Masters on 1 Feb 2015 was an epic battle between the South Korean players Cho "Maru" Seong Ju and Lee "Life" Seung Hyun. As of 4 Feb 2016, this match had been watched 1,771,150 times on YouTube. Fans and organizers alike described the showdown between the Terran and Zerg races as a "dream" final.

Longest period of domination in *StarCraft II*

As of 4 Feb 2016, Terran player "Mvp", aka Jung Jong Hyun (KOR), had a "period-points" score of 6,222. This total is based on players' ratings across multiple leaderboards, as calculated by the *StarCraft II* statistics site Aligulac.

FACT! In Dec 2015, *StarCraft: Brood War* legend Lee "Flash" Young Ho (KOR) announced his retirement from pro gaming, aged just 23. Fans had nicknamed him "God".

3 Number of playable races in *StarCraft II*: the Terran, Protoss and Zerg.

Highest-earning *StarCraft II* player

Despite announcing his "retirement" last year, 24-year-old Jang "MC" Min Chul (KOR) had earned $503,931 (£348,124) from competing in 107 *StarCraft II* tournaments, as of 4 Feb 2016. He had achieved 16 first-place finishes, most recently at the 2015 Red Bull Battle Grounds in Washington, DC, USA.

Longest-running eSports game

Debuting at the PGL Season 3 on 12–14 Nov 1998, the original *StarCraft* (plus its expansion *Brood War*) had been a regular fixture in pro gaming for 17 years 72 days by 4 Feb 2016. The RTS game's most recent tournament was the VANT36.5 National Starleague, which ran from 28 Oct 2015 to 23 Jan 2016.

Most eSports tournaments for a videogame

As of 4 Feb 2016, *StarCraft II: Wings of Liberty* (2010) had been the subject of 3,366 eSports tournaments. According to eSportsearnings, 1,474 players had collectively won $18,234,791 (£12,506,072), making the game the third most lucrative eSports title behind *Dota 2* and *League of Legends*. In Nov 2015, Kim "sOs" Yoo Jin (KOR, inset) won the WCS Global Finals for the second time at BlizzCon.

Most Actions Per Minute in a videogame

Actions Per Minute (APM) refers to how many times a player clicks their mouse or uses their keyboard during a minute of gaming action. Although Blizzard no longer tracks the APM in pro matches, *StarCraft* players have clocked peak APMs of more than 1,000 during intense battles. That's the equivalent of performing an action up to 17 times every second!

FACT! Pro *StarCraft* players are reported to train for as many as 10 hours a day, with players often living together in "Team Houses" to improve their bonding and discipline.

7 Number of official pro *StarCraft II* teams in South Korea.

Most pro eSports tournament victories by a female gamer

As of 9 Mar 2016, Sasha "Scarlett" Hostyn (CAN) had earned $116,185 (£81,614) from competing in 64 *StarCraft II* tournaments, winning 14 of them. *The New Yorker* once hailed her as "the most accomplished woman in eSports". In 2015, Sasha announced plans to start playing the MOBA *Dota 2* (Valve, 2013).

Youngest competitive *StarCraft II* player

Born on 28 Jul 1997, Terran player Cho "Maru" Seong Ju (KOR) was 13 years 41 days old when he won his first televised *StarCraft II* match, competing in the 2010 TG Sambo Intel Open Season 1 on 7 Sep. He participated in the event's preliminaries from 28 Aug 2010, just one month after turning 13. As of 4 Feb 2016, "Maru" was playing for the South Korean team Jin Air Green Wings.

FIGHTING GAMES

While they lack the epic prize pools of MOBAs, fighting game tournaments have been popular since the 1990s. Fast, skill-based gameplay is key to their appeal.

Most entrants in an eSports fighting tournament

Since its inception in 1996, the dedicated fighting tournament Evolution Championship Series (EVO) has grown in size and stature every year. Featuring an open-entry system, the 2015 event attracted 7,101 competitors to Las Vegas, USA, on 17–19 Jul. Contests were waged in nine games including *Tekken 7* (Bandai Namco, 2015) and *Killer Instinct* (Microsoft, 2013). The *Ultra Street Fighter IV* (2014) tournament was the most subscribed, with 2,227 combatants battling to reign supreme in Capcom's revered fighter.

Most EVO Championship Series titles held on a single game

In his fighting game career, Justin Wong (USA) won the *Marvel vs. Capcom 2: New Age of Heroes* (Capcom, 2000) event at EVO a record six times – in 2002, 2003, 2004, 2006, 2008 and 2010. While *Marvel vs. Capcom 2* has not been contested at EVO since 2011, Justin did manage to snare top prize at EVO 2014 – only this time playing *Ultimate Marvel vs. Capcom 3*.

Most Capcom Pro Tour ranking points (cumulative)

Across the 2014 and 2015 seasons, Olivier "MD Luffy" Hay (FRA) amassed 2,645 points in key *Ultra Street Fighter IV* tournaments, as recognized by Capcom. The fighting ace also holds the record for **most Capcom Pro Tour ranking points in one season**, racking up 1,921 points in 2014.

Largest screen in a gaming tournament

A supersized screen measuring 35.72 x 29.57 m (117 x 97 ft) – about half the size of a basketball court – was used at a qualifying event for the *Tekken* European Championships, staged at the Panasonic IMAX Theatre in Sydney, Australia, in Sep 2012.

14,157 Number of attendees at the 2015 EVO Championship Series.

FACT! The fighting community website Shoryuken is named after a move from the *Street Fighter* series. It translates as "Rising Dragon Fist".

$250,000 Prize pool for the 2015 *Ultra Street Fighter IV* contest, the Capcom Cup, which was staged on 6 Dec that year.

Largest live audience for a competitive fighting game match

Some 248,000 Twitch viewers saw Yusuke Momochi (JPN, right), fighting as Evil Ryu, defeat Bruce "GamerBee" Hsiang (TPE) in the *Ultra Street Fighter IV* final at EVO 2015 on 19 Jul that year. Streamed live from Las Vegas, USA, the match provided further drama when Momochi's fight-stick broke.

Most podium places in fighting games (female)

In a career that began in 2001, "Kayane", aka Marie-Laure Norindr (FRA), had achieved 57 top-three finishes in fighting tournaments, as of 11 Feb 2016. Most of Kayane's successes have been for Namco's *SoulCalibur* series and *Super Street Fighter IV* (Capcom, 2010).

Largest Super Smash Bros. tournament
An epic 1,926 gamers competed on *Super Smash Bros. for Wii U* (2014) at the EVO Championship Series at the Bally's/Paris Las Vegas Casino in Nevada, USA, on 17–19 Jul 2015, making it the biggest contest of its kind. Its title was won by Gonzalo "ZeRo" Barrios (CHL, below right).

Longest winning streak in *Super Smash Bros.* tournaments

Between Nov 2014 and Oct 2015, Gonzalo "ZeRo" Barrios (CHL, below) won an incredible 53 tournaments in a row on *Super Smash Bros. for Wii U* (Nintendo, 2014). The ace's winning streak ended at the MLG World Finals on 18 Oct 2015, when he was defeated by American gamer Nairoby "Nairo" Quezada.

FACT!
A video of Kenneth "KBrad" Bradley (USA) performing the finishing move of WWE's Stone Cold Steve Austin at CEO 2015 went viral. The feat earned a shout-out from the wrestler himself!

Most eSports tournament results (single player)
US *Super Smash Bros.* supremo "Mew2King" (aka Jason Zimmerman) had achieved "top-placed" prize finishes in 339 pro eSports tournaments, as of 11 Feb 2016, amassing earnings of $141,488 (£97,656). His bio at eSportsearnings reveals that his gaming style relies on an in-depth testing of game mechanics, including character weight, knockback and physics.

Most *Tekken* tournament championships
As of 28 Jan 2016, eSports player Ariel "FightingGM" Capellan (USA) had won 19 major tournaments in the *Tekken* franchise, as recognized by the organizers of EVO. His victories included three Winter Brawl titles, two Summer Jam titles and Absolute Battle 2015.

ESPORTS ROUND-UP

eSports isn't just about MOBAs: racers, sports games and – especially – shooters have been muscling in and gaining in stature on the high-stakes gaming circuit.

Largest prize pool for a single-player eSports tournament

A prize pool of £410,000 (£296,805) was put up by the CPL World Tour Finals – open to individuals rather than teams – in New York, USA, on 20–22 Nov 2005. The tournament saw one-to-one duelling on the FPS *Painkiller* (DreamCatcher, 2004). Winner Johnathan "Fatal1ty" Wendel (USA) walked away with a $150,000 (£87,295) first prize.

Longest absence for an eSports tournament

A quarter of a century after the inaugural Nintendo World Championships took place across 29 US cities in 1990, the second was staged at E3 2015 in Los Angeles, California, USA, on 14 Jun. The comeback contest saw gamers compete in *Mario Kart 8* (2014), *Splatoon* (2015) and the then-unreleased *Super Mario Maker* (2015). It was won by John "John Numbers" Goldberg (USA).

Longest winning streak in *Counter-Strike*
Swedish team Ninjas in Pyjamas (above) have twice recorded 23-match winning streaks in the FPS *Counter-Strike* (1999), according to data from GosuGamers. The first was from 21 Sep 2012 to 12 Feb 2013, when they lost during the group stage of StarLadder StarSeries' Season 5. The second began on the same day as that defeat, when they beat Russian Roulette (DEU) in the same competition. The run ended on 7 Apr 2013, when they lost to Virtus.pro (RUS) in the tournament's play-offs.

Highest-rated player on *World of Tanks* (PC)

On *World of Tanks* (Wargaming, 2010), "Dodoma" (USA) held a chart-topping "PR" score of 11,960 as of 11 Mar 2016.

Highest-earning *Splatoon* team

After heats around Japan, Ikata Tama Kids (JPN) triumphed at the grand final of the *Splatoon* Koshien in Tokyo on 30–31 Jan 2016. The team were rewarded with the lion's share of the competition's prize pot, reported to be worth over $1,000,000 (£701,828). At least 400,000 viewers watched on the Japanese streaming site Niconico.

FACT! On 25 Aug 2015, Betway became the **first major bookmaker to launch a dedicated global eSports portal.** Among the first bets available was for *Hearthstone* (2014) to be part of the 2030 Winter Olympics, at odds of 99 to 1.

3 High schools in Sweden that, in summer 2015, announced they would offer eSports classes in the coming terms, with subjects to include *DotA* and *Counter-Strike*. Magnus Alehed, headmaster of a school in Karlstad, told the press: "We aim to kill the myth that it has to be a bad thing."

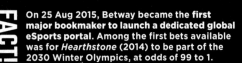
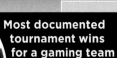

Most documented tournament wins for a gaming team

"I wanted to help develop the videogame culture through competitive gaming," said Isaiah "Triforce" Johnson (above left). That mission was truly accomplished when his Empire Arcadia team (both USA) – despite its shifting line-ups – netted 2,000 tournament victories, as recorded on 14 May 2015. Over the years, the team has included stars such as Justin Wong.

Q&A with Empire Arcadia's Isaiah "Triforce" Johnson

When was the team formed?
In 2001. The first tournaments we entered were a mix of retro and arcade games like *Tetris* and *Super Street Fighter II* at Chinatown Fair arcade. Now we try to keep it diverse: *Marvel vs. Capcom 2*, *Gears of War 2*, *Super Smash Bros. Melee*, *Hearthstone*, *Call of Duty*, *FIFA*, *Tetris*...

What are your historic victories?
We won *Injustice: Gods Among Us* and *Ultimate Marvel vs. Capcom 3* at EVO 2013, *Gears of War 2* at the World Cyber Games in 2009 and *Super Smash Bros. Brawl* at Major League Gaming in 2010. More recently, we won the CyberBox eSports League *FIFA 16* championship and represented Jamaica in *Hearthstone* for the Americas Tour 2015.

How do you view eSports today?
Games such as *League of Legends* and *Dota 2* have taken eSports to the next level; much as *StarCraft* and *Halo* did in the first decade of the 21st century, and *Quake* and *Doom* in the late 1990s. We've been building a *League of Legends* team since 2015 and have shifted our focus from retro, fighting and shooting games to MOBA and RTS titles.

Most watched *Counter-Strike* eSports tournament

Some 27 million Twitch users tuned in for the ESL One Cologne *Counter-Strike: Global Offensive* (Valve, 2012) tournament on 22–23 Aug 2015. The thrilling contest was held at the Lanxess Arena in Cologne, Germany (main picture), and was won by the Swedish team Fnatic (below).

Viewing figures peaked at 1.3 million – the **most concurrent viewers for a *Counter-Strike* tournament**.

28 Years between the release of the first *Metal Gear* (Konami) in 1987 and ESL's launch of the *Metal Gear* Online Global Championships in December 2015 – the **longest time for an eSports debut by a videogame series.**

10 YEARS OF *GAMER'S*
Founded on 10 Nov 1981 in Ottumwa, Iowa, USA, Twin Galaxies is the **first videogame adjudicator**. It sought to turn gaming into an international sport.

Highest-earning *Counter-Strike* player

Winning $366,061 (£257,324) from *Counter-Strike* and its sequel *Counter-Strike: Global Offensive* at 170 events, as of 11 Mar 2016, has made Patrik "f0rest" Lindberg (SWE, above) the biggest money-winner across the series.

This success has helped make Sweden the **highest-earning *Counter-Strike* country**. Its players had won $5,436,162 (£3,821,370) from all of its games, as of 11 Mar 2016.

Most eSport tournaments for a racing game

Between 28 Jun 2006 and 12 Dec 2015, there were 94 major tournaments across four incarnations of *TrackMania* (Digital Jesters, 2003). The most commonly played by pro gamers was *TrackMania Nations Forever* (2008), with 40 events between 27 Nov 2011 and 31 Mar 2013, and a total of $111,875 (£73,557) prize money paid out. As of 11 Mar 2016, it remained the most common racing name on the competitive circuit.

GOSUGAMERS

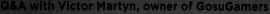

The rise in popularity of eSports has been aided by a new wave of websites dedicated to covering the phenomenon. Such publications cover everything from the biggest and smallest competitions to the nuances of each game's often-complex rules. Few have done a better job of keeping digital sports fans informed and educated as GosuGamers. Run by former pro player Victor Martyn (right), it's one of the most popular dedicated eSports websites on the planet.

Q&A with Victor Martyn, owner of GosuGamers

What are the origins of GosuGamers?
It was built by a Swedish gamer in 2001 or 2002 when he was just 13 years old. At that time, the site was a hub for the Swedish *StarCraft* community, but it broadened into other games and countries. I bought the site in May 2010 and have been involved ever since. None of the founding staff members remain today.

You're a former pro gamer. What triggered the switch to website management?
I was a pro gamer in South Korea for three years between 1999 and 2002, but I returned to Sweden hoping to follow a more traditional career path. However, while I was studying I launched an online business and used some of the money that I had made to acquire GosuGamers. My decision to return to eSports was driven by my passion for it.

What kind of eSports events do you cover?
We do a mix of online and on-site coverage, attending tournaments in many countries. For that purpose, we have correspondents across the world. Each game has its own section on the site, with its own dedicated team.

Has GosuGamers changed much?
The tech and the way we consume eSports has changed. In 2010 it was a big thing to download and watch replays of matches. That was one of our most important features,

with users downloading replays for *Warcraft III*, *DotA* and *StarCraft: Brood War*. Now everyone watches live streams on Twitch and YouTube. Replays have ballooned from 1 MB to 200 MB with the inception of *Dota 2*, while *League of Legends* doesn't even have replays at all! We've had to stay mobile and meet changes in consumption and audience behaviour.

How do you decide which games to cover?
Mostly, it comes down to deciding whether a game has potential, what its current quality is, and whether or not our staff have an interest in it.

In your opinion, what will be the next big game in eSports?
I think Blizzard's *Overwatch* (inset) will be a huge eSports title. It seems to be converging a lot of different genres that have been overlooked, such as action-orientated FPS games, namely *Quake*, and combining that brilliantly with the better elements of a MOBA.

Predicted global viewing figures for eSports
eSports was watched by 188.3 million fans in 2015 according to SuperData, with figures predicted to rise further by 2017.

KEY:
1 = 10 million viewers
SOURCE: SuperData

238.1 M

218.4 M

188.3 M

100.6 M

2014	2015	2016	2017

Predicted growth in eSports revenue
Industry experts estimate that eSports will generate more than $1 billion in revenue by 2019. This sum would be generated by media sales, merchandising, online advertising, brand partnerships and game-publisher investment. (Source: Gamesindustry.biz)

2019

$1.072 billion (predicted)

GosuGamers' top-ranked eSports teams

GosuGamers uses its own system to decipher which teams and players are the world's best. Of course, in this fast-moving sport things can swiftly change. Here's how they ranked as of 6 Apr 2016...

Dota 2

1. Evil Geniuses Dota2 (USA, above)
2. Team Secret (Europe)
3. Fnatic.Dota2 (MYS)
4. Team Liquid (Europe)
5. EHOME (CHN)

League of Legends

1. SKT T1 (KOR, above)
2. G2 Esports LoL (Europe)
3. Immortals (USA)
4. EDward Gaming (CHN)
5. ahq e-Sports Club (TPE)

Counter-Strike: Global Offensive

1. Fnatic (SWE, above)
2. Natus Vincere (UKR)
3. Luminosity Gaming (BRA)
4. Astralis (DNK)
5. Ninjas in Pyjamas (SWE)

Heroes of the Storm

1. MVP Black (KOR, above)
2. eStar Gaming (CHN)
3. Cloud9 HotS (USA)
4. EDward Gaming HotS (CHN)
5. Natus Vincere HotS (Europe)

Meet some of the GosuGamers team...

Reggie Woo, Senior Editor for *League of Legends*

Favourite *League of Legends* match?
That would have to be Unicorns of Love vs Fnatic during Week 8 of the 2015 EU LCS Spring Split.

Why was that?
It showed how exciting a single professional game can be. Fnatic were so close to killing the enemy "Nexus", but weren't able to. That let Unicorns of Love bounce back and take the game.

Andreea Esanu, *Dota 2* Editorial Section Leader

Favourite *Dota 2* match?
The International 3 – Grand Finals.

Why is eSports journalism important to you?
It's still in its early development, and lacks true models and professionals that could take this sort of job to the next level. With all the community commitment and dedication I truly believe we can change the way that the eSports press is regarded.

What's most exciting about the future of eSports?
It's almost unbelievable how fast and how far the eSports industry has got with almost no support from any "mainstream" media. We're now at a point where eSports are not even dependent on this sort of attention.

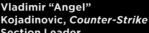

Vladimir "Angel" Kojadinovic, *Counter-Strike* Section Leader

Favourite *Counter-Strike* match?
Fnatic vs Team LDLC during DreamHack Winter 2014.

What impact did that match have on you?
The joy I felt while watching it was definitely comparable to the joy that I always feel cheering for my favourite sports club. My memories of that match will remain forever.

ACTION-ADVENTURE

The staple of any gaming diet, action-adventures have brought us blockbuster plots, epic set-pieces and heroes such as Link and Nathan Drake. No genre has sold better.

Released in 2015, *LEGO Dimensions* was the toy giant's long-anticipated debut to the toys-to-life genre. In classic brick-building style, gamers get to collect interactive figurines, which they can then assemble and customize before transporting into the game itself. To date, characters have hailed from such mighty franchises as *Batman* and *Jurassic World*.

Fastest time to assemble characters in *LEGO® Dimensions'* starter pack

The figurines for Wyldstyle, Gandalf and Batman (all pictured) were assembled in a record 32 sec by "Leon Ip" in Solihull, West Midlands, UK, on 9 Jan 2016.

The young gamer – whose dad, rather helpfully, is an architect – also set the record for the **fastest time to build the Batmobile figurine in *LEGO Dimensions***: 1 min 13 sec, on 4 Mar 2016.

ACTION-ADVENTURE ROUND-UP

Arguably the "granddaddies" of most modern games, action-adventures are a mix of everything you could wish for: gripping narratives, fiendish puzzles and explosive action!

Fastest completion of *Rise of the Tomb Raider*

Tomb Raider speed-runner "TheArtisticBallistic" (CHE) completed a glitched run through Crystal Dynamics' 2015 instalment in just 1 hr 14 min 36 sec on the PC. The super-fast time was verified by Speedrun.com on 5 Mar 2016.

First 100% completion of *Titan Souls*

Acid Nerve's indie title *Titan Souls* was released on 14 Apr 2015. "DeGarmo2" earned a Platinum Trophy for completing the PS4/PSV version three days later, at 1:06:40 a.m. on 17 Apr 2015 – incredibly, just two seconds ahead of the next gamer!

Fastest completion of *The Last of Us: Left Behind*

Greg "The Thrillness" Innes (UK) raced through Naughty Dog's 2014 DLC in just 5 min 58 sec on 4 Jun 2015.

A prologue to the original game, *Left Behind* had a GameRankings score of 89.94% as of 9 Mar 2016 – the **most critically acclaimed DLC for an action-adventure game**.

Fastest completion of *Shadow of the Colossus*

Japanese gamer "Shirapon" sped through the PS3 version of Fumito Ueda's monster-inhabited classic *Shadow of the Colossus* in just 1 hr 31 min 7 sec on 11 Dec 2015, as verified by Speedrun.com. The sparse, atmospheric adventure is the unofficial predecessor to the upcoming *The Last Guardian* (2016), with both titles sharing a fondness for huge character models. In *The Last Guardian*'s case, gamers can look forward to meeting the gigantic "pet" Trico.

LARA CROFT

TOMB RAIDER SERIES

Originally known as	Lara Cruz
Profession	Archaeologist
Main weapon	Bow and arrow
Back-up weapons	Pistol, climbing axe
Games (inc. spin-offs)	20

★ TO PROMOTE *RISE OF THE TOMB RAIDER*, EIGHT PEOPLE TOOK PART IN A STREAMED "SURVIVAL BILLBOARD" CHALLENGE, BRAVING SIMULATED HARSH WEATHER ON THE LEDGE OF A BILLBOARD IN LONDON, UK. THE WINNER LASTED FOR OVER 20 HR.

43 Number of "ghosts" – hard-to-find images hidden within a game – for eagle-eyed gamers to spot in *Metal Gear Solid* (Konami, 1998). The spectral images are the game's designers.

FACT! In Naughty Dog's *The Last of Us*, an apocalypse might have hit the USA but one creature seems to be thriving – giraffes! Apparently symbols of lost innocence, the long-necked animals can be spotted in the shape of toys and ads, or even seen milling around in scenes inspired by *Jurassic Park*.

First motion-capture animation in a videogame

Using a technique known as rotoscoping, Jordan Mechner (USA) filmed his brother performing the acrobatic moves eventually seen in *Prince of Persia* (Brøderbund, 1989), tracing over the frames to create smooth animated motions.

With $335,154,643 (£213,973,000) in box-office receipts from May 2010, *Prince of Persia: The Sands of Time* is the **highest-grossing live-action game-to-film transfer**.

Most uses of a cardboard box in a videogame

Ever since Solid Snake used one to evade his enemies in the first *Metal Gear* (Konami, 1987), the humble cardboard box has become a running joke throughout the series. In *Metal Gear Solid V: The Phantom Pain* (Konami, 2015), it is put to no less than 12 different uses – including a shield, toboggan and a pin-up board for posters.

Fastest completion of *The Legend of Zelda: Ocarina of Time*
On 10 Jul 2015, "skater82297" stunned the gaming world with a time of 17 min 45 sec. Using the classic *Zelda* tactic of running backwards and playing the Japanese version for faster-scrolling subtitles, he became only the second gamer to complete it in under 18 min, beating the mark set by "Jodenstone" (SWE) on 16 Mar 2015.

Most critically acclaimed game on Metacritic

With a Metacritic score of 99% as of 14 Mar 2016, *The Legend of Zelda: Ocarina of Time* (Nintendo, 1998) is a hair's breadth from perfection. Link's classic adventure is the only title ever to achieve that score, ahead of gaming heavyweights *Grand Theft Auto IV* (Rockstar Games, 2008), *Tony Hawk's Pro Skater 2* (Activision, 2000) and *SoulCalibur* (Namco, 1999), all on 98%.

10 YEARS OF *GAMER'S*

The **longest cutscene in a game** – a non-interactive sequence to explain the story between levels – is 27 min, in *Metal Gear Solid 4: Guns of the Patriots* (Konami, 2008).

Largest cosplay costume based on a videogame (single person)

Ruby Taki (JPN) of US-based cosplay group Pro Voltage spent eight months making a jaw-dropping Metal Gear REX from *Metal Gear Solid* (Konami, 1998). Her creation is 215 cm (7 ft) tall, 190 cm (6 ft 2 in) wide and measures 250 cm (8 ft

Fastest completion of *Uncharted: Drake's Fortune*

On 18 Mar 2016, French speed-runner "Erims" hared through Naughty Dog's 2007 action-adventure in 42 min 29 sec. "Really bad run," Erims moaned, despite shaving 27 sec off his previous time. The run was achieved on the PS4 version, which was released as part of *The Nathan Drake Collection* in 2015.

SANDBOX ADVENTURES

The biggest evolution in the action-adventure genre is the advent of "sandbox" environments, enabling gamers to roam large, open worlds with new-found freedom.

Best-selling action-adventure game series

With global sales of 157.5 million units as of 11 Feb 2016, Rockstar's open-world franchise *Grand Theft Auto* (*GTA*) is the best-selling series in its genre, according to VGChartz.

The **best-selling action-adventure game** is *GTA V* (2013), which had sold 51.96 million copies as of the same date.

Most critically acclaimed open-world game

As of 11 Feb 2016, the PS3 version of 2008 crime romp *GTA IV* held a mighty GameRankings score of 97.04%, very narrowly topping its successor – *GTA V*, at 97.01%.

Longest marathon on an action-adventure game

Tony Desmet, Jesse Rebmann and Jeffrey Gammon (all BEL) played the periodic thriller *Assassin's Creed: Brotherhood* (Ubisoft, 2010) for a hand-numbing 109 hr at the GUNKtv World Record Gaming Event in Antwerp, Belgium, on 18–22 Dec 2010.

Fastest completion of *Middle-earth: Shadow of Mordor*

American speed-runner and Twitch user "FearfulFerret" completed the hugely acclaimed Tolkien action-fest *Middle-earth: Shadow of Mordor* (Warner Bros., 2014) in 1 hr 56 min 35 sec on 19 Nov 2014. This any% run was completed on the PC version and is ranked at Speedrun.com.

Most signatures for a videogame petition
A petition appealing for *GTA V* to be released for PC had gained 728,144 signatories on Change.org by 11 Jun 2014. Targeting developer Rockstar, it pleaded: "It's a big shame not seeing the newest iteration of the game being released on the most powerful platform." *GTA V* finally hit PCs in Apr 2015.

FACT! Courtesy of a mod created by "popos1", gamers can drive the world's **smallest production car** in *GTA V* – a Peel P50, whose real-world counterpart is just 134 cm (53 in) long and 99 cm (39 in) wide.

99 Voice actors in 2013's *Saints Row IV* (Deep Silver). The over-the-top open-world game features aliens, gangsters and former WWE legend "Rowdy" Roddy Piper.

First 3D open-world action-adventure

A military-themed third-person game, *Hunter* is widely credited as the first action-adventure to provide open-world gameplay in 3D. Players controlled a soldier as they executed a number of covert missions. The game, released in 1991 for Atari ST and Amiga, was designed by Paul Holmes for Activision.

JACOB FRYE

ASSASSIN'S CREED: SYNDICATE

Occupation	**Master Assassin**
Nationality	**English**
Age	**21**
Skills	**Eagle vision, free-running**
Tools	**Hidden Blade, rope-launcher**

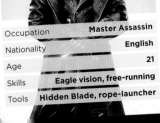

Highest vertical range in a land-based videogame

The highest playable point in *Just Cause 3* (Square Enix, 2015) measures in at 3,015 m (9,891 ft) above sea level, creating the highest known vertical range of any land-based game using an approximate real-world scale. In it, players pilot choppers, skydive and – most satisfyingly of all – soar around in a wingsuit like a supercharged eagle.

8

D.I.C.E. awards won by *Middle-earth: Shadow of Mordor* in 2015, including Outstanding Innovation in Gaming.

10 YEARS OF *GAMER'S*

Assassin's Creed II has secured the **most magazine covers for a videogame** – a total of 127 between Apr 2009 and Apr 2010.

Fastest entertainment property to gross $1 billion

When *GTA V* was released for home consoles on 17 Sep 2013, it smashed the $1 bn-grossing record in just three days. Developers Rockstar claimed that $800 million (£500 m) was made in one day alone.

Most money pledged for a videogame on Kickstarter

Announced at E3 on 15 Jun 2015, *Shenmue III* (Ys Net) went on to raise $6,333,296 (£4,066,048) on Kickstarter. It had earlier set the record for **fastest $1 million pledged for a videogame**, reaching that milestone in just 1 hr 44 min. Shown right is *Shenmue* series director Yu Suzuki.

Thank You!!!

Shenmue III
Keep Those You Love!!

GUINNESS WORLD RECORDS

CERTIFICATE

The most money pledged for a Kickstarter videogame is $6,333,296 (£4,066,048) and was achieved by Shenmue 3 (Japan) from 16 June to 17 July 2015

OFFICIALLY AMAZING

RECORD HOLDER

SUPERHERO GAMES

Superheroes are effectively ready-made gaming stars, capable of incredible feats and embroiled in out-there plots. Inevitably, they have fronted some epic videogame titles.

Most Marvel movies condensed into a videogame

Action-adventure title *LEGO® Marvel Avengers* (Warner Bros., 2016) spans the epic events covered in no less than six feature-length films: *Captain America: The First Avenger* (2011), *The Avengers* (2012), *Iron Man 3* (2013), *Thor: The Dark World* (2013), *Captain America: The Winter Soldier* (2014) and *Avengers: Age of Ultron* (2015).

10 YEARS OF GAMER'S ...

The **most prolific vide...** game superhero ...ne appearances, is Spider-Man, with 37 hea...ut *Spider-Man* to ranging from his 1982 de...-Man: Unlimited. 2014's mobile title Spid...

Most licensed superheroes

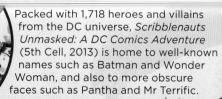

Packed with 1,718 heroes and villains from the DC universe, *Scribblenauts Unmasked: A DC Comics Adventure* (5th Cell, 2013) is home to well-known names such as Batman and Wonder Woman, and also to more obscure faces such as Pantha and Mr Terrific.

Most lines of dialogue in a superhero game

Brooding adventure title *Batman: Arkham Knight* (Warner Bros., 2015) features 36,160 lines of dialogue, amounting to more than 60 hr of audio. Reprising the voice of Batman from the other games in the *Arkham* franchise is US actor Kevin Conroy.

51

Episodes of *Viewtiful Joe*'s TV series

Fastest completion of *The Incredible Hulk*

Troy "Hellfire7777777" Spence (USA) Hulk-smashed his way through classic SNES/MegaDrive platformer *The Incredible Hulk* (U.S. Gold, 1994) in 19 min 35 sec, according to Speed Demos Archive. The run was completed on 21 Nov 2009 and was played on the Arcade setting, which is the most difficult.

Most critically acclaimed superhero videogames

Game	Publisher	Version	Score
Batman: Arkham City (2011)	Warner Bros.	PS3	95.94%
Batman: Arkham Asylum (2009)	Eidos	Xbox 360	92.34%
Viewtiful Joe (2003)	Capcom	GC	91.19%
Marvel vs. Capcom 2: New Age of Heroes (2000)	Virgin	DC	90.15%
Batman: Arkham Knight (2015)	Warner Bros.	PS4	88.45%
Freedom Force (2002)	EA	PC	87.88%
Spider-Man (2000)	Activision	PS	86.53%
Freedom Force vs The 3rd Reich (2005)	Irrational	PC	86.07%
Marvel vs. Capcom 3: Fate of Two Worlds (2011)	Capcom	Xbox 360	85.9%
Viewtiful Joe 2 (2004)	Capcom	GC	85.87%

Source: GameRankings. Figures accurate as of 8 Feb 2016.

Longest-running superhero MMO

City of Heroes, the **first superhero MMORPG**, ran for 8 years 217 days before closing on 30 Nov 2012. Its developer Cryptic Studios also released the free2play *Champions Online* on 1 Sep 2009. As of 3 Mar 2016, it had run for 6 years 184 days, making it the **longest-running superhero MMO still active**. The game is based on the *Champions* table-top role-playing game.

FACT!

Krypton's surviving son Superman has the distinction of being the **first official videogame superhero**, headlining his own eponymous title on the Atari 2600 way back in 1979.

10,000

Buildings in the virtual Metropolis that appear in 2006 film tie-in *Superman Returns*. The city covers ...

SUPERMAN

SUPERMAN SERIES

Videogame debut	1979
Nationality	Krypton/USA
Headline game appearances	14
Powers	Flight, strength, icy breath

Most Spider-Men and Spider-Women in a videogame
Set across the vast Marvel multiverse, Gameloft's mobile outing *Spider-Man: Unlimited* (2014) features a veritable army of 77 Spidey-people to battle evil. The game is an endless runner that revolves around the Green Goblin's bid to overthrow Spidey's "regular" earthly dimension by using a portal.

FOR FUN VIDEOS OF *GTA V* SUPERHERO MODS, HEAD TO THE "TYPICAL GAMER" YOUTUBE CHANNEL. IT FEATURES POPULAR DO-GOODERS ROMPING AROUND ROCKSTAR'S EPIC CRIME GAME. A VID OF THE FLASH ALONE HAS 11-MILLION-PLUS VIEWS!

Most official superhero costumes in a videogame

As of 29 Feb 2016, US-based developer Gazillion Entertainment had released 404 superhero outfits for its MMORPG *Marvel Heroes 2016*. Each is officially adapted from either a comic-book or movie source. They include 23 costumes for Iron Man, 19 for Spider-Man, 14 for the Hulk and eight for the Fantastic Four's Thing.

TOYS-TO-LIFE

By using devices known as "hubs" or "portals", special figurines can be teleported into games. The popular toys-to-life genre has also inspired feverish collecting.

First toys-to-life videogame

Although *Skylanders: Spyro's Adventure* (Activision, 2011) popularized the toys-to-life phenomenon, it was actually Mattel's 2007 PC title *U.B. Funkey* that first used a portal to insert additional toy-based characters into a videogame. Disappointing sales led to the series being discontinued in 2010.

Most expensive amiibo figure

Thanks to a factory defect, this ultra-rare amiibo of *Super Mario*'s perennial damsel in distress, Princess Peach, appeared with missing legs – a flaw that only increased her value. On 9 Dec 2014, the factory-sealed toy fetched a reported $25,100 (£16,091) on eBay.

Most actors reprising TV and film roles in a videogame

LEGO® Dimensions (Warner Bros., 2015) saw 24 actors reprising roles they had previously played. This included the 12th Doctor Who, Peter Capaldi (left), original *Ghostbusters* (1984) stars Dan Aykroyd and Ernie Hudson, and Michael J Fox from *Back to the Future* (1985).

Most licences in a single videogame

Released on 27 Sep 2015, LEGO's first foray into the toys-to-life genre promised to "fuse many fan-favourite universes together". *LEGO Dimensions* lived up to the billing, featuring characters from 11 franchises that are independent of LEGO including *The Lord of the Rings*, DC Comics, *Jurassic World*, *Scooby-Doo!*, Portal, *The Wizard of Oz* and *The Simpsons*.

10 YEARS OF GAMER'S

The **rarest** *Skylanders* were given away at E3 2011 – 600 Spyro, Gill Grunt and Trigger Happy toys in packaging marked "Bring me to life at the Activision E3 booth."

30

Games based on toy franchises developed by UK studio TT Games, the **most prolific developer of toy videogames.**

In Mar 2015, a consignment of *Splatoon* special editions, complete with rare Inkling Squid amiibo, was hijacked on its way from Nintendo's European HQ to GAME's UK warehouse, leaving the company unable to meet its orders.

FACT!

15

Minutes it took for the US retailer Walmart to sell out of 3,000 exclusive Gold Mario amiibo, in Feb 2015.

Most critically acclaimed toys-to-life game

Set on the Cloudbreak Islands, *Skylanders: Swap Force* (2013) for Xbox 360 had a GameRankings rating of 84.68% as of 14 Mar 2016, more than any other game requiring figurines to play.

Highest-altitude freefall videogame session

As part of the European launch of *Skylanders: Trap Team* on 10 Oct 2014, a group of skydivers dubbed "Skytrappers" played the game in freefall at 12,500 ft (3,810 m).

Largest collection of *Skylanders* memorabilia

Christopher Desaliza of Pace in Florida, USA, has amassed a collection of 4,100 unique *Skylanders* items, as verified on 27 Jan 2015.

First amiibo figurine of an indie-game character

On 27 Aug 2015, the spade-wielding hero of *Shovel Knight* (Yacht Club Games, 2014) was unveiled as a new amiibo figurine. The figurine unlocked a special "Co-op" mode on the Wii and exclusive challenge stages on both the 3DS and Wii.

First game to use wearable technology to unlock content

The MagicBand is a wristband that allows visitors to Walt Disney World Resort in Florida, USA, to enter the Magic Kingdom. It also enables users to unlock extra content for the "Toy Box" mode in various *Disney Infinity* titles when the user places the MagicBand on the game's Infinity Base device.

Smallest dev team on a toys-to-life videogame
Combining Jenga-style tabletop stacking with a digital strategy element, *Fabulous Beasts* (Sensible Object, 2016) was the brainchild of an indie studio of just five people. Development was aided by crowdfunding support on Kickstarter, which pledged $237,979 (£168,360).

HE PLAYS *SKYLANDERS*. HE UNBOXES. HE IS SCARED BY HIS DAD JUMPING OUT ON HIM AT HALLOWEEN. EVAN IS AN 11-YEAR-OLD YOUTUBE SENSATION WITH MORE THAN 4 MILLION SUBSCRIBERS TO CHANNELS "EVANTUBEHD" AND "EVANTUBERAW".

Largest game hardware accessories brand (current)

Since the first *Skylanders* gamer plugged Spyro the Dragon into the "Portal of Power", Activision's series has helped to establish the toys-to-life game as a vibrant new genre. The rewards have been remarkable: according to market research by Euromonitor, *Skylanders* earned an astonishing revenue of $541,200,000 (£383,393,000) in 2014 alone, ahead of *Disney Infinity*'s $365,700,000 (£235,416,000).

CAPTAIN FALCON

AMIIBO FIGURE

amiibo number	18
Game debut	*F-Zero* (1990)
Occupation	Bounty hunter
Alias	Bart Lemming
Arch-enemy	Black Shadow

GRAPHIC ADVENTURES

Celebrated for their teasing puzzles and compelling storytelling, graphic adventures are for those who like their gameplay cerebral, gently paced and utterly gripping.

10 YEARS OF *GAMER'S*

Appearing on 13 computer platforms and consoles across multiple generations, the original *Myst* (1993) is the **most ported** graphic adventure videogame.

Most critically acclaimed "art" game

The rise of independent gaming studios, coupled with a wider availability of dev tools, led to many developers experimenting more freely with game design.

As of 9 Feb 2016, the most critically acclaimed game described as "art" was the PS4 version of *Journey* (2015), which had scored 94.8% on GameRankings based on 25 reviews.

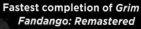

Most awards won by an indie game

The PS3 original of the desert adventure *Journey* (thatgamecompany, above, 2012) bagged 118 awards in 2012–13. Highlights included *IGN*'s Number One PSN Game of All Time, *GameSpot*'s Overall Game of the Year, multiple gaming BAFTAs, and CNN citing it among its 10 Best Video Games of 2012.

Longest-running graphic adventure protagonist

Guybrush Threepwood appeared in five *Monkey Island* games from 15 Oct 1990 to 8 Dec 2009: a total of 19 years 54 days. George and Nico of the *Broken Sword* series are closing the gap, with 17 years 199 days between their first and most recent appearances.

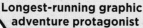

"MANNY" CALAVERA

GRIM FANDANGO

Debut	**1998**
Age	**Unknown**
Nationality	**Mexican**
Job	**Travel agent for the deceased**
Enemy	**Domino Hurley**

198

Cups of tea in *Everybody's Gone to the Rapture* (The Chinese Room, 2015) – the **most cups of tea in a videogame**.

Longest gap between an original game and its remake

Announced to nostalgic fervour in 2014, Tim Schafer's remastered remake of his own *Day of the Tentacle* (LucasArts) was set for release in Mar 2016 – at least 22 years 250 days after the original's 25 Jun 1993 debut. The much-loved point-and-click adventure saw three awkward teens fighting a purple tentacle.

Fastest completion of *Grim Fandango: Remastered*

Gamer "Caffeinated_Fox" (BRA) completed Tim Schafer's Mexican-themed yarn *Grim Fandango* (2015) in 1 hr 21 min 30 sec on 26 Jan 2016.

Fastest completion of *Life is Strange*

On 6 Feb 2016, Brazil's "Roxy_Rose" played through all episodes of psychic thriller *Life is Strange* (Square Enix, 2015) in 5 hr 31 min 53 sec. She described it as the longest speed-run she'd ever done.

Fastest completion of *Maniac Mansion*

Lucasfilm's 1987 adventure *Maniac Mansion* was completed by Kyle "Mr K" Halversen in just 6 min 49 sec on 13 Aug 2012.

The goat puzzle in Revolution's 1996 title *Broken Sword: The Shadow of the Templars* is regarded as one of the hardest videogame puzzles of all. In 2012, fans celebrated by creating the "Order of the Goat" guild.

FACT!

36

Number of fairytale or folklore characters in *The Wolf Among Us* (Telltale, 2013), including the Big Bad Wolf.

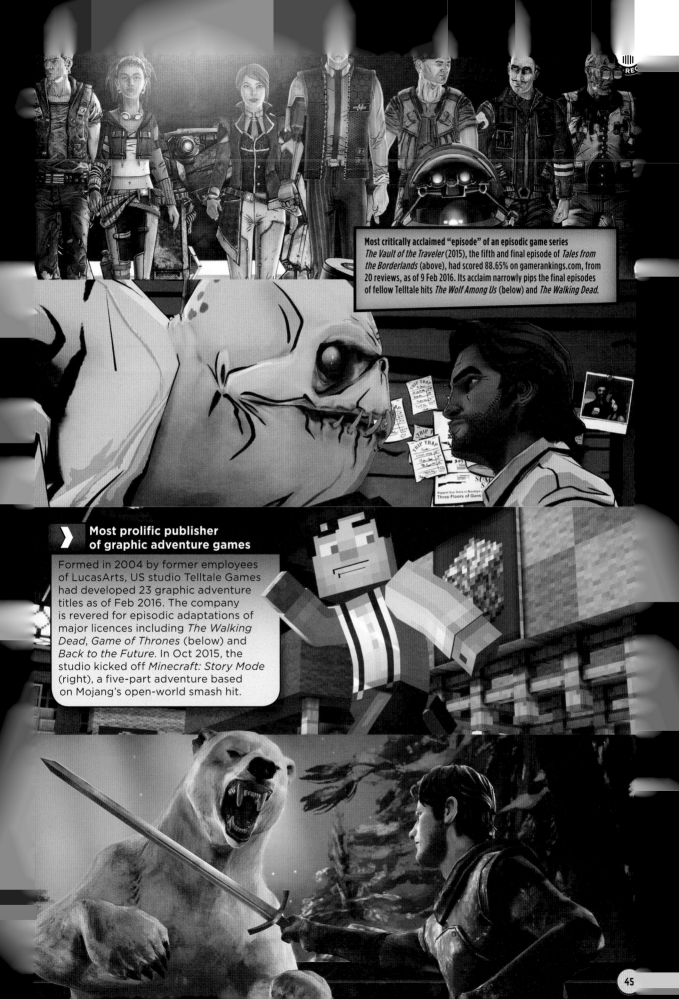

Most critically acclaimed "episode" of an episodic game series
The Vault of the Traveler (2015), the fifth and final episode of *Tales from the Borderlands* (above), had scored 88.65% on gamerankings.com, from 20 reviews, as of 9 Feb 2016. Its acclaim narrowly pips the final episodes of fellow Telltale hits *The Wolf Among Us* (below) and *The Walking Dead*.

❯ Most prolific publisher of graphic adventure games

Formed in 2004 by former employees of LucasArts, US studio Telltale Games had developed 23 graphic adventure titles as of Feb 2016. The company is revered for episodic adaptations of major licences including *The Walking Dead*, *Game of Thrones* (below) and *Back to the Future*. In Oct 2015, the studio kicked off *Minecraft: Story Mode* (right), a five-part adventure based on Mojang's open-world smash hit.

HORROR GAMES

Blending terror with action and adventure is a match made in gaming heaven. Jump-scares, strange locales and grisly villains all bode well for unsettling gaming experiences.

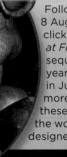

Most game sequels

Following its initial release on 8 Aug 2014 for PC, the point-and-click survival horror *Five Nights at Freddy's* had three full-sized sequels released in less than a year, its fourth iteration arriving in Jul 2015. Making this feat even more impressive was the fact that these creepy indie romps were the work of just one man – games designer Scott Cawthon (USA).

Largest collection of *Silent Hill* memorabilia

Since kick-starting her collection in 1999, Whitney Chavis (USA) has amassed 342 different items of memorabilia from Konami's seminal survival horror series *Silent Hill*. The hoard includes posters, figures, dolls and movie props.

Most "cash" collected in *Dying Light*

As of 1 Mar 2016, US gamer "NYPD1993" had amassed $6,322,292 on the Xbox One version of Techland's open-world zombie game. Meanwhile, Italy's "APOGEUS12" achieved the **most kills in Dying Light (console)**, notching up a zombie body count of 212,449 by the same date.

Fastest "Nightmare" completion of *Alien: Isolation*

German gamer "Metzix" finished the PC version of Sega's sci-fi chiller *Alien: Isolation* (2014) in just 2 hr 41 min 38.89 sec (with loads), a feat ranked at Speedrun.com on 6 Feb 2016. "I'm happy and unhappy at the same time," he said of his record-breaking run, complaining that an android's head had become "invisible".

6

Videogame appearances for the iconic *Alone in the Dark* investigator Edward Carnby.

47

Unique death animations for poor Leon S Kennedy in the eerie, Spain-set classic *Resident Evil 4* (Capcom, 2005).

The panned Atari 2600 movie spin-off *The Texas Chainsaw Massacre* (Wizard Games, 1983) featured the first playable videogame villain in Leatherface.

FACT!

Most expensive videogame package

Techland released a collector's "Spotlight Edition" of *Dying Light: The Following* (2016) through UK retailer GAME for $10 m in Feb 2016. The special, one-bundle-only package offered a supporting role in a proposed *Dying Light* film, acting lessons, stuntman training, an off-road driving course, first-class flights and accommodation, the chance to voice a game character, and, finally, four signed copies of the game itself.

Most critically panned dialogue in a videogame

The *Resident Evil* (1996) line "Here's a lockpick. It might be handy if you, the master of unlocking, take it with you" has appeared in at least 10 "worst dialogue" features, lists and polls, including those published by *Electronic Gaming Monthly*, IGN and Audio Atrocities. So infamous and ironically revered is *Resident Evil*'s original dialogue that in Oct 2015 a modder restored the game's original words to its 2015 remake.

Fastest completion of *SOMA*

Gamer "Sychotixx" (USA) finished *SOMA* (Frictional Games) – one of 2015's most acclaimed horror titles – in just 1 hr 1 min 12 sec (without loads) on 8 Nov 2015.

JILL VALENTINE
RESIDENT EVIL

Videogame debut	1996
Year of birth	1974
Nationality	USA
Skills	Firearms, lockpicking, bombs
Enemies	Umbrella Corp & "zombies"

Longest script for a graphic adventure game
Screenwriters Graham Reznick and Larry Fessenden (both USA) wrote 1,000 pages of dialogue for *Until Dawn* (2015), reduced from an initial 10,000-page outline. The script's epic length was in part owing to the game's extended development period. It was originally announced as an action title back in 2012.

Most scripted jump-scares in a graphic adventure

PS4 chiller *Until Dawn* (Supermassive, 2015) features a nerve-shredding 86 scripted jump-scares, with around 35 in a single play-through. The game's frights include books flying off shelves and traps springing shut. Such is the game's propensity for jolts that some 400 video compilations had been made by YouTubers within one month of its release. Shown here is Ashley, one of eight protagonists in the game. She is played by US actress Galadriel Stineman.

FIVE NIGHTS AT FREDDY'S IS ONE OF THE MOST POPULAR VIDEOGAMES ON YOUTUBE, WITH MANY FAN-MADE VIDEOS TO ITS NAME. THE TRIBUTE SONG "FIVE NIGHTS AT FREDDY'S 1 SONG – THE LIVING TOMBSTONE" HAD BEEN VIEWED 68,908,333 TIMES AS OF 9 MAR 2016.

BATMAN COSPLAY

Cosplayer Julian Checkley (UK, pictured) made a huge splash on the gaming festival circuit by building – and wearing – a Batman suit based on that in *Arkham Origins* (Warner Bros., 2013). A special FX master by trade, Checkley spent three months in his studio in Ireland loading up his mega-creation with 23 working gadgets – the **most functioning gadgets on a cosplay suit.** "I was wracking my brain trying to devise gadgets that not only looked fun but would also have great visual appeal," he said. Some of Julian's gizmos are shown below.

NBC-rated (nuclear, bacterial, chemical) bat-respirator: fits into cowl

Gauntlet video screen: relays images and information to Batman

Bat-comms: a multi-channel and multi-frequency two-way radio

Gauntlet-mounted, four-barrel fireball shooter: fires at 4–5 m (13–16 ft)

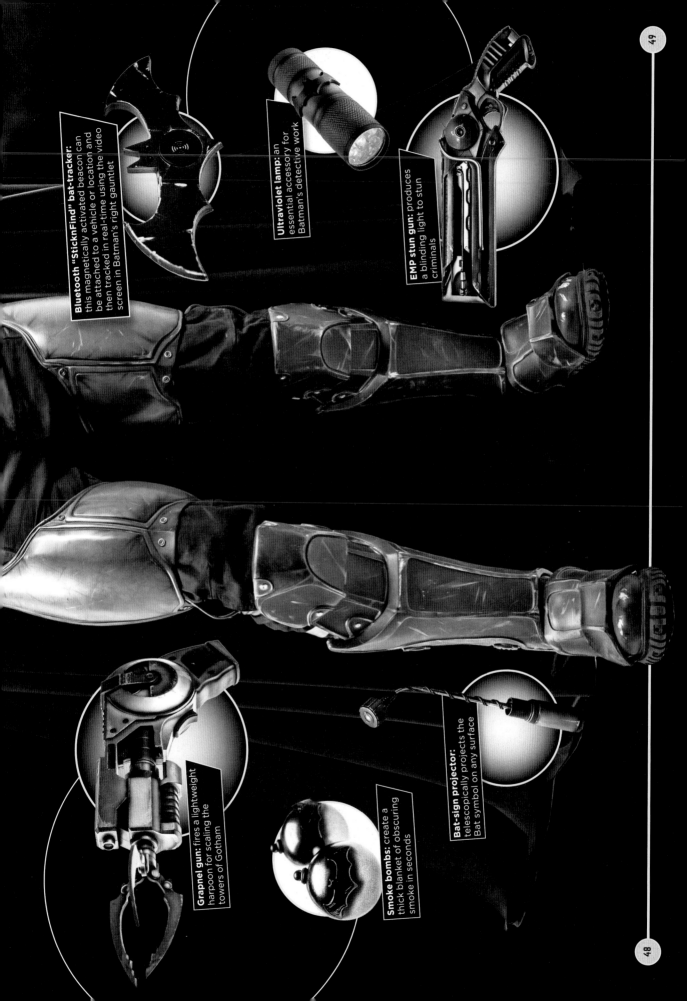

Bluetooth "SticknFind" bat-tracker: this magnetically activated beacon can be attached to a vehicle or location and then tracked in real-time using the video screen in Batman's right gauntlet

Ultraviolet lamp: an essential accessory for Batman's detective work

EMP stun gun: produces a blinding light to stun criminals

Grapnel gun: fires a lightweight harpoon for scaling the towers of Gotham

Smoke bombs: create a thick blanket of obscuring smoke in seconds

Bat-sign projector: telescopically projects the Bat symbol on any surface

Truly great games never grow old. Retro platformers, vintage puzzlers and arcade icons are as popular as ever, with new generations now discovering them on the move.

⌄ Largest game ported to the Sinclair ZX81

Released in 1983, Cinematronics' technical marvel. Using state-of-the-art (and incredibly expensive) LaserDisc technology, it was able to display the action not only in colour, but also with smooth movie-like animation. Back then, ordinary gamers were plugging away on machines such as the Sinclair ZX81, which couldn't possibly run such a beautiful game... or could it?

On 30 Apr 2015, programmer Jim Bagley (UK) managed, with the aid of add-on hardware and cunning coding, to get the game running on his ZX81. His port clocked in at 15,824,610 bytes (15 MB) on a system where most games were less than 16,384 bytes (16 KB).

Q&A with Jim Bagley

What made you port *Dragon's Lair*?
People said this couldn't be done, which made it a challenge.

Why couldn't it be done before?
The ZX81 had no way of loading a game as big as *Dragon's Lair*. It loaded its programs from audio tapes. They could theoretically hold about 120 KB of data, but in practice the ZX81's tiny amount of RAM – no more than 16 KB – meant the system struggled with anything that was more than a few kilobytes in size.

How did you make it work?
I used an expansion module called ZXpand that gives the machine 32 KB of RAM and lets it load files from an SD card (which gave me enough storage space for *Dragon's Lair*). Even with these expansions it was a real challenge getting the game to work: I ended up having to write my own custom video converter for the ZX81.

Dragon's Lair was a unique experiment in interactive story-telling – part game, part movie. Gameplay was limited to timed button presses, which triggered different animations (drawn by former Disney animator Don Bluth) to advance the story of Dirk the Daring (below) and his quest to rescue Princess Daphne from the dragon Singe. To adapt this game for the ZX81, Jim Bagley had to first convert the video from colour to black-and-white, then reduce the resolution from 720 x 480 pixels to 128 x 96.

PLATFORM GAMES

Since *Mario Bros.* debuted in 1983 and fully introduced pudgy plumber Mario, platformers have been gaming staples. Now independent hits such as *Spelunky* are carrying the torch.

THE SPELUNKER

SPELUNKY

Attack moves	**Whipping, jumping**
Basic gear	**Ropes, bombs**
Likes	**Gold, damsels in distress**
Dislikes	**Bats, yetis, ghosts**
Nicknames	**Iowa Jack, Indie, Derek**

Longest-running comic

Archie Comics' *Sonic the Hedgehog* debuted in Jul 1993 and had notched up 279 issues by Mar 2016. Charting battles against bad guys such as Doctor Eggman, the comic led to spin-offs *Knuckles the Echidna* (1997–2000) and *Sonic Universe* (2009–present).

10 YEARS OF GAMER'S

Playing Atari's cancelled ...arfield (1983), US gamer Tom Duncan ea...ed an astonishing 23,418,862,404,272,676,8...4 points – verified on 7 Jul 2008 as the highe... game score ever.

Fastest completion of *Ori and the Blind Forest*

On 7 Feb 2016, Swiss gamer "Ikewolf" braved dark forests and ancient dangers to finish Moon Studios' 2015 fantasy adventure in 23 min 14 sec.

The game is also the **most critically acclaimed indie game on Xbox One**, with a GameRankings score of 88.52%.

197

Number of unique weapons in the *Ratchet & Clank* series as of 17 Feb 2016 (not counting upgrades and mods).

Longest-running fan convention for a videogame character

The UK's "Summer of Sonic" became, in 2008, the first official fan convention to celebrate Sega's icon. Repeated for the next five years, it helped spawn the "Sonic Boom" event in the USA. In 2013, tickets moved faster than Sonic himself, reportedly selling out in just 15 sec.

Fastest single-segment completion of *Super Meat Boy*

Ultra-hard indie *Super Meat Boy* (Team Meat, 2010) was a hit on PC and consoles. On 1 Jan 2015, "Vorpal" (USA) raced through the PC version in just 17 min 43 sec.

First commercial game developed with an indigenous culture

Upper One's atmospheric *Never Alone* (2014) was a collaboration with the Alaskan non-profit organization Cook Inlet Tribal Council. The game follows Iñupiat girl Nuna and her arctic fox through Alaskan folk stories.

Seminal platformers *Donkey Kong* (1981) and *Mario Bros.* (1983) were both designed by the same man: Shigeru Miyamoto. In a 2009 survey of 9,000 game developers, 3,000 people hailed him as their "ultimate development hero".

FACT!

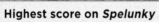

Highest score on *Spelunky*

Jamie "Kinnijup" White (USA) hit $3,404,400 in 5 hr 30 min on 10 Oct 2015. "Never anticipated that people would use the ball and chain to mine out entire levels," creator Derek Yu tweeted.

The **fastest any% completion** is by "Spelunky God", who used the perilous teleporter to finish in 1 min 41 sec on 16 Aug 2015.

18

Playable cameos from other games in *Super Meat Boy* (2010) – the **most crossover characters in a platform game.**

Shortest game release

The Great Giana Sisters (1987, above left) was on sale for one week before publisher Rainbow Arts withdrew it, owing to its resemblance to Nintendo's *Super Mario Bros.* (1985, above right). The game spread and won fans via illegal copies, but original versions remain rare.

Fastest marathon runner dressed as a videogame character

Neil Light (UK) finished the London Marathon in 3 hr 9 min 28 sec on 26 Apr 2015 as Sonic the Hedgehog. Promising to run as fast as Sonic himself, Neil smashed the record set by Dan McCormack and Nash Pradhan (both UK), who finished the 2012 London Marathon in 3 hr 29 min 41 sec dressed as the blue blur's rivals Mario and Luigi.

Most cutscenes in a platform game
Jak II: Renegade (Sony, 2003) can lay claim to 131 cutscenes (non-interactive sections that break up the gameplay). With 51 in the first act alone, they total nearly 1 hr 40 min. *Jak and Daxter* games are known for their involved stories and funny dialogue, more in keeping with an RPG or action-adventure game than a platformer.

Fastest any% completion of *Shovel Knight*

Indie hit *Shovel Knight* is a 2D side-scrolling platformer starring a spade-wielding warrior and featuring gameplay heavily influenced by the 1980s golden age of the NES. On 27 Jan 2016, Swedish gamer "Smaugy" raced through the game in just 44 min 32 sec.

Smaugy also set the record for the **fastest 100% completion of *Shovel Knight***: a time of 1 hr 7 min 29 sec, achieved on 22 Dec 2015.

SUPER MARIO BROS.

Publisher: Nintendo
Debut: 1983
Games: 180+

Developer: Nintendo
Series sales: 324.82 million
Rivals: *Ratchet & Clank, Sonic*

The **most prolific video game character** ... red in 202 titles, ... including cameos (but ... and rereleases), as of Mar 2016.

Largest gathering of people dressed as Mario

A total of 250 fans dressed as the moustachioed plumber convened at an event organized by the Red Star Macalline Furniture Mall in Chifeng City, China, on 18 Aug 2010. The many folks dressed as Luigi (Mario's slimmer brother) didn't count towards the final total.

Best-selling gaming character

Created in 1981 by Shigeru Miyamoto (JPN, left), Mario had been responsible for 555.35 m sales as of 16 Feb 2016, according to VGChartz. The total includes Mario's core platformers, party games and sports spin-offs.

Most critically acclaimed videogame

Set in the not-so-dark recesses of space, the Wii's *Super Mario Galaxy* (2007) carries a record-breaking GameRankings score of 97.64% from 78 reviews. This also makes it the **most critically acclaimed platformer**. "You haven't played anything like *Galaxy*," enthused *Nintendo Life*.

Largest collection of *Super Mario* memorabilia

Verified in Tokyo, Japan, on 15 Jul 2010, the collection of official *Super Mario* goodies owned by Mitsugu Kikai (JPN) features 5,441 individual items. Included in the super-fan's colourful haul are posters, stationery and "cuddly" toys of such series stalwarts as Mario, Luigi, Yoshi, Princess Peach and Toad.

31

Different types of "Boo" (enemy ghosts) across the Mario series, from Atomic Boo to Sleepy Boo.

On 4 Aug 2015, US *Mario* super-fan "pannenkoek2012" offered a $1,000 (£640) bounty for anyone able to recreate and record a mystery glitch in the Tick Tock Clock stage of *Super Mario 64* (1996).

FACT!

21

Number of bosses to defeat in the 2010 sequel *Super Mario Galaxy 2*. The baddies include Whomp King and Cobblegut.

Highest score on *Nintendo Campus Challenge 1991*

Chris Bidwell (USA) recorded a score of 11,765,000 in the super-rare NES game *Nintendo Campus Challenge 1991*, as verified by Twin Galaxies on 26 Sep 2015. *Nintendo Campus Challenge 1991* was a competition cartridge containing three minigames of *Super Mario Bros. 3*, *Pin*Bot* and *Dr. Mario* (see below). Interestingly, Nintendo fan Chris was also a finalist at the Nintendo World Championships at E3 2015.

Rarest *Super Mario* game

In 1991, Nintendo toured US campuses with *Nintendo Campus Challenge*. After this national tournament, all the cartridges were destroyed save one, which was retained by a Nintendo employee and sold to US collector Rob Walters at a 2006 New York garage sale. In 2009, the game was resold on eBay for $20,100 (£12,350).

Fastest completion of *Super Mario Galaxy 2*

Finnish gamer "Vallu" speed-ran *Super Mario Galaxy 2* (2010) on the Wii on 26 Feb 2016, defeating its princess-pilfering antagonist Bowser in just 3 hr 1 min 57 sec.

WARIO

MARIO SERIES

Debut	1992
Occupation	Antagonist
Special traits	Evil grin, scary laugh
Ambitions	To own a castle
appearances	80+

Longest time to collect a coin in a *Mario* game
In 2002, gamers discovered a mystery coin in *Super Mario 64*, located beneath the ground in the Tiny-Huge Island course. In Jun 2014, some 18 years after the game's Jun 1996 release, "pannenkoek2012" (USA) used tool assistance to collect "The Impossible Coin" before anyone else.

Fastest completion of *Super Mario Bros.*

On 14 Jan 2016, Twitch user "darbian", aka Brad M (USA), blasted through the 1985 NES mega-classic *Super Mario Bros.* in 4 min 57.427 sec. The run pipped his own previous record of 4 min 57.627 sec, which he'd set some months earlier. Speaking via his YouTube channel, "darbian" estimates that the fastest time a human can complete the game (without tools) is 4 min 57 sec exactly.

RETRO GAMES

Decades after their first release, retro arcade classics such as *Donkey Kong* and *PAC-Man* retain legions of fans and provoke fierce and long-lasting rivalries between players.

Rarest game
It is believed that there is only one copy in existence of *Gamma-Attack* (Gammation, 1983) for the Atari 2600. Recent valuations of this ultra-rare sci-fi shooter have placed it at $20,000–$50,000 (£13,000–£32,000).

Largest human PAC-Man
On 21 May 2015, a total of 351 participants gathered in front of the Tokyo Tower in Minato, Tokyo, Japan, to form a giant PAC-Man in an event organized by Sony Pictures Entertainment Japan. Each participant had to dress in bright yellow and form the iconic open-mouthed shape of Namco's original character from 1980.

Highest score recorded in an arcade game
As verified on 27 Feb 2008 by Twin Galaxies, gamer Rodrigo Lopes (BRA) recorded an incredible score of 13,617,120,714,066,509,824 points playing *Giga Wing 2* (2000), a conversion of an arcade shooter for the Sega Dreamcast.

Shortest development for a film tie-in
Widely derided as one of the worst games ever made, Atari's 1982 film tie-in *E.T. the Extra-Terrestrial* had to be programmed in just five weeks in order to release the game in time for the Christmas market.

Most awards won by a game documentary
Directed by Seth Gordon, *The King of Kong: A Fistful of Quarters* (2007) followed rivals Billy Mitchell and Steve Wiebe (both USA) as they attempted to set *Donkey Kong*'s highest all-time score. The film won 11 "Best Documentary" awards and gained nominations at six other ceremonies.

10 YEARS OF GAMER'S

On 15 Jan 1984, Tim McVey (USA) became the **first person to score one billion points in a game**. He used just one quarter during his 44-hr 45-min stint playing *Nibbler*.

581

Arcade games at Weirs Beach, New Hampshire, USA – making this the **largest video arcade**, as of 12 Jan 2016.

*Q*Bert* (1982) is a cube-hopping arcade classic. But would it have been as successful had it been released under its development title *Snots and Boogers*?

FACT!

255

Total extra lives *Asteroids* players can collect before the number of icons shown on screen will slow down the game.

Highest score on *Space Invaders* achieved by mind control
In 2006, scientists at Washington University in St Louis, USA, devised a hands-free system of playing the classic game using brain power alone. An (ECoG) grid was attached to a teenager's brain and linked to specially adapted Atari software. Controlling the on-screen cursor by imagining the movements in his head, the boy reached the third screen of the game and amassed 5,000 points in the process.

Largest *Space Invaders* artwork
Dutch duo Leon Keer and Remko van Schaik created an anamorphic street painting themed on *Space Invaders*. The artwork measured 150 m² (1,614 sq ft) and was made for the "Art on Science Project" at the EPFL campus in Lausanne, Switzerland, on 17 Mar 2014.

PAC-MAN

PAC-MAN

Previous name	Puck-Man
Residence	Mazes
Likes	Pac-dots, mazes
Dislikes	Ghosts
Pets	Chomp-Chomp the dog

Largest *PAC-Man* game
With a staggering total of 4,014,144,000 pixels across 62,721 mazes, *The World's Biggest PAC-Man* lives up to its name. Developed by Australia's Soap Creative agency, it went live on 12 Apr 2011.
Measured on 7 Jan 2015, the **largest life-sized PAC-Man maze** was 580.86 m² (6,252 sq ft). It was built by Anheuser-Busch, Mosaic, Energy BBDO, and Bandai Namco Games America (all USA).

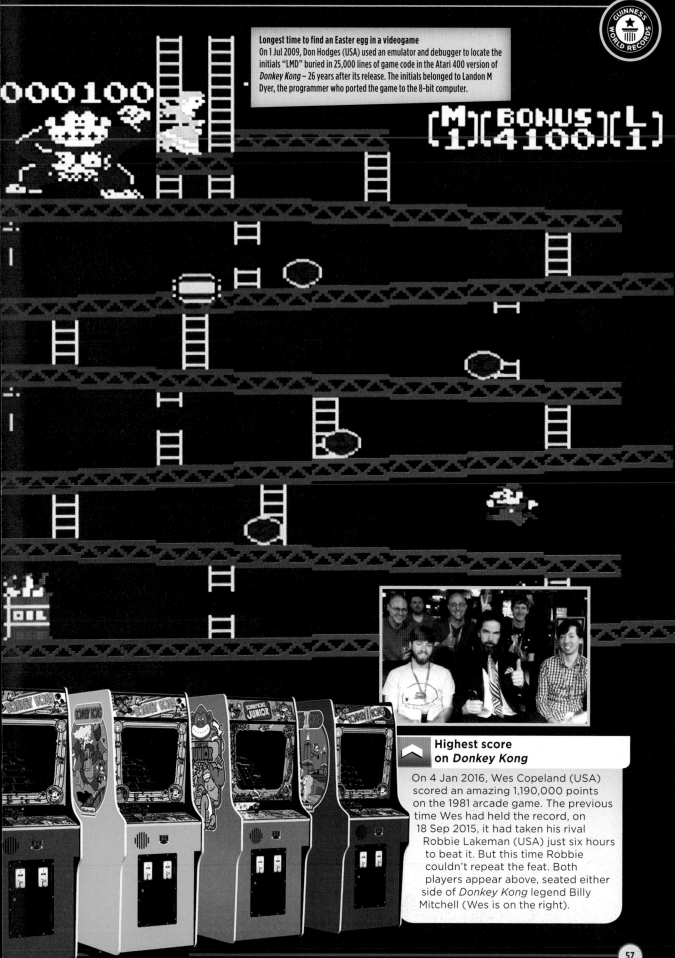

000100

[M] [BONUS] [L]
[1] [4100] [1]

Longest time to find an Easter egg in a videogame
On 1 Jul 2009, Don Hodges (USA) used an emulator and debugger to locate the initials "LMD" buried in 25,000 lines of game code in the Atari 400 version of *Donkey Kong* – 26 years after its release. The initials belonged to Landon M Dyer, the programmer who ported the game to the 8-bit computer.

Highest score on *Donkey Kong*

On 4 Jan 2016, Wes Copeland (USA) scored an amazing 1,190,000 points on the 1981 arcade game. The previous time Wes had held the record, on 18 Sep 2015, it had taken his rival Robbie Lakeman (USA) just six hours to beat it. But this time Robbie couldn't repeat the feat. Both players appear above, seated either side of *Donkey Kong* legend Billy Mitchell (Wes is on the right).

PUZZLE GAMES

From *Lemmings* to *Limbo*, some of the most addictive and accessible games have been puzzlers. Simple concepts meld with intelligent design, ensuring the genre has wide appeal.

Fastest completion of *The Talos Principle* (all Sigils)

An innovative game with a philosophical twist, *The Talos Principle* (Devolver Digital, 2014) is a big hit with speedrunners. On 17 Jan 2016, Twitch user "Azorae" (USA) acquired every Sigil on the PC version in 51 min 57 sec. On the same day, Azorae achieved the Messenger ending in exactly 13 min.

Largest architectural videogame display

A skyscraping version of Alexey Pajitnov's iconic 1984 title *Tetris* was played on the 29-storey Cira Centre in Philadelphia, USA, on 5 Apr 2014. Developed by game designer Professor Frank J Lee (USA), it measured 11,111.2 m² (119,600 sq ft) – more than 1.5 times bigger than a soccer pitch.

Most theme parks based on a videogame

As of Mar 2016, there were 11 active *Angry Birds* fun parks. Two can be found in the UK, while China, Malaysia, Russia and Spain each have one. The rest are located in Finland (home of the game's creator Rovio), with the biggest situated at the Särkänniemi adventure park. *Angry Birds* began life as a mobile puzzler in 2009 but has since grown into a huge entertainment franchise, with an animated movie.

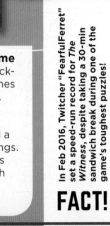

Most acclaimed iOS videogame

Utilizing simple controls with pick-up-and-play design, puzzle games are ideal for hand-held formats. As of 19 Feb 2016, the highest-rated iOS game was *Monument Valley* (ustwo, 2014), which held a score of 90.05% at GameRankings. The arty puzzler calls on players to navigate Princess Ida through a world of optical illusions and fiendish architecture.

10 YEARS OF GAMER'S

Popularized by a 198... Game Boy bundle, *Tetris* has the **most varia**... of a videogame. As of 18 Mar 2015, some ... official versions were recognized by ... e Tetris Company.

650

Approximate number of puzzles in Jonathan Blow's *The Witness* (2016). Its creator said they would take 80 hr to solve.

Largest game of *Minesweeper*

Using 24 linked HD TVs to create a playing board of 718 x 262 tiles, video company CineMassive (USA) unveiled an epic game of *Minesweeper* on 10 Aug 2015. Their creation – dubbed *Minesweeper Super Challenge* – featured 188,116 tiles infested with 38,799 mines.

Fastest completion of *Kula World*

On 16 Jul 2015, "adeyblue" (UK) rolled his beach ball through *Kula World* (Game Design Sweden AB, 1998) in 38 min 37 sec, as verified by SpeedDemosArchive. A cult puzzle game, *Kula World* was originally released for PlayStation.

Fastest completion of *World of Goo*

Nigel "ridd3r" Martin (UK) completed 2D Boy's sticky, physics-based puzzler *World of Goo* (2008) in 53 min 41 sec. His single-segment run was verified by SpeedDemosArchive on 7 Sep 2009.

In Feb 2016, Twitcher "FearfulFerret" set a speed-run record for *The Witness*, despite taking a 30-min sandwich break during one of the game's toughest puzzles!

FACT!

Most played mobile game (current)
According to figures from SuperData, the mobile version of *Candy Crush Saga* was the most played mobile videogame of 2015. Activision's puzzler enjoyed an average of 182,892,377 monthly active users (MAU) – that's more people than the current population of Russia.

SAGA

First gamer in space
In 1993, Russian cosmonaut Aleksandr A Serebrov (1944–2013) became the first gamer in space when he played Nintendo's 1989 version of *Tetris* during a trip to the *MIR* space station. "During flight, in rare minutes of leisure, I enjoyed playing Game Boy," he confessed in an autographed note. In total, both he and his Game Boy spent 196 days in space. The hand-held console and the game were auctioned by Bonhams in 2011.

Largest acquisition of a game studio

On 2 Nov 2015, Activision Blizzard announced that it was buying King Digital Entertainment – creator of *Candy Crush Saga* (2012) – for $5.9 bn (£3.8 bn). The deal, completed on 23 Feb 2016, was heralded by a visit to the New York Stock Exchange by *Candy Crush*-styled mascots (above left). The acquisition was more than double the sum of $2.5 bn (£1.65 bn) that Microsoft paid for *Minecraft* developer Mojang one year earlier.

BLINDFOLDED SPEED-RUNS

For some players, completing a game is just the beginning. Can it be done again? How quickly can you do it? How difficult can you make it? Speed-runs can take different forms – any%, 100%, single-segment – but *blindfolded* speed-runs are the quirkiest and most demanding challenge of all. They require unbelievable timing, intense concentration, and an astonishing knowledge of the game.

Perhaps because of their difficulty, blindfolded runs are proving very popular on Twitch and YouTube. Charity gaming marathons such as Awesome Games Done Quick (AGDQ) provide a great platform for attempts – although audience cheers can present a problem for blindfolded speed-runners desperately listening out for audio cues...

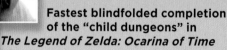

Q&A with Jacob Criminski, aka "Shenanagans"

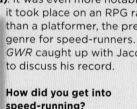

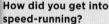

Taking part in a race against "Keizaron" at the Summer Games Done Quick event on 1 Aug 2015, "Shenanagans" (USA, inset left) romped to the end of the 1996 Game Boy title in 25 min 53 sec – the **fastest blindfolded completion of *Pokémon Blue* (glitched)**. It was even more notable as it took place on an RPG rather than a platformer, the preferred genre for speed-runners. *GWR* caught up with Jacob to discuss his record.

How did you get into speed-running?
It was completely on a whim. Myself and another runner, "eddaket", wanted to race something but couldn't think of anything fun to race. We decided to try the first blindfolded *Pokémon Blue* "No Save Corruption" race. With zero practice, it took us around 30–40 min.

How much training did you have for the record-breaking *Pokémon Blue* completion?
Surprisingly, not very much. I've played through this game hundreds of thousands of times so I have most of it memorized. After

attempting it with the blindfold three-to-four times I was consistently getting times of 23–28 min.

How were you able to navigate the game?
Audio cues play a massive role. We need exactly 16 Tackles and 36 Growls remaining when we leave the forest to do a major glitch. We use audio cues to track our Tackle and Growl counts during battles. Audio cues also helped us figure out our locations on the map, as a sound plays when you bonk into a wall.

What was the biggest challenge?
Keeping track of everything; knowing what your health, power points, items and location are can be fairly overwhelming. The underflow menu at the end is also a pretty difficult menu, as you can randomly get different items causing different effects.

Any tips for others wanting to attempt a game blindfolded?
Practise! Start out by mastering the game normally. Learning audio cues can be very useful when starting out. Don't get too frustrated. It can be really hard at first, but after some practice you will progress.

Fastest blindfolded completion of the "child dungeons" in *The Legend of Zelda: Ocarina of Time*

On 10 Jan 2015, "Runnerguy2489" (USA) successfully navigated the first three dungeons of the N64 classic in 1 hr 26 min 56 sec while blindfolded. The feat was achieved in front of a live audience as part of the 2015 AGDQ event. "Runnerguy2489" used glitches, sound cues, side-hops, backflips and his familiarity with the levels to complete the challenge.

...st blindfolded ...letion of "The ...t" in *Super Meat Boy*

...ng the spinning sawblades of the fiendish ...ndie platformer requires flawless timing ...rmal runs. But "MattyIce3131" (USA) was ...o complete the Forest levels blindfolded in ...min 2 sec on 24 Jun 2014, at the Summer ...s Done Quick event.

Fastest blindfolded completion of *Super Mario World*

On 23 Jun 2015, crack *SMW* speed-runner "PangaeaPanga", aka Alex Tan (USA, right), completed the game blindfolded in an incredible 23 min 14 sec. He had begun practising his attempt only eight days earlier, mapping out the best route before memorizing musical cues to know when to jump and fire. "This run features three deaths, getting lost briefly in Starworld, baby Yoshi eating the goal tape, and entertaining spectators to keep the hype up for when I was too concentrated on the run," he said.

Fastest blindfolded completion of WVBA Championship in *Mike Tyson's Punch-Out!!*

At the 2014 AGDQ event on 10 Jan, "Sinister1" (USA, left) managed to punch his way to the title in the 1987 NES boxing classic in a time of 28 min 21 sec. His impressive victories included a super-speedy pummelling of Von Kaiser in 38 sec. Eventually, "Sinister1" met his match when he fought the game's final boss – Mike Tyson himself. Despite "Sinister1" landing several blows on the eponymous ring titan, Tyson prevailed.

UGC GAMES

The craving for "user-generated content" (UGC) games has exploded in recent years. Creative sandbox titles and level editors let us build worlds, make games and even ride pigs!

Most views for a dedicated *Minecraft* video channel

*Minecraft*er DanTDM (aka Daniel Middleton, UK) started his YouTube channel "TheDiamondMinecart" as a part-time hobby while studying at university. Since its launch on 14 Jul 2012, his fun-infused channel had accrued 6,284,997,560 views from 1,811 videos, as of 24 Mar 2016. Despite the popularity of fellow YouTube megastars such as "stampylonghead", "Sky Does Minecraft" and "CaptainSparklez", DanTDM has been watched more than any other specialist *Minecraft* host.

UGC ROUND-UP

Level editors such as *Super Mario Maker* and *LittleBigPlanet* may offer slick platforming action, but their biggest reward comes from letting you create the games yourself.

Most starred *Super Mario Maker* UGC creator

As of 21 Mar 2016, a Japanese gamer known as "Chagama" had netted 1,194,891 stars from fellow *Super Mario Maker* players. The course-making maestro designed 45 levels in the Wii U game including "Anime Medley-Automatic" and "Pokémon N Final Battle".

The **most shared *Super Mario Maker* level** is "Ice Cap Cave" by "ƒ¢ıٮQuøte" (USA), which had been shared 262 times.

Most "world records" in *Super Mario Maker*

"World records" in *Super Mario Maker* refers to the number of fastest clear times that a player has achieved when attempting the community's user-created levels. As of 21 Mar 2016, "Izumi" (JPN) held a lofty 2,049 world records in the game.

First player to publish a level on *LittleBigPlanet*

Molecule's *LittleBigPlanet* (2008) is awarded to players once they've made and published their own level. According to PSNprofiles, "RiotPelaaja" (USA) won this UGC accolade on 20 Sep 2008 – more than a month before the game's commercial release.

Longest marathon on *LittleBigPlanet 2*

Gamers David Dino, Lauren Guiliano and Sean Crowley (all USA) played the 2011 platformer/game-maker for 50 hr 1 min on 17–19 Jan 2011. This mammoth session took place in the Sony Style PlayStation Lounge in New York City, USA.

Most hearted *LittleBigPlanet* level
As of 22 Mar 2016, "Little Dead Space" (left) by DarknessBear had won 317,000 hearts since being published in Nov 2008 – that's more than any user-made level across all three *LBP* games. The level riffed on EA's space horror *Dead Space*, which was released in the same year.

FACT! *Minecraft*'s influence continues to spread far and wide. In Jan 2016, Square Enix released *Dragon Quest Builders*, a sandbox spin-off set in the JRPG's fictional world of Alefgard.

8.9 MILLION

Number of bricks in the "LEGO Worlds Island" level from *LEGO® Worlds* – the most LEGO bricks in a single videogame level.

Most viewed *LEGO Worlds* fan video

Released for Steam early access in Jun 2015, LEGO's *Minecraft* challenger *LEGO Worlds* (TT Games, 2016) attracted the interest of a number of star *Minecraft* YouTubers. As of 2 Mar 2016, the most watched *LEGO Worlds* fan video was "Lego Worlds - Cake Castle (1)" by "stampylonghead" (UK), which had been viewed 4,500,477 times since it was uploaded on 2 Jun 2015.

Most starred course on *Super Mario Maker*

Super Mario Maker invites players to design their own platform levels and then share them with fellow *Mario* fans to tackle and judge. As of 21 Mar 2016, the user-generated level "Automatic Mario Kart" by Japanese gamer "Sasae Tamae" had won 169,742 stars – or likes – from fellow players.

The **fastest completion of "Automatic Mario Kart"** (above) was 24.897 sec, achieved by "Danger" (USA), according to the official site SuperMarioMakerBookmark.nintendo.net.

SACKBOY
LITTLEBIGPLANET

Size	Small!
Species	Sackperson
Skills	Grabbing, climbing, telekinesis
Number of costumes	100+
Game appearances	14

◀ Most hearted *LittleBigPlanet 3* adventure

Inspired by the creepy indie series *Five Nights at Freddy's*, the user-made *LittleBigPlanet 3* adventure "FNAF1 | FNAF2 | FNAF3" (above) by "Mooserick" had won 8,054 "hearts" from *LBP3* fans, as of 22 Mar 2016. "HOLY MOLY!!!! It's scary but cool," observed one reviewer. The Adventure Crater is a new area for *LBP3* (Sony, 2014) that allows players to craft larger creations consisting of up to 15 linked levels.

204,755 Number of mischievous pink rabbits that HyperLiger deployed in a *Mazecraft* maze (above left). The developer's maze-building app was released in Aug 2015.

10 YEARS OF *GAMER'S*

Between 2009 and 2012, Sony's *LittleBigPlanet* series scooped four game BAFTAs for three of its titles – the **most BAFTA wins for a platform series**.

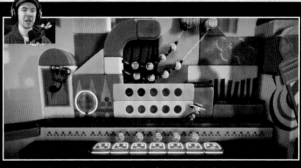

Most viewed *Terraria* video

Re-Logic's 2D game *Terraria* is often compared to *Minecraft* because, like Mojang's blocky behemoth, players can use it to build and create things. A video of *Minecraft* YouTuber "stampylonghead" (UK) playing *Terraria* for the first time had been viewed 6,327,989 times as of 20 Apr 2016. Both *Terraria* and *Minecraft* were first released in 2011.

Most viewed level review for *LittleBigPlanet*

While players can browse the official *LBP* site to find new user-made content, many gamers turn to YouTube for recommendations. As of 20 Apr 2016, the video "JACKSEPTICEYE LEVELS | Little Big Planet 3 #5" had been viewed 3,327,899 times. In it, the Irish YouTuber "jacksepticeye" (top left) tackles fan-made *LBP3* levels that were designed in his honour.

MINECRAFT

Publisher: Mojang
Debut: 2011
Games: 1 (exc. *Story Mode*)

Devs: Markus "Notch" Persson
Series sales: 22.66 million
Rivals: *LEGO® Worlds, Terraria*

Most watched gaming video

the four-and-a-half-minute "Revenge – A Minecraft Original Music Video", created by "CaptainSparklez", aka Jordan Maron (USA), had been viewed a staggering 160,312,315 times on YouTube as of 21 Feb 2016.

Largest *Minecraft* spacecraft

Featuring more than 5,043,664 blocks, a supersized recreation of the titular starship from the sci-fi series *Battlestar Galactica* by Ragnur Le Barbare (FRA) had been downloaded 21,190 times from the Planet Minecraft website as of 24 Feb 2016. It earned 754 diamonds (likes) in approval.

Farthest distance ridden on a pig in *Minecraft*

Washington-based gamer L J Pegross (USA) hitched a ride on a passing pig and didn't get off until 667 km (414 mi) later! This porcine marathon, uploaded on 25 Feb 2013, beat the previous record by 536 km (333 mi).

First exhibition of real-world art in *Minecraft*

The Tate gallery group's DLC *Tate Worlds* reimagines art as *Minecraft* maps. Launched in Nov 2014, it features Christopher Nevinson's *Soul of the Soulless City* (above), André Derain's *The Pool of London* and Peter Blake's *The Toy Shop*.

Longest journey in *Minecraft*

In Mar 2011, Kurt J Mac (USA, right) began a quest for the Far Lands at the edges of the game's terrain. As his audience grew, he started to raise money for charity, only measuring his distance when he reached fundraising milestones. On 28 Mar 2016 he was 2,723 km (1,692 mi) from Spawn – only 21.78% of the way there!

Full of minigames, roleplays and parodies, Sky Does Minecraft is the most subscribed *Minecraft* YouTube channel, with 11,794,783 fans as of 25 Feb 2016.

A jaw-dropping Microsoft HoloLens version of *Minecraft* was previewed at E3 in Los Angeles, California, USA, on 15 Jun 2015. *The Guardian* played it and observed: "The future of gaming is right in front of your eyes."

FACT!

363

Number of splash texts (phrases selected at random from the game's files) featured on the title screen as of 25 Feb 2016.

Most wood collected in 3 minutes in *Minecraft* (console)

Enkil Fernando Ceron Alvarez (MEX) collected 99 wood blocks at the Legends of Gaming event in London, UK, on 5 Sep 2015.

Minecraft's **tallest staircase built in 1 minute (console)** rises ?? blocks, built first by Alastair "Ali-A" Aiken (UK) on 11 Jun 2015 and then matched by Tristen Geren (USA) on 22 Nov 2015.

Most downloaded *Minecraft* project

Featuring 650 custom skins from the *Minecraft* community, the epic multi-genre challenge map "Diversity 2", by "qmagnet", had been downloaded 1,741,045 times from Curse.com, as of 23 Feb 2016.

Largest original fictional world in *Minecraft*

In Jul 2011, Aerna server users began crafting the mother of all *Minecraft* worlds. By late 2014, the 84-GB fantasy world measured 102,400 x 51,200 blocks. It spanned multiple continents and covered 2,000 sq mi (5,240 km²), with detailed landmarks, sprawling towns and an array of cultures.

Largest real-world place created in *Minecraft* at full scale

The Danish Geodata Agency published a 1:1 scale recreation of Denmark in Apr 2014, using around a terabyte-gobbling 4 trillion blocks. Players could explore the entire 43,000-km² (16,602-sq-mi) country. The project survived sabotage on 7 May 2014, when cyber vandals smuggled in dynamite and blew up a small area.

First working computer built in *Minecraft*

"theinternetftw" built a working 16-bit arithmetic logic unit from powerful redstone. A video of it, uploaded on 28 Sep 2010, earned the approval of "Notch" himself.

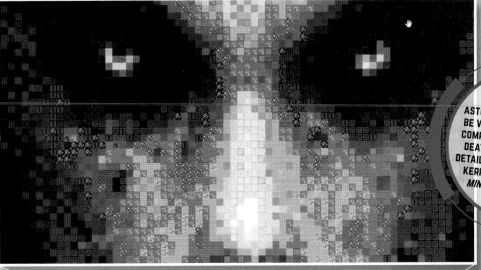

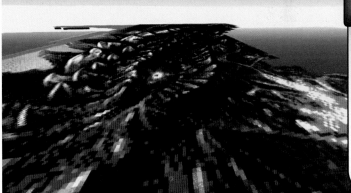

Largest pixel art in *Minecraft*

Created by Swedish gamer "Thorlar Thorlarian", this incredible piece of pixel art took 165 days to build before its completion on 19 Jun 2015. Crafted from 1,128,960 blocks, it depicts *StarCraft*'s Sarah Kerrigan flanked by *World of Warcraft*'s "Dragon Aspect" Deathwing (left) and ruler of Hell, Diablo, from the series of the same name (right). The piece was so large that Thorlar had to use a plug-in to zoom out far enough to see what he was making.

MINECRAFT

The sandbox game that became a commercial juggernaut rumbles on, with users entranced by its building blocks and limitless possibilities. A movie version is now in the works.

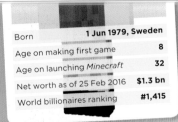

MARKUS "NOTCH" PERSSON

MINECRAFT

Born	1 Jun 1979, Sweden
Age on making first game	8
Age on launching *Minecraft*	32
Net worth as of 25 Feb 2016	$1.3 bn
World billionaires ranking	#1,415

(sidebar, vertical text) **10 YEARS OF *GAMER'S*** ...er 2,622 players on 1 Aug 2011, rendering the game barely playable but securing the record for **most concurrent players in one *Minecraft* world.**

Best-selling PC videogame

According to figures on the Mojang website, *Minecraft* had sold 22,670,361 copies for PC/Mac platforms alone as of 25 Feb 2016, including physical sales and digital downloads. That equates to a creeper-quelling one every 6 sec since the game's release on 18 Nov 2011.

Largest gathering of people dressed as "Steve"

On 12 Sep 2015, 337 "Steve" fans came together at MineVention, hosted by O'Brien Event Management (IRL) in Peterborough, UK. The origin of *Minecraft*'s first controllable player is shrouded in mystery: his nickname "Steve" is an in-joke on his lack of an *actual* name.

Most popular female games YouTuber

A "true geek" who loves to "make people smile", Tiffany "iHasCupquake" Herrera (USA) had 4,396,662 subscribers to her YouTube channel, as of 11 Apr 2016. She specializes in creative and cultural content, with an emphasis on gaming, especially *Minecraft*. She also features "geek baking" and DIY videos.

Most viewed videogame unboxing video

Few concepts baffle outsiders more than "unboxing" videos, in which consumers unpack products to give their reviews. But that hasn't stopped "MINECRAFT Papercraft Overworld Deluxe Set – Unboxing & Review" – uploaded by "EvanTubeHD" on 3 Jan 2014 – attracting 16,566,767 views as of 25 Feb 2016.

6

Disney parks on the MCMagic server, which also houses the **largest real-world theme park recreated in *Minecraft*.**

A Japanese gamer set fire to his room during a *Minecraft* session by playing with a cigarette lighter. A video of the live stream, in Oct 2015, reportedly earned more than 3 million views within 24 hours.

FACT!

10 MILLION

Number of users of the *Minecraft* beta who registered from Dec 2010 to Jul 2011, making it the **most popular videogame beta.**

Longest *Minecraft* marathon

Twitcher and YouTuber Joe Kelly (UK) played *Minecraft* for 35 hr 35 min 35 sec on his PC, on 10–13 Oct 2015. Motivated by his love for the game but using it as an opportunity to raise money for Cancer Research, he beat the 24 hr 10 min of previous record holder Martin Fornleitner (AUT).

Smallest version of *Minecraft*

On 2 Dec 2009, "Notch" revealed a working version of *Minecraft* that took up only 2.52 KB of disk space. Named *Minecraft 4k*, this game was his entry in a contest for games no larger than 4 KB.

Most popular *Minecraft* server network

A block-rocking 34,434 gamers played *Minecraft* concurrently on the Mineplex network on 28 Jan 2015. Mineplex's MMO-style experience is enabled by multiple servers that communicate to stop the game grinding to a halt.

Most widely used videogame in schools

Minecraft is one of the few commercial videogames to be adapted specifically for classrooms. According to TeacherGaming LLC, their version – dubbed *MinecraftEdu* – is used in more than 7,000 schools in at least 40 countries.

At Minecon 2015, eager fans seized the chance to cosplay their favourite *Minecraft* characters, interact with the exhibits, watch live shows on the big screen and meet the staff of Guinness World Records.

01:40 **MINECON** LONDON 2015 01:40

Largest convention for a single videogame

Minecon 2015, held at London's ExCeL (UK) on 4–5 Jul, swiftly sold out its 10,000 tickets, effortlessly surpassing all previous Minecons. It also outdid any other fellow conventions dedicated to one game, including Summer of Sonic and EVE Fanfest – the latter of which recorded 4,000 attendees for *EVE Online*'s 10th anniversary in 2013. Started in 2010, Minecon celebrates all things *Minecraft* with a host of blocky activities.

SUPER MARIO MAKER

Publisher: Nintendo
Debut: 2015
Games: 1 (for Wii U)

Developer: Nintendo
Series sales: 2.88 million
Rivals: *LittleBigPlanet*

Q&A with "PangaeaPanga"

How long have you been into *Mario* games?
Since I was a little kid!

You'd uploaded 25 courses in *Super Mario Maker*, as of 22 Mar 2016. How long do they usually take to design?
Each level takes roughly 4–5 hr to design, with my longest level – "Saved by the Shell" – taking me 24 hr, and the shortest being 2 hr.

What makes your levels so difficult?
It's the precise sequence of inputs that a player needs to make in order to overcome the obstacles that I create, such as shell-jumps or mid-air springboard jumps. If the inputs are done wrong, it almost always results in death.

Your courses aren't just tough, they're also extremely popular. Do you have any tips for designing a fun, challenging level?
I would say focus more on putting in tough tricks and movements rather than spamming enemies or spikes everywhere. Try to find the right balance between fairness and frustration.

How long does it usually take for someone to beat one of your courses?
On average, the first clear of a "Pit of Panga" level occurs around a day after I upload it. However, "P-Break" and "U-Break" did not get cleared by anyone until a week after.

You have a bit of history with super-difficult *Mario* challenges. What can you tell us about that?
I've been making hard *Mario* levels ever since 2008. Prior to *Super Mario Maker*, I was most famous for creating the "Item Abuse" series of three ridiculously hard *Super Mario World* levels. "Item Abuse 3" has consistently been named by players and games journalists as the hardest *Super Mario World* level ever made.

Is your next ambition to make an even more difficult level in *Super Mario Maker*?
Ha, that is top secret!

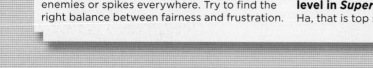

"PIT OF PANGA: P-BREAK" HAD BEEN VIEWED 3,733,701 TIMES ON YOUTUBE AS OF 22 MAR 2016, BUT IT'S NOT THE MOST VIEWED *SMM* VIDEO. THAT ACCOLADE FALLS TO "LOS NIVELES IMPOSIBLES DE MARIO I SUPER MARIO MAKER" BY "ELRUBIUSOMG" (ESP), WITH 10,354,147 VIEWS.

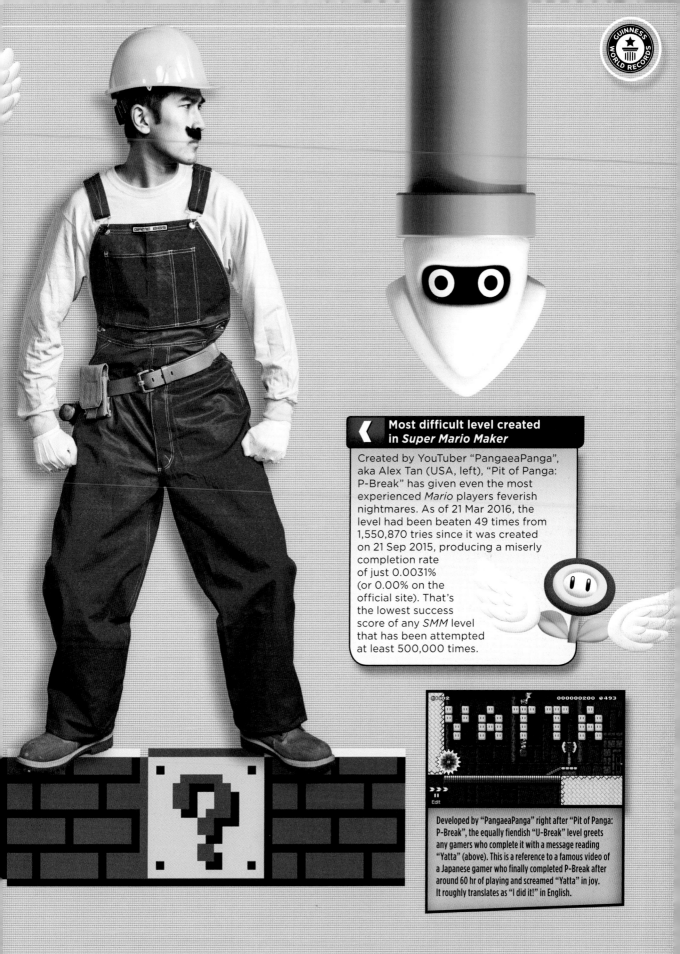

Most difficult level created in *Super Mario Maker*

Created by YouTuber "PangaeaPanga", aka Alex Tan (USA, left), "Pit of Panga: P-Break" has given even the most experienced *Mario* players feverish nightmares. As of 21 Mar 2016, the level had been beaten 49 times from 1,550,870 tries since it was created on 21 Sep 2015, producing a miserly completion rate of just 0.0031% (or 0.00% on the official site). That's the lowest success score of any *SMM* level that has been attempted at least 500,000 times.

Developed by "PangaeaPanga" right after "Pit of Panga: P-Break", the equally fiendish "U-Break" level greets any gamers who complete it with a message reading "Yatta" (above). This is a reference to a famous video of a Japanese gamer who finally completed P-Break after around 60 hr of playing and screamed "Yatta" in joy. It roughly translates as "I did it!" in English.

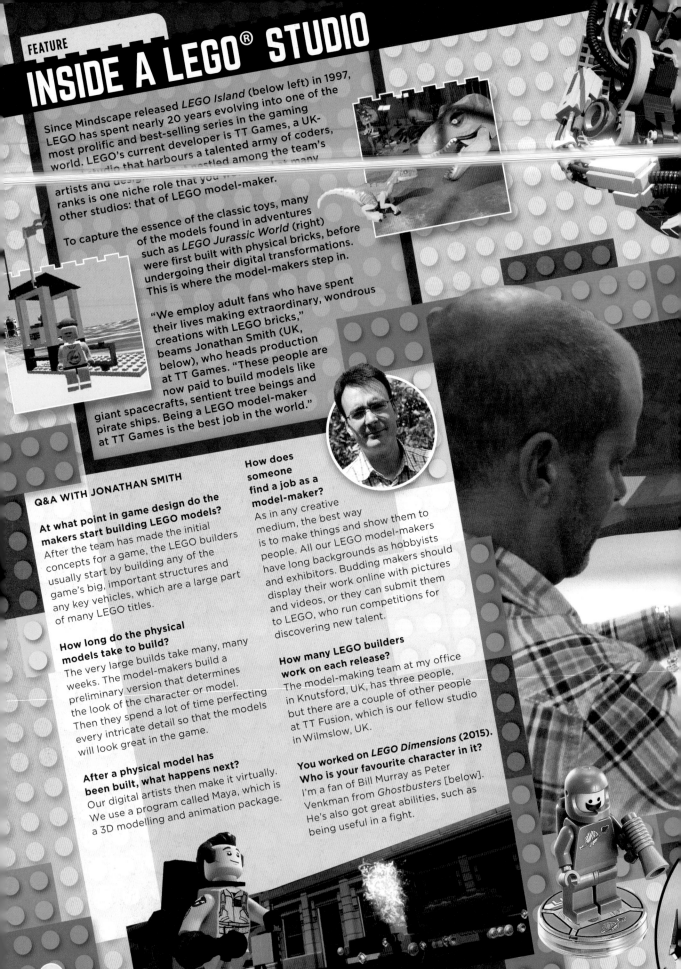

INSIDE A LEGO® STUDIO

Since Mindscape released *LEGO Island* (below left) in 1997, LEGO has spent nearly 20 years evolving into one of the most prolific and best-selling series in the gaming world. LEGO's current developer is TT Games, a UK-studio that harbours a talented army of coders, artists and designers. But nestled among the team's ranks is one niche role that you wouldn't find in many other studios: that of LEGO model-maker.

To capture the essence of the classic toys, many of the models found in adventures such as *LEGO Jurassic World* (right) were first built with physical bricks, before undergoing their digital transformations. This is where the model-makers step in.

"We employ adult fans who have spent their lives making extraordinary, wondrous creations with LEGO bricks," beams Jonathan Smith (UK, below), who heads production at TT Games. "These people are now paid to build models like giant spacecrafts, sentient tree beings and pirate ships. Being a LEGO model-maker at TT Games is the best job in the world."

Q&A WITH JONATHAN SMITH

At what point in game design do the makers start building LEGO models?
After the team has made the initial concepts for a game, the LEGO builders usually start by building any of the game's big, important structures and key vehicles, which are a large part of many LEGO titles.

How long do the physical models take to build?
The very large builds take many, many weeks. The model-makers build a preliminary version that determines the look of the character or model. Then they spend a lot of time perfecting every intricate detail so that the models will look great in the game.

After a physical model has been built, what happens next?
Our digital artists then make it virtually. We use a program called Maya, which is a 3D modelling and animation package.

How does someone find a job as a model-maker?
As in any creative medium, the best way is to make things and show them to people. All our LEGO model-makers have long backgrounds as hobbyists and exhibitors. Budding makers should display their work online with pictures and videos, or they can submit them to LEGO, who run competitions for discovering new talent.

How many LEGO builders work on each release?
The model-making team at my office in Knutsford, UK, has three people, but there are a couple of other people at TT Fusion, which is our fellow studio in Wilmslow, UK.

You worked on *LEGO Dimensions* (2015). Who is your favourite character in it?
I'm a fan of Bill Murray as Peter Venkman from *Ghostbusters* [below]. He's also got great abilities, such as being useful in a fight.

GLaDOS

A villainous artificial intelligence from Valve's classic puzzler *Portal*, GLaDOS (Genetic Lifeform and Disk Operating System) can also be found causing mayhem in *LEGO Dimensions*. The character was voiced in both series by Ellen McLain (USA).

Game: *LEGO Dimensions*	
Model specifications	
Total parts:	1,968
Height:	45.34 cm (1 ft 48 in)

Dalek Emperor

A fearsome despot from the *Doctor Who* franchise, the Dalek Emperor is the supreme ruler of the Dalek Empire and also the heftiest of all Daleks in size. He appeared as a non-playable boss in *LEGO Dimensions* and can be encountered in the "*Doctor Who*: Skaro" world.

Game: *LEGO Dimensions*	
Model specifications	
Total exterior parts:	8,689
Height:	75 cm (2 ft 46 in)
Diameter:	1.2 m (3 ft 93 in)

Tallest LEGO model in a videogame

The Barad-dûr tower from *LEGO The Lord of the Rings* (2012) is the tallest structure built for a LEGO game. This ominous, sky-piercing entity – the fortress home to Middle-earth baddie Lord Sauron – stood at 2.5 m (8 ft 2 in) tall and used a total of 53,673 bricks. The tower was first imagined by J R R Tolkien in his classic book trilogy *The Lord of the Rings*, and is recognizable for the Eye of Sauron, which keeps watchful guard from the building's highest tower.

Game: *LEGO The Lord of the Rings*	
Here is how the 53,673 bricks were used to build the Barad-dûr tower.	
Top section:	5,046
Mid section:	6,311
Base top:	8,759
Base bottom:	7,145
Base bottom ground:	18,128
Path with towers:	4,882
Large tower x 2:	3,402
Total parts:	53,673
Height:	2.5 m (8 ft 2 in)

FIGHTING GAMES

From the side-scrolling brawlers of yesteryear to the grand tournament play of *Street Fighter*, fighting games dazzle with their martial artistry and memorable characters.

As of 2016, Ryan Hart had won more than 450 fighting game tournaments in 20 countries, coming out on top playing *The King of Fighters*, *Tekken*, *Virtua Fighter*, *Mortal Kombat* and *Street Fighter*.

Most consecutive opponents on *Street Fighter V*

On 16 Feb 2016, to celebrate the launch of the latest instalment of Capcom's classic fighting series, eSports pro Ryan Hart (UK) played *Street Fighter V* for 10 hr 36 min without breaks at a GAME store in Manchester, UK. To qualify for the record, Ryan needed to win 90% of his bouts, but he went even better than that, completing an incredible clean sweep of 260 consecutive opponents.

FIGHTING ROUND-UP

From the brutal one-on-one challenge of *Tekken* and *Mortal Kombat* to the chaotic melees of *Super Smash Bros.*, the rules remain the same: KO your opponent before they KO you...

Most crowdfunded fighting game

[...]2D fighter *Skullgirls* (2012) raised $828,768 (£521,477) from 15,860 backers when an Indiegogo campaign was launched in Feb 2013. The game's developer Lab Zero Games had hoped to raise $150,000 (£94,383) for a new DLC character, but the extra backing allowed them to create even more DLC.

Strongest recorded hit in *Super Smash Bros. for Wii U* (without items)

In a YouTube video published on 3 Sep 2015, the Austrian team known as "Beefy Smash Doods" demonstrated a mammoth strike that inflicted 158% of damage. The intricate combo lasted 8 sec and involved four players in an orchestrated move in which an airborne log was swatted with a baseball bat – twice!

Lowest-rated fighting game

Ubisoft's Kinect-controlled brawler *Fighter Within* (2010) had a GameRankings rating of just 24.68% from 31 reviews, as of 16 Feb 2016. The Digital Fix called it a "disaster", describing the multiplayer as "a tragic, so-bad-it's-almost good comedy of errors".

Rarest console fighting game

There are believed to be only five copies in existence of the European PAL version of SNK's *Kizuna Encounter* (1996) for the Neo Geo. If you are lucky enough to find a cartridge, it could fetch up to $12,500 (£7,740). Copies of the NTSC version are considerably cheaper.

Longest gold trophy achievement in a fighting game

To win the "My Kung Fu is Stronger" gold trophy in *Mortal Kombat* (2011), gamers need to play the game for a minimum of 672 hr (28 days). They have to win 2,800 fights, land 4,200 X-rays, spill 280,000 litres of blood and fight as each character for 24 hr.

Cutesy, crowdfunded indie fighter *Them's Fightin' Herds* (Mane6) was originally planned as a game based on the TV series *My Little Pony: Friendship is Magic* – until a legal threat prompted a redesign.

FACT!

3.5 MILLION

Number of words in *Super Smash Bros.* fan-fiction *The Subspace Emissary's Worlds Conquest* by AuraChannelerChris.

Most critically acclaimed 3D fighting game

Released in 1999, the weapons-based fantasy fighter *SoulCalibur* (Namco) is still king of the pile when it comes to critical acclaim. The Dreamcast game scored [...] reviews at Metacritic, and 96.56% based on 25 reviews at GameRankings. IGN called it "The number one reason to buy a Dreamcast". On GameRankings, it is the sixth most acclaimed game overall.

Most critically acclaimed film based on a videogame

As of 17 Feb 2016, the big-screen adaptation of fighting series *Mortal Kombat* (1995), starring Robin Shou, boasted an aggregated review score of 58% at Metacritic. This edged out 2010's *Prince of Persia: The Sands of Time*, which scored 50%.

PRO *SUPER SMASH BROS.* LEGEND GONZALO "ZERO" BARRIOS (CHL) IS NOT ONLY A CHAMPION GAMER; HE'S ALSO A POPULAR YOUTUBER. HIS CHANNEL "ZERO" HAD 153,676 SUBSCRIBERS AND 27,182,734 VIEWS AS OF 22 FEB 2016.

Most gaming genres covered by a film licence

Since the original film hit big screens in 1993, *Jurassic Park* has spawned games in nine distinct genres. These include shooters, virtual park builders, a point-and-click adventure, an RTS, and perhaps most curiously of all, a one-on-one fighting game featuring dinosaurs called *Warpath: Jurassic Park*. The game was published by Electronic Arts in 1999.

Most knockouts on *Super Smash Bros. Melee*

On 16 May 2015, "anthony11293", aka Jeremy Anthony (USA), achieved an amazing 56 KOs in a single match in St Louis, Missouri, USA. A *Super Smash Bros. Melee* specialist, he snatched the record from Shawn Alvarez (USA), who had set the previous best of 42 KOs just 13 days earlier.

Most moves for a *Tekken* character
In the 2011 game *Tekken Tag Tournament 2* (Bandai Namco), the jaguar-masked combatant King II boasted 176 fighting moves. King (pictured) has appeared across the series in two guises, first as a Catholic priest who is killed by Ogre, and then as an orphan trained by the original King.

JIN KAZAMA

TEKKEN

Height	5 ft 11 in
Weight	75 kg
Birthplace	Yakushima, Japan
Fighting style	Mishima-style karate
Aliases	Fatal Lightning

❯ Best-selling fighting series (excluding crossovers)

An early 3D fighter title, *Tekken* (Namco, 1994) has evolved into one of the most enduring names in gaming. As of 17 Feb 2016, the iconic series boasted lifetime sales of 33.91 million units, according to VGChartz. The latest iteration, *Tekken 7*, was released in arcades in 2015. A notable addition to the fighting roster was Akuma (above), *Street Fighter*'s mysterious self-proclaimed "Master of the Fist".

The **best-selling *Tekken* game** is *Tekken 3* (Sony), released for the original PlayStation in 1998. The game has sold a total of 7.16 million units.

STREET FIGHTER

Publisher: Capcom
Debut: 1987
Games: 16 canonical games

Developer: Capcom
Series sales: 33.33 million
Rivals: *Mortal Kombat, Tekken*

M BISON

Birthday	17 Apr
Game debut	1991 (*Street Fighter II*)
Fighting style	Psycho power
Aim	World domination
Dislikes	Incompetent underlings

Most popular character in *Ultra Street Fighter IV*

The 2014 update to *Street Fighter IV* offered five new characters for selection. Yet according to EventHubs, *Street Fighter* stalwart Ryu remained the character competitive players turned to the most. As of 8 Mar 2016, he had racked up 3,382 usage points, with taekwondo expert Juri in second place with 2,201, and *Final Fight's* Cody in third with 2,158.

Best-selling fighting game (including crossovers)

Street Fighter and its rival *Tekken* have spent years slugging it out to see who is champion of the fighting-game world. Including crossover successes such as *Marvel vs. Capcom* and *Capcom vs. SNK*, *Street Fighter* boasted formidable series sales of 40.01 million, as of 8 Mar 2016.

Most viewed competitive videogame match

Viewers of the 2004 EVO *Street Fighter III: 3rd Strike* competition were treated to a thrilling battle between Daigo "The Beast" Umehara (JPN) and Justin Wong (USA), with Umehara's Ken somehow snatching victory from a seemingly hopeless position. As of 8 Mar 2016, the bout had been viewed an incredible 5,385,142 times on YouTube.

Most viewed *Street Fighter IV* fantasy fight

On 18 Sep 2015, YouTuber "Richie Branson" used a PC mod to adapt the characters of Cammy and Balrog to resemble UFC fighter Ronda Rousey and boxer Floyd Mayweather Jr. The resulting bout, "Street Fighter IV: Mayweather vs. Rousey Edition", had been viewed 680,111 times by fight fans as of 8 Mar 2016.

FACT! In Nov 2015, fans launched a petition asking Capcom not to censor a risqué taunt by Rainbow Mika in *Street Fighter V*. It had received 8,656 signatures as of 5 Apr 2016.

1,499,811

Views of Necalli's *Street Fighter V* reveal trailer on YouTube, as of 5 Apr 2016. The long-haired Necalli was a new character in the series.

Largest collection of *Street Fighter* memorabilia

"I honestly don't know what the world would look like without *Street Fighter*," Canada's Clarence Lim (below) told the 25th anniversary documentary *I Am Street Fighter* (2014). His record-setting collection of *SF* memorabilia consisted of 2,723 individual items, as of 29 Jun 2014.

Highest-ranked *Ultra Street Fighter IV* player

Evil Geniuses member Yusuke Momochi (JPN) won 10,885 points from 22 tournament competitions during the calendar year up to 8 Mar 2016, according to rankings produced by prominent fighting-game website Shoryuken.com. Daigo Umehara (JPN) sat in second with 10,215 points.

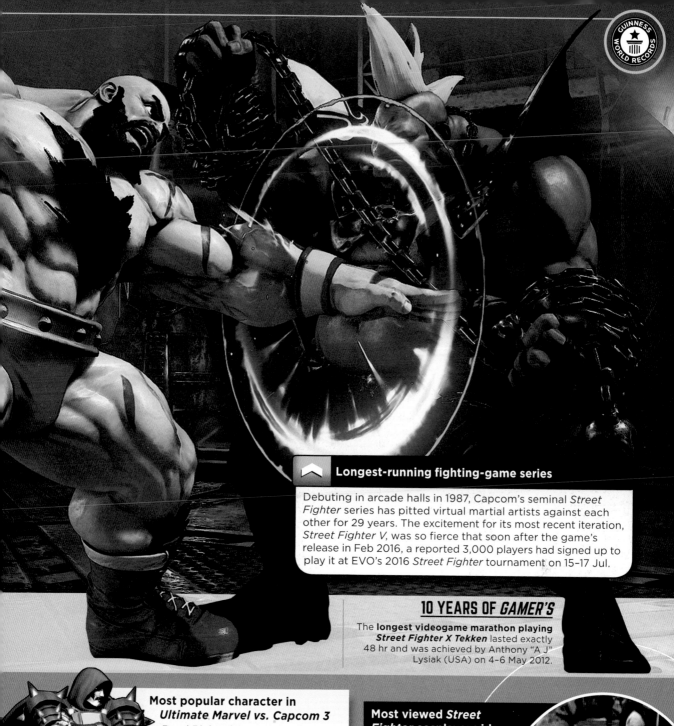

Longest-running fighting-game series

Debuting in arcade halls in 1987, Capcom's seminal *Street Fighter* series has pitted virtual martial artists against each other for 29 years. The excitement for its most recent iteration, *Street Fighter V*, was so fierce that soon after the game's release in Feb 2016, a reported 3,000 players had signed up to play it at EVO's 2016 *Street Fighter* tournament on 15–17 Jul.

10 YEARS OF *GAMER'S*

The **longest videogame marathon playing** *Street Fighter X Tekken* lasted exactly 48 hr and was achieved by Anthony "A J" Lysiak (USA) on 4–6 May 2012.

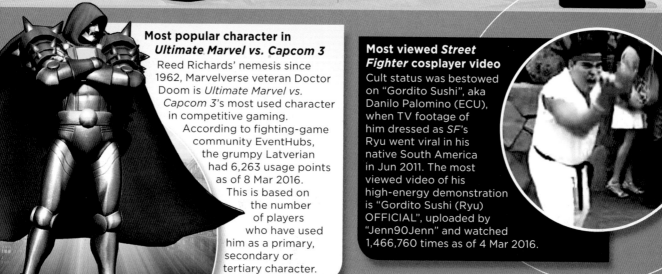

Most popular character in *Ultimate Marvel vs. Capcom 3*

Reed Richards' nemesis since 1962, Marvelverse veteran Doctor Doom is *Ultimate Marvel vs. Capcom 3*'s most used character in competitive gaming.
According to fighting-game community EventHubs, the grumpy Latverian had 6,263 usage points as of 8 Mar 2016. This is based on the number of players who have used him as a primary, secondary or tertiary character.

Most viewed *Street Fighter* cosplayer video

Cult status was bestowed on "Gordito Sushi", aka Danilo Palomino (ECU), when TV footage of him dressed as *SF*'s Ryu went viral in his native South America in Jun 2011. The most viewed video of his high-energy demonstration is "Gordito Sushi (Ryu) OFFICIAL", uploaded by "Jenn90Jenn" and watched 1,466,760 times as of 4 Mar 2016.

COMBAT SPORTS

The more sober cousin of OTT fighters such as *Street Fighter*, combat sports games typically feature sizeable career modes and gameplay that is realistic and technical.

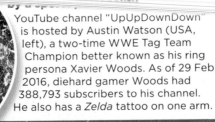

Most popular games channel

YouTube channel "UpUpDownDown" is hosted by Austin Watson (USA, left), a two-time WWE Tag Team Champion better known as his ring persona Xavier Woods. As of 29 Feb 2016, diehard gamer Woods had 388,793 subscribers to his channel. He also has a *Zelda* tattoo on one arm.

Best-selling boxing game on a single format

Released in 1987 for the NES, legendary slug-fest *Mike Tyson's Punch-Out!!* powered its way to sales of 3.02 million units, according to VGChartz. The **best-selling boxing game (multiple platforms)** is EA's *Fight Night Round 3* (2006), which had sold 5.55 million across five formats by 29 Feb 2016.

5,385,036

Views of Bruce Lee taking on UFC's Mike Easton in *EA Sports UFC* – the **most watched UFC videogame fight**, as of 29 Feb 2016.

Fastest victory in *WWE 2K16*

Bunny-costumed gamers "oKILL3R JESUSo" and "XxNeroDreXelxX" secured victory in an extreme-rules tornado tag-team match on *WWE 2K16* (2K Sports, 2015) that lasted just 15 sec on 7 Nov 2015. Their speedy success was uploaded to the "WWE Network Gaming" channel on YouTube.

Most videogame appearances by a real-life martial artist

"Godfather of mixed martial arts" Bruce Lee (HKG) had starred in 12 games as of 29 Feb 2016. This includes Datasoft's 1984 action platformer *Bruce Lee*, the 1994 film spin-off *Dragon: The Bruce Lee Story* (top left), a grappling stint in *Virtual Pro Wrestling 64* (1997) and a bonus unlockable character role in *EA Sports UFC* (2014, left).

10 YEARS OF GAMER'S

Fire Pro Wrestling Returns (Spike, 2005) featured 327 wrestling likenesses from a variety of global organizations – the largest roster in a combat sports videogame.

In a video recorded for the YouTube channel "Hot Pepper Gaming", Xavier Woods, aka Austin Watson, reviewed *Street Fighter V* while eating a plate of mouth-scorching Habanero peppers. Big ouch!

FACT!

22

Number of venues in 2K's 2008 boxing game *Don King Presents: Prizefighter*, from a gym to Madison Square Garden.

KING HIPPO

MIKE TYSON'S PUNCH-OUT!!

From	Hippo Island, South Pacific
Highest boxing rank	Major circuit #2
Wins	18
Losses	10
Wins by knockout	18

Largest roster in a WWE wrestling game
Released in Oct 2015, *WWE 2K16* featured a selection of some 120 current and classic wrestlers. In addition, fans pre-ordering the game were treated to two playable versions of Arnold Schwarzenegger (right) in his guise of iconic movie cyborg The Terminator. "I'll be back," he once said – and indeed he was.

First fighting game

The first game to feature one-on-one brawling was Sega's *Heavyweight Champ* in 1976. The coin-op title featured a boxing-glove controller that allowed players to strike and block high or low punches.

Fastest completion of *WWE 2K15* using all Superstars

German gamer "LPer93" grappled his way through *WWE 2K15* (2K Sports, 2014) using the full roster of Superstars in a time of 3 hr 4 min. The run was recorded on his Twitch channel on 7 Jul 2015 and listed at Speedrun.com.

Longest-running wrestling game series

Since its debut for the PC Engine in 1989, the Japanese series *Fire Pro Wrestling* (Spike Human Entertainment) has been turning out sequels and spin-offs for more than 23 years. Its most recent ring-bound romps were the social network game *Fire Pro Wrestling in Mobage* in 2011 and *Fire Pro Wrestling* for the Xbox 360 in 2012.

First all-female cast in a fighting game

Released for the Mega Drive, Asmik's 1990 wrestling romp *Cutie Suzuki No Ringside Angel* featured only female characters. The game – exclusive to Japan – was named after pro wrestler Cutie Suzuki, aka Yumi Harashima.

Most prolific developer of combat sports games

Excluding cross-platform ports of the same game, developer Yuke's (JPN) has made 41 combat sports games between the release of *Power Move Pro Wrestling* in 1996 and *WWE 2K16* (pictured) in Oct 2015. The studio's titles included the female wrestling game *Rumble Roses* (2004), the robo-boxing movie tie-in *Real Steel* (2011), and multiple entries in the *WWE* and *UFC Undisputed* series.

BEAT-'EM-UPS

Whether you're battling bare-knuckled through hordes of bad guys or hacking and slashing with weapons, the golden rule of beat-'em-ups remains: the more enemies the better!

10 YEARS OF GAMER'S

The **most ubiquitous** videogame ninja is Ryu Hayabusa, the star of Tecmo's Ninja Gaiden series had appeared in 27 different games as of 6 Mar 2016.

Largest combo goal in a side-scrolling beat-'em-up
A 2013 title developed and published by DrinkBox Studios, *Guacamelee!*'s hero is Juan, a murdered farmer brought back to life as a Mexican wrestler. To earn the Never Ending Combo Trophy/Achievement, players must use ... perform a sequence of no fewer than 200 moves.

KRATOS
GOD OF WAR

Nickname	"Ghost of Sparta"
Weapons	Blades of Chaos
Likes	Vengeance, God-slaying
Dislikes	Ares
Funniest alter ego	Spud of War

Best-selling hack-and-slash series
The electrifyingly brutal *God of War* series (Sony, 2005–15) follows antihero Kratos as he carves a bloody path through the world of Greek mythology, chopping up Olympians with his pair of chained blades. As of 6 Mar 2016, it had racked up global sales of 24.61 million units according to VGChartz.
The original *God of War* is the **highest-rated hack-and-slash**, with its GameRankings score of 93.58% from 91 reviews placing it narrowly ahead of Capcom's 2001 *Devil May Cry*, with 92.6% from 70 reviews.

10
Number of iconic fighting soundtracks composed by Japan's Yuzo Koshiro, including *Streets of Rage 1–3*.

Most moves for a character in a beat-'em-up
Capcom's *God Hand* (2006) mixes hard-boiled action with lots of zany comedy. Its hero, martial artist Gene (left), uses his divine fists to perform combination attacks built upon moves comprising 114 individual techniques. The game's designers had wanted to make a title for "hardcore" gamers, hence its many complex combos.

First beat-'em-up with all-female heroes
Released for the Mega Drive and Super Famicom and rarely seen outside of Japan, Angel's *Sailor Moon* (1993) let gamers play as one or two of five female fighters. The game might look cute, but it is considered to be one of the most bruising examples of the genre.

Devil May Cry was originally conceived as a new iteration of *Resident Evil*, until developers realized that the prototype did not fit with its survival-horror counterparts and deserved its own series.

FACT!

Smallest beat-'em-up hero
Despite standing only 1 ft (30 cm) high upon his haunches, Nando the rabbit becomes a playable character in the competitive fighting mode of 2D side-scrolling cult classic *Guardian Heroes* (Sega, 1996).

Fastest 100% completion of *Battletoads* (all stages)
Mexico's Piotr "TheMexicanRunner" Delgado Kusielczuk completed Tradewest's notoriously difficult 1991 NES beat-'em-up in 24 min 19 sec, knocking nearly 10 min off the existing record in the process. The run was verified by Speed Demos Archive on 3 Apr 2014.

Lowest-rated videogame
As of 6 Mar 2016, GameCube beat-'em-up *Charlie's Angels* (Ubisoft, 2003) had a GameRankings rating of 23.74% from 23 reviews – the lowest rating of any videogame in any genre. Full throttle? Stuck in reverse, more like.

Most hero death animations in a videogame
The dark and fiendishly difficult *Bayonetta* (PlatinumGames, 2009) has 48 different post-death animations for defeated gamers to savour, the most dramatic of all being "Armageddon", in which Earth itself explodes into pieces.

Best-selling hack-and-slash
Tackling levels taken directly from scenes from the first two films in Peter Jackson's *Lord of the Rings* trilogy (2001–03), players of *The Lord of the Rings: The Two Towers* (EA, 2002) had to master individual attack combos in order to beat back the forces of Sauron. As of 6 Mar 2016, the game had sold 6.65 million copies, according to VGChartz.

Most prolific publisher of beat-'em-ups

Since 1989's release of the arcade classic *Final Fight*, Capcom has published 44 beat-'em-up titles across all platforms. Early arcade titles *Dynasty Wars* (1989) and *Dungeons & Dragons: Tower of Doom* (1993) helped define the genre, while later home-console blockbusters *Devil May Cry* (whose fourth instalment special-edition is pictured here) and *Onimusha Soul* (2012) added complexity and smoother gameplay.

SUPERDATA

The way we buy games is radically shifting. It's no longer a case of buying physical discs from retailers: many gamers now download titles from digital distributors such as Steam, PlayStation Store and Xbox Games Store. The rise of the free2play (F2p) model has also led to a change in the way games can make money. US company SuperData tracks digital game sales for the global market, as well as analysing trends in esports and virtual reality. Some of the company's most telling data is shared on these pages.

Q&A with Joost van Dreunen (right), CEO of SuperData

What is SuperData?
We're the leading providers of data and insights on digital games and playable media. By collecting the transaction data of more than 48 million spending gamers, we can report on the monthly performance of games, genres and markets.

How much of a shift has there been towards downloading games?

Digital distribution has made it possible for small developers to successfully launch games in an arena that was previously dominated by just a few publishers. New digital-only platforms such as social, mobile and MMO have also exploded. Worldwide, digital games are about five times larger than retail.

Who are the most popular distributors of digital games?
For mobile it's Apple and Google. For PC games it's Steam. A key challenge in covering digital game sales is reconciling this fragmented market.

Have recent sales charts been misleading owing to them not including digital sales?
Yes, the emphasis on retail-based game sales gave the impression that interactive entertainment was a dying industry. Underneath that, however, has been the rising tide of digital.

What metrics do you track?
The core group includes full game downloads, revenues, monthly active users (MAU), conversion rate and average revenue per paying user.

How long will it be before digital sales will be the most dominant way to buy games?
For some platforms, digital is already king. Premium PC titles have leaned digitally for some time. Platforms with no retail equivalent like mobile are obviously all digital. But the console market has been slower to adapt for cultural and infrastructural reasons.

Which countries have the biggest digital markets?
Emerging markets, especially Brazil, India and China, have digital markets that are vastly larger than retail.

SUPERDATA
playable media & games market research

SUPERDATA STATS
Based: **New York, USA**
Year founded: **2009**
Full-time employees: **15**
Countries tracked: **50**
Gamers tracked: **48 million**

STEAM

Countries ranked by digital videogames revenue for 2015

	Country	Revenue
1	China	$13.15 bn
2	USA	$13.06 bn
3	Japan	$11.85 bn
4	South Korea	$3.19 bn
5	UK	$2.67 bn
6	Germany	$2.37 bn
7	Brazil	$1.83 bn
8	France	$1.61 bn
9	Russia	$1.60 bn
10	Italy	$1.14 bn

Worldwide digital sales growth since 2010

Mobile games

Year	MAU	Revenue
2010	1,195,642,770	$5,902,871,737
2011	1,412,651,158	$7,488,774,876
2012	1,614,459,600	$12,883,392,538
2013	2,012,287,459	$19,299,431,200
2014	2,216,533,322	$24,119,513,918
2015	2,519,342,539	$30,149,587,706

Correct as of 31 Mar 2016

Console games (digital sales)

Year	MAU	Revenue
2010	n/a	n/a
2011	n/a	n/a
2012	163,288,709	$4,360,287,995
2013	182,503,536	$4,750,023,667
2014	204,270,983	$5,546,637,074
2015	208,334,566	$6,238,669,087

Correct as of 31 Mar 2016

% of US gamers using mobile apps to watch eSports in 2015

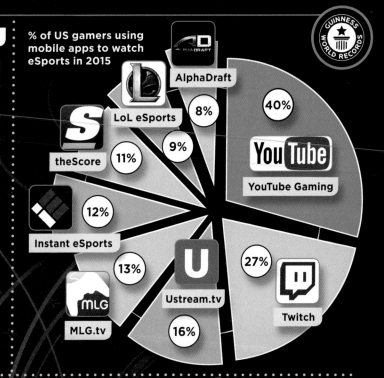

- AlphaDraft — 8%
- LoL eSports — 9%
- theScore — 11%
- Instant eSports — 12%
- MLG.tv — 13%
- Ustream.tv — 16%
- Twitch — 27%
- YouTube Gaming — 40%

Most watched eSports mobile titles in the USA in 2015

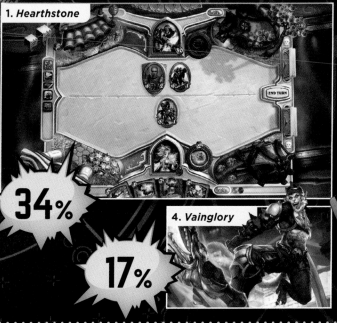

1. *Hearthstone* — 34%

4. *Vainglory* — 17%

2. *World of Tanks Blitz* — 30%

3. *Million* — 19%

Predicted eSports revenue for 2015

- Sponsorships and advertising: $578.6 m (£390.2 m)
- eSports betting and fantasy sites: $55.8 m (£37.6 m)
- Prize pools: $53.8 m (£36.2 m)
- Amateur and micro-tournaments: $27.7 m (£18.6 m)
- Merchandise: $17 m (£11.4 m)
- Ticket sales: $15.9 m (£10.7 m)

RACING

A favourite in old-school arcades, racing games have evolved and diversified. Whether they're playing ultra-realistic sims or cartoon racers, gamers love putting the pedal to the metal.

MKTV
MARIO KART TELEVISION

YOSHI'S

Longest marathon on *Mario Kart* (series)

On 4–5 Jul 2014, Harry Twyford, Josh Alexander, Matt Smith and James Hickman (all AUS) played the *Mario Kart* series on the Wii, Wii U and Nintendo 64 for 35 hr 45 min at Brauer College in Warrnambool, Victoria, Australia. They had practised for six months, including one 10-hr marathon training session that ended in disaster when one member threw up and the rest fell asleep!

RACING SIMS

Know your downforce from your DRS? Developers of racing sims go to extraordinary lengths in order to create the most realistic and authentic driving experience possible.

Best-selling driving sim series
EA's *Need for Speed* may have the edge in the overall driving ~~~~~~~, with 101.6 million units sold, but no driving sim can touch *Gran Turismo* with its series sales of 72.1 million as of 28 Apr 2016. Impressively, Sony's *GT* games have only been released for PlayStation consoles, unlike the multi-platform *NFS*.

Most critically acclaimed racing game
Launched in Japan on 23 Dec 1997, the original *Gran Turismo* for PlayStation remains the critical benchmark for racers, with a GameRankings rating of 94.95% as of 16 Mar 2016.

Best-selling Formula 1 videogame
~~~~ have been popular since the 1980s. However, the best-selling digital take of this high-octane motorsport is Codemasters' *F1 2011*, which had sold 2.43 million copies as of 16 Mar 2016. Predecessor *F1 2010* is second on the podium, with sales of 2.28 million according to VGChartz.

First racing game with dashboard instruments
The racer *netKar Pro* (Kunos Simulazioni, 2006) was the first videogame to include a fully interactive dashboard of the type typical of flight sims.

FACT! *Gran Turismo* designer and producer Kazunori Yamauchi has showcased his driving skills on real-life circuits, competing in the 24 Hours Nürburgring team race in 2010–12 and 2014.

19,000 Number of pink flamingos featured at the Chilean track "Chungara Lake" in *Driveclub*. Incredibly, each flamingo in the supersized flock behaves independently of the others.

Most podium finishes for a gamer in a real-life driving competition
Since winning the 2008 GT Academy, Lucas Ordóñez (ESP) had secured 20 podium finishes in real-life race competitions as of 14 Mar 2016, according to his career stats at driverdb.com. Highlights include first place in the 2013 Blancpain Endurance Series – GT3 Pro-Am Cup, and second place in the GT4 European Cup in 2009.

Longest-running PlayStation franchise
With the release of *Gran Turismo 6*'s Track Path Editor app on 30 Sep 2015, Sony's racing sim series had been gracing PS platforms for a period of 17 years 281 days. At Paris Games Week in Oct 2015, Polyphony Digital unveiled a teaser for the next instalment in the franchise, *Gran Turismo: Sport*, confirming that the game would also support Sony's new virtual reality hardware.

First racing game to win a "Game of the Year" BAFTA
In 2001, Sony's PS2 smash *Gran Turismo 3: A-spec* picked up the console "Game of the Year" award at the prestigious BAFTA Games Awards. As of Mar 2016, it was still the only racer to win a "top" British Academy Award. BAFTA has been recognizing videogames since 1998.

Most "stakeholders" involved in a racing game

Developed by Slightly Mad Studios, *Project CARS* (Bandai Namco, 2015) was put together with the assistance of racing fans, who became involved through the WMD funding portal. Eighty-thousand so-called "stakeholders", mainly fans and enthusiasts, put their hands in their pockets, raising a total of €3.75 m (£2.99 m). Pro racer Nicolas Hamilton (above), brother of Formula 1 champion Lewis, was brought on board to advise the *Project CARS* dev team on car handling to ensure the most authentic drive possible.

26 Different locations in *Forza Motorsport 6*, including five new circuits – Brands Hatch, Daytona, Indianapolis 2014, Rio de Janeiro and Watkins Glen.

10 YEARS OF *GAMER'S*

In China and Japan, the first editions of *Gran Turismo 4* came with the **largest instruction guide for a racing game**. The guide was 212 pages long and featured a car index and professional tutorials.

Longest draw distance in a racing game

Draw distance is a computer-graphics term that measures the maximum distance of objects in a three-dimensional scene. The hyper-detailed *Driveclub* (Sony, 2014) boasts a draw distance of 200 km (124 mi). It uses high-resolution data collected by NASA to simulate Earth's curvature and to accurately map the stars in the night sky. Even the clouds are 3D models.

Most drivable surfaces in a game

Forza Motorsport 6 (Microsoft, 2015) features a total of 148 individual driving surfaces, with each surface's friction uniquely affected by multiple weather variables. Key to that are the refined rain effects and 3D puddles.
The exclusive Xbox One title is also the **most critically acclaimed racer for an eighth-generation platform**. It had scored 88.63% at GameRankings as of 7 Mar 2016.

ARCADE RACERS

From melting tyres at improbable speeds, to flying upside down in futuristic cars, arcade racers let you live out your high-speed fantasies, no matter how crazy they may be.

Fastest lap on *Ridge Racer* (high level)

Namco's 1993 classic, considered one of the first "must-haves" for the original PlayStation. Gamer Alex T Trammell (USA) clocked a scorching lap time of 1 min 0.757 sec, as verified by Twin Galaxies on 21 Jun 2005.

First racing game to win "Game of the Year" at the Golden Joystick Awards

In 1988, *OutRun* beat Activision's *The Last Ninja* and Taito's beat-'em-up *Renegade* to the coveted Game of the Year title at the long-running British videogame awards ceremony – and remained the only racing game to have done so, as of 9 Mar 2016.

"SMOOTH MCGROOVE" IS A YOUTUBER WHO PERFORMS ACAPELLA VERSIONS OF VIDEOGAME SONGS. HIS "F-ZERO – MUTE CITY ACAPELLA", BASED ON A TRACK FROM THE FUTURISTIC RACER, HAS BEEN VIEWED MORE THAN 2 MILLION TIMES!

Fastest lap of "Klies Bridge" in *WipEout 64*

Making cunning use of programming glitches in the gameplay, Wouter Jansen (NLD) flew round the anti-gravity track in exactly 13 sec, a time verified by Speed Demos Archive on 28 Mar 2009.

Fastest lap time in *Daytona USA*

Brian Ho (USA) completed a circuit of Sega's 1993 arcade racer in just 45.62 sec on "Time Attack" mode, as verified by Twin Galaxies on 18 Jul 2009.

Largest licensed soundtrack in a racing game

Developed by French studio Ivory Tower, *The Crew* (2014) features 120 licensed songs from artists as diverse as Arctic Monkeys and Mozart. There is also an original score by Joseph Trapanese (USA), who has composed for movies including *Oblivion* and *Tron: Legacy* alongside Daft Punk.

FACT! In 1987, some home-computer versions of *OutRun* came bundled with a cassette featuring the original arcade soundtrack, as the hardware wasn't sophisticated enough to replicate it.

51 Number of high-performance cars available in the 2015 *Need for Speed* reboot – all customizable, naturally...

Most prolific racing-game series

The *Need for Speed* series had amassed 26 titles as of 16 Mar 2016, dating all the way back to 1994. It has appeared on 3DO and iOS, while 2015's *Need for Speed: No Limits* was released exclusively for mobile platforms. Underlining its place in pole position, the series is also the **best-selling driving-game series**, with worldwide sales of 101.6 million as of 28 Apr 2016, according to VGChartz.

Highest score on *OutRun*

Richard Jackson (USA) scored 52,897,690 points on Sega's 1986 arcade racer, as verified by Twin Galaxies on 21 Feb 1987.

The **highest score on *Turbo OutRun* (arcade)**, the sequel to *OutRun*, was set by Martin Bedard (CAN) with 52,087,460 points, verified on 29 May 2008.

First racing-game soundtrack CD
The launch of the original *WipEout* (Psygnosis, 1995) was accompanied by a CD featuring cutting-edge electronica music by artists such as Orbital, Leftfield and the Chemical Brothers. A follow-up soundtrack, *WipEout 2097*, accompanied the game of the same name in 1996.

Longest-running futuristic racing-game series

Between the release of its PlayStation launch title (for Europe) in Sep 1995 and the PS Vita game *WipEout 2048* in Jan 2012, the *WipEout* series had been burning anti-gravity matter for 16 years 4 months. Developer Studio Liverpool (formerly Psygnosis) subsequently closed, but in Sep 2015 a Sony executive refused to rule out the possibility of a new title.

682

Speed in km/h (423.7 mph) reached by YouTuber Fernando Moretti in a nitro-powered Ford GT in a *Need for Speed: Carbon* video uploaded on 4 May 2007 – the **fastest speed by a real-world car in a videogame.**

10 YEARS OF *GAMER'S*

On 1 Sep 1982, Todd Rogers (USA) set a time of 5.51 sec on *Dragster* (Activision, 1980). Over 33 years later the time still stood, making it the **longest-standing videogame record** recognized by GWR.

Most money earned in *Crazy Taxi*

Hitmaker's 1999 open-world racer challenges gamers to accumulate fares by delivering passengers to their destination as quickly as possible. J C Padilla (USA, inset) showed off some serious cabby skills in the game's sun-scorched Californian setting. As verified by Twin Galaxies on 7 Jul 2010, the gamer earned $106,833.09 (£70,404.09) in fares.

Most critically acclaimed kart-racer

Mario Kart might dominate the kart market, but *Crash Team Racing* (SCEA, 1999) has the critics' seal of approval with a GameRankings score of 91.78%.

Donkey Kong: Barrel Blast (Nintendo, 2007) could only score 43.94%, making it the **lowest-rated kart-racer**.

MARIO KART

Publisher: Nintendo
Debut: 1992
Games: 8 (plus 3 coin-ops)

Developer: Nintendo
Series sales: 108.98 million
Rival: *Crash Team Racing*

DONKEY KONG

MARIO KART

Species	A very large gorilla
Number of karts	16
Strengths	Bashing into small karts
Weaknesses	Poor acceleration
Likes	Bananas

Best-selling Wii U game

With global sales of 6.79 million as of 28 Apr 2016, *Mario Kart 8* is the Wii U's biggest seller. Sales of the console itself as of that date were 12.98 million, meaning that more than 52 per cent of Wii U owners have the game.

Fastest time for *MK 8*'s "Animal Crossing" track

"Flarena" (USA) finished three laps of the "Animal Crossing" track in 1 min 36.29 sec on 28 Mar 2016. The track – inspired by the Nintendo game of the same name – was among several new ones featured on DLC for *Mario Kart 8*, released on 23 Apr 2015.

Longest-standing *Mario Kart* lap record

Multiple *Mario Kart* record holder Karel "KVD" van Duijvenboden (NLD) set the fastest lap for the "Ghost Valley" track in the NTSC version of *Super Mario Kart* on 29 Dec 2006. As of 28 Apr 2016, his 11.65-sec run remained a record after 9 years 121 days.

Most heats in a kart videogame competition

Mario Kart event "The Grand Wii" was held on 5–12 Apr 2008. Run by GAME, it featured 30 regional heats in the UK. Winners went to the final, to battle it out for a Mario-themed VW Beetle.

Longest-running kart videogame series
When *Mario Kart 8* arrived in Japan on 29 May 2014 (a day later in Europe and North America), the series cemented its position as gaming's longest-running kart-racing franchise: 21 years 275 days had elapsed since *Super Mario Kart* made its debut on 27 Aug 1992.

FACT! PAC-Man notched up roles in all three *Mario Kart Arcade GP* games. The yellow fellow was joined in the first two by his wife, Ms. PAC-Man, and red ghost Blinky. They were the first characters from a non-Nintendo game to appear in the series.

19 *Mario Kart 8* records held by Japanese gamers as of 27 Apr 2016, according to mkwrs.com – more than any other nation.

Most live-action parodies of a racing game

As of 12 Apr 2016, YouTube boasted at least 17 live-action *Mario Kart* parodies, featuring cosplayers driving through public spaces. Among the most viewed are "MARIO IN REAL LIFE LONGBOARDING, RUNNING FROM SECURITY PRANK (CHASED By security)" by "JOOGSQUAD PPJT" (above) and "Mario Kart FlashMob" by "Base37" (left). In the latter, actors dressed as *Mario Kart* characters hare around the floors of one of London's Westfield shopping centres.

Fastest 32-track 200cc speed-run in *MK 8*

When Nintendo's fastest-ever karts were added to *Mario Kart 8* in Apr 2015, 200cc records became musts for track addicts. On 7 Feb 2016, "MBisonFuté" (FRA) guided Donkey Kong around 32 tracks in just 1 hr 4 min 1 sec, as verified by Speedrun.com. "What a great run," he commented. "Only Piranha Plant Slide [the second course of the Lightning Cup] was awful."

Best-selling racing series

Outselling major racing sims and arcade racers alike, the *Mario Kart* series had sold 108.98 million units as of 28 Apr 2016. By comparison, *Gran Turismo* and *Need for Speed* had shifted 72.1 and 101.6 million respectively.

Sales of 35.78 million make *Mario Kart Wii* (2008) the **best-selling racing videogame** and third all-time best-seller, after *Wii Sports* and *Super Mario Bros.*

405

Number of historic and current *Super Mario Kart* records held by Karel van Duijvenboden (NLD), as of 24 Mar 2016.

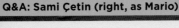

10 YEARS OF *GAMER'S*

The **most viewed fan film based on a racing game** is "MARIO KART (REMI GAILLARD)". As of 29 Apr 2016, it had been watched 67,827,239 times.

Most *Super Mario Kart* World Championship trophies

The *Super Mario Kart* World Championship tournament has been held in France since 2002. Gamers compete in four events, such as GP 150cc and Battle Mode. As of 28 Apr 2016, Florent Lecoanet (FRA) had won eight gold and two silver trophies. Only in his first year (2005) did he fail to finish first or second.

Q&A: Sami Çetin (right, as Mario)

The British founder of the time-trial page mariokartplayers.com/smk is a five-time runner-up and one-time winner at the *Super Mario Kart* World Championships.

How did you start with the game?
I was 10: my sister bought it for me. The handling mechanics were perfect. I had a vision of knowing the world's best players and going to events. But there was no internet then. It was just a crazy dream.

Then the *Super Mario Kart* World Championships happened...
I was very nervous at my first one. But I won the title once, in 2012.

What would you tell gamers who want to be pro at *Super Mario Kart*?
Play harder tracks often; your driving accuracy improves, which helps on easier tracks. And you can watch strategy videos online – we didn't have those in the 1990s. Set realistic goals: don't try to replicate the fastest strategy straight away.

And you hold world records too...
Yes: Mario Circuit 1 Time Trial, the first track in *Super Mario Kart*, in 57.90 and 55.97 sec for the PAL and NTSC versions, respectively.

25 YEARS OF *MARIO KART*

Since the release of the first *Super Mario Kart* in 1992, the series has had millions of virtual racers dodging banana skins and firing red shells at one another. Few games can match its sense of addictive fun and pure adrenaline thrill. As the power of consoles has increased, Nintendo has continued to improve the *Mario Kart* blueprint, adding new features and facets of gameplay. And with talk ~~of~~ ... for ~~the~~ ... ~~up~~coming NX console, it could be a long time before this series reaches the finishing line...

THE MASTERMIND BEHIND *MARIO KART* IS NINTENDO'S CREATIVE GENIUS SHIGERU MIYAMOTO. SINCE JOINING THE COMPANY IN 1977, HE HAS CREATED BOTH *SUPER MARIO BROS.* AND *ZELDA*, AND PRODUCED EVERY *MARIO KART* CONSOLE TITLE TO DATE.

1992

Super Mario Kart
The first *MK* title begins with eight racers and 20 tracks. It marries the fun of Mario with serious kart-racing gameplay using power slides and hopping.

1996

Mario Kart 64
Mario Kart arrives on the N64 boasting four-player split-screen thrills, 3D courses with elevation changes, and Wario and Donkey Kong as characters.

START

2001

Mario Kart: Super Circuit
Released exclusively for the Game Boy Advance, the third *Mario Kart* entry is the first to appear on a hand-held console.

2003

Mario Kart: Double Dash!!
The GameCube title is notable for its two-player karts. One character drives while a second collects items and weapons.

2008

Mario Kart Wii
The sixth console title makes full use of the Wii's unique motion-sensing controls. It introduces motorbikes to the series.

2011

Mario Kart 7
Innovations in the Nintendo 3DS title include stereoscopic 3D graphics, hang-glider add-ons, and underwater sections on some of its tracks.

2005

Mario Kart DS
The second title for hand-helds features Retro Cups, in which players race over old courses. It also adds online multiplayer and customizable karts.

2013

Mario Kart Arcade GP DX
Mario's third arcade title features a "Team Mode" that lets two karters create one larger vehicle, with a driver and a "gunner".

FINISH

2016

Uploaded on 6 Apr 2016 by "The Pixel Kingdom", mash-up video "SUPER MARIO ROCKET LEAGUE" has *Mario Kart*-ers causing havoc in the vehicle-based soccer title *Rocket League*.

2014

Luigi's "death stare" while overtaking in *Mario Kart 8* becomes an internet meme. It is nominated for "Best Gaming Moment" at the 2014 Golden Joystick Awards.

2014

Mario Kart 8
Wii U users can enjoy new antigravity track sections and all-terrain vehicles. Race highlights can now be edited and uploaded to YouTube.

2016

Car manufacturer Tesla sneak in a *Mario Kart* Easter egg for their Model S and X cars. It lets drivers turn their dashboard display into the iconic Rainbow Road track.

RHYTHM & PARTY

From instrument-based rivals *Guitar Hero* and *Rock Band* to the fancy footwork fun of *Just Dance*, music games flex the fingers and stretch the legs of gamers and non-gamers alike.

Crazy

Funky

Longest marathon on a videogame

Record-smasher Carrie Swidecki (USA) played *Just Dance 2015* (Ubisoft, 2014) for a toe-toughening 138 hr 34 sec on 11–17 Jul 2015. Having set new dance marathon records four years in a row, Carrie this time broke the overall gaming marathon record, beating by almost 3 hr the time set by Okan Kaya (AUS), who played *Call of Duty: Black Ops II* for 135 hr 15 min 10 sec in 2012.

RHYTHM GAMES

They've got the music, you've got the moves – these games are great for budding dancers, would-be guitarists and even, thanks to *Crypt of the NecroDancer*, dungeon-crawlers.

INDIE FAN "PEWDIEPIE" WAS BLOWN AWAY BY THE INVENTIVE *CRYPT OF THE NECRODANCER*. HIS YOUTUBE VIDEO "AMAZING RYTHM GAME! – CRYPT OF THE NECRODANCER... ...EEN 2,251,222 TIMES AS OF 20 APR 2016, AMASSING 102,585 LIKES.

Best-selling dance videogame series

Crammed with Katy Perry hits and more crazy colours than a *Candy Crush* convention, Ubisoft's *Just Dance* had moved a massive 58.08 million copies across multiple platforms as of 31 Mar 2016, according to VGChartz.

Just Dance 3 (2011) is the **best-selling dance game**, with a total of 12.87 million units sold for the Wii, PS3 and X360.

5

Nickelodeon Kids' Choice "Best Videogame" awards won by the *Just Dance* series, as of the 2016 ceremony.

Longest-running instrument videogame series

Konami's *GuitarFreaks* hit arcades in 1998. The most recent version – *AC GITADORA Tri-Boost* – was released 17 years later, on 21 Apr 2015. It features 791 songs by the likes of Babymetal. Tub-thumpers can opt for sister game *DrumMania*, which debuted in 1999.

Most viewed *Just Dance* music video

"Just Dance Kids 2 – The Gummy Bear Song (Wii Rip)" had been viewed 71,149,634 times as of 31 Mar 2016 – that's an average of more than 30 times per min since it was uploaded by YouTuber "beyre83" on 20 Nov 2011. Its popularity is partly due to the presence of Disney's *Girl Meets World* actress Sabrina Carpenter. Other YouTube uploads of the same clip take its total views close to 90 million.

Fastest completion of *Beat Sneak Bandit*

Simogo's 2012 iOS title combines rhythm-based action with stealth, making it eye-catchingly original. On 2 Jan 2014, "Rebcart" (USA) beat his way to the end in just 21 min 49 sec.

Fastest play-through of *Crypt of the NecroDancer*

Part rhythm-action game, part dungeon-crawler, *Crypt of the NecroDancer* was developed by Brace Yourself Games and released by Klei Entertainment in 2015. As of 31 Mar 2016, "incnone" (USA) held pole position on the game's leaderboard, having completed its "Story Mode" in just 17 min 44 sec.

Rhythm-game legend ParRappa the Rapper (a rapping dog) comically befriends rapper 50 Cent in the stop-motion TV show *Robot Chicken*. The comedy sketch has been viewed more than 90,000 times on YouTube.

FACT!

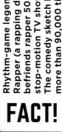

Fastest *Dance Dance Revolution* song *Dance Dance Revolution X3*'s (2011) relentless banger "Tohoku EVOLVED" peaks at a whopping 1,020 beats per min as players progress through the song. The increased rate of bpm refers to the on-screen arrows that a player has to match with their moves. The beat of the actual song does not literally speed up.

Youngest gamer to achieve a perfect score on *Dance Dance Revolution*

Ryota Wada (JPN) was aged just 9 years 288 days when he secured a flawless "AAA" rating on the "Expert" difficulty level of Konami's *Dance Dance Revolution*. He mastered the song "Hyper Eurobeat" – by Konami's resident composer Naoki Maeda – at his home in Wakayama, Japan, on 29 Aug 2010.

Longest marathon on a karaoke videogame

Julian Hill (UK) played *SingStar* (Sony, 2004) for a lung-busting 24 hr 21 min 25 sec on 13–14 Apr 2012. Fundraising for London's Great Ormond Street Hospital, Take That fan Julian began with the British pop group's "Greatest Day" and finished with their "Rule the World". He livestreamed the entire attempt, taking requests from internet users in exchange for donations to the charity.

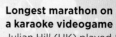

Best-selling dance mat series

More than 130 versions of Konami's *Dance Dance Revolution* have been released in arcades and on home consoles. As of 31 Mar 2016, its overall series sales amounted to 21.67 million. The original debuted on 21 Nov 1998. A total of 17 years 129 days elapsed before the most recent game, *Dance Dance Revolution A*, hit Japanese arcades on 30 Mar 2016, making it the **longest-running dance mat series**.

ROCK BAND

Publisher: Harmonix/MTV
Debut: 2007
Games: 7

Developer: Harmonix/EA
Series sales: 27.88 million
Rival: *Guitar Hero*

10 YEARS OF *GAMER'S*

...ating of 92.44%
from 47 reviews, *Rock ...*
...d 3 is the **most**
critically acclaimed inst
...ment game and
the **most critically acclaim...**
...d rhythm game.

First band-specific *Rock Band* game

Rock Band's roster consists mainly of songs from a range of artists, but the "Fab Four" got their very own edition with *The Beatles: Rock Band*. Issued on 9 Sep 2009, in the wake of the first band-specific edition of rival *Guitar Hero* (2008, for Aerosmith; see p.102), it was endorsed by former Beatles Paul McCartney and Ringo Starr.

First gamer to reach 1,000,000,000 fans on *Rock Band 3*

On 21 Nov 2010, after just 26 days of gameplay, *Rock Band 3* muso Josh Ray (USA) had gained 1,011,627,907 virtual fans. He broke the billion mark by playing the solo to Europe's 1986 chart-topper "The Final Countdown" without missing a note. Josh is now "looking to start a real band and become a musician".

First song to sell more on Xbox than iTunes

Mötley Crüe (bassist Nikki Sixx, right) let loose "Saints of Los Angeles" simultaneously on digital stores and via Xbox Live for *Rock Band* players on 11 Apr 2008. The heavy metal quartet's song shifted 47,000 units in its first week on Xbox, outselling downloads of the iTunes and Amazon versions by almost five to one.

113

Buttons representing every possible finger position on *Rock Band 3*'s Fender Mustang PRO-Guitar controller.

Lawsuits flew between Harmonix and Konami when the latter launched *Rock Revolution* in 2008. A settlement was agreed, but *Rock Band* was the sales winner over its poorly reviewed rival.

FACT!

18

Headbanging classics in 2008's *AC/DC Live: Rock Band Track Pack*, including "Back in Black".

Longest marathon drumming on *Rock Band*

A muscle-mangling 26-hr 40-min marathon was achieved by Sean "Phr34k" Feica (CAN) in Ontario on 26–27 Jul 2008. He played all 243 songs on *Rock Band* at the time, in order of difficulty, and (of which 56 were full combos). At the end, he encored with the appropriately titled "Still Alive" (by Jonathan Coulton), better known as *Portal*'s end theme.

RETAILING AT $179.99 AND FEATURING EXTENSIVE USE OF HALL & OATES' "SAY IT AIN'T SO", THE *ROCK BAND* BOARD GAME WAS UNVEILED BY HARMONIX WITH A YOUTUBE AD – "THE NEW GAME FROM HARMONIX REVEALED!" – ON 1 APR 2012. IT WAS, OF COURSE, A SPOOF.

Highest cumulative disc scores on *Rock Band 4*

A cumulative disc score refers to the points achieved across all 65 tracks that feature on the game disc. As of 29 Mar 2016, the following players held records for their chosen instruments:

• **guitar**: "a drunk taco" (12,806,592)
• **bass**: "TheRealZachBraff" (10,877,075)
• **drums**: "bookreader52" (USA) (12,832,389)
• **pro drums**: "PedroRVD" (ECU) (13,796,026)
• **vocals**: "Cdrock7" (USA) (11,748,212)
• **harmonies**: "Valkrinos" (10,048,202)
• **band**: "Peacemaker27" (USA) (26,011,521).

Most "Expert" full combos in *Rock Band 4* (guitar)

A full combo involves players performing an entire song to perfection, without fluffing a single note. As of 29 Mar 2016, virtual axe-wizard "CURS06" had achieved 1,046 full combos on the game's "Expert" setting.

As of the same date, budding frontman "BansheeMan55" had wailed his way to 988 full combos – the **most "Expert" full combos on *Rock Band 4* (vocals)**.

Highest individual score recorded on *Rock Band 4*

American gamer "vic699" scored a powerful 847,954 playing bass on Iron Maiden's "Powerslave" – *Rock Band 4*'s highest individual score as of 29 Mar 2016.

Maiden were also responsible for the **most difficult song in the first *Rock Band*** – their hit "Run to the Hills" was rated nine for difficulty on guitar, vocals, drums and bass.

Most downloadable songs for a rhythm game
Although constantly changing due to the arrival of new DLC, as of 6 Apr 2016, the *Rock Band 4* Music Store had 1,845 songs to download. Its vast, eclectic repertoire catered for all musical tastes, with artists as diverse as U2, Ed Sheeran, Royal Blood, Sam Hunt, Opeth, Outkast and shock-rock legend Marilyn Manson (right).

Longest downloadable song in a *Rock Band* game

"2112" by Canadian prog rockers Rush is so long that it filled a whole side of a vinyl record on its original release in 1976. On *Rock Band 4*, it's an endurance-testing 20 min 27 sec, or 618 bars and 1 beat. Inevitably, the epic also holds the record for **most gems playable in one song on *Rock Band 4*** – its 13,453 total betters even DragonForce's finger-melter "Through the Fire and Flames".

GUITAR HERO

Publisher: Activision
Debut: 2005
Games: 7

Developer: Various
Series sales: 61.6 million
Rivals: *Rock Band*

Youngest gamer to 5-star "Through the Fire and Flames" on "Expert" difficulty

First appearing in *Guitar Hero III: Legends of Rock* (2007), "Through the Fire and Flames" by UK metal-heads DragonForce is regarded as one of the toughest *Guitar Hero* tracks in existence. On 24 Nov 2007, Ben Eberle (USA) mastered it aged just 9 years 167 days.

Highest guitar-part score on a *Guitar Hero* game

On 17 Jun 2014, "Thabeast721" scored 1,063,377 while playing *Guitar Hero: Metallica*'s epic "Mercyful Fate" – as of 30 Mar 2016, the highest score on any *Guitar Hero* game.

Highest score for a vocal part on *Guitar Hero Live*

Performing the "Expert"-level vocal track of "Berzerk" by Eminem, "parzrevenge" achieved a score of 368,755 on 20 Oct 2015. It was still unbeaten, as of 30 Mar 2016.

Most viewed fan film based on an instrument game

Posted to YouTube "Blaze IDIUc Comedy" on 25 Jun 2008, "Worlds most impossible gh3 song!!" had been viewed an incredible 30,150,277 times as of 30 Mar 2016. The video features BloodBlitz attempting a play-through of an ultra-tough custom song on the PC version of *Guitar Hero III* titled "Do not try this song!!". He does well to emerge with a score of 498 out of 2,340, with 21% of the notes hit. The clip is by far the most popular of the 143 he has uploaded.

Highest score on *Guitar Hero Live*

On 11 Jan 2016, "Lo11o2" scored 663,622 playing the "Expert"-level guitar part of "I Will Wait" by Mumford & Sons – the highest recorded score on any *GH Live* song on any level, as of 30 Mar 2016. Lo11o2 hit more than 1,000 consecutive correct notes during the course of the song.

DANNY JOHNSON (USA) IS A LEGEND OF THE VIRTUAL FRETBOARD AND HOLDS SEVERAL GWR TITLES FOR *GUITAR HERO* HIGH SCORES. HIS YOUTUBE CHANNEL "GUITARHEROPHENOM" SHOWS HE'S NO SLOUCH ON REAL INSTRUMENTS, TOO.

FACT! Scientists at Johns Hopkins University in Maryland, USA, used adapted *Guitar Hero III* controllers while developing prosthetic limbs. The controllers helped to calibrate the electrical signals generated by the residual muscles of amputees.

3 Baseball games missed by pro pitcher Joel Zumaya (USA) in 2006 – he was benched by the Detroit Tigers owing to a wrist injury caused by playing *Guitar Hero*!

First band-specific *Guitar Hero* game

Released in Europe on 27 Jun 2008, *Guitar Hero: Aerosmith* featured the iconic riffwork of the US rock band behind songs such as "Livin' on the Edge" and "Walk This Way". The game took wannabe rock behemoths on the journey from tiny club venues to packed-out arenas. It was later followed by similar titles featuring US groups Metallica and Van Halen.

Longest continuous custom note streak in *Guitar Hero*

Performing a player-made track in *Guitar Hero: Warriors of Rock* (2010), Jeremy Durand (USA) achieved a custom streak of 7,500 continuous notes on 14 Feb 2015. This feat of sustained tapping excellence and endurance was streamed live on his Twitch channel.

GUINNESS WORLD RECORDS

OTE
REAK

Best-selling rhythm game series

As of 31 Mar 2016, Activision's *Guitar Hero* series had sold 61.6 million units according to VGChartz. That figure put the series roughly 3 million ahead of its nearest rival, Ubisoft's *Just Dance*, which boasted overall sales of 58.08 million.

The **best-selling rhythm game** across multiple platforms is 2007's *Guitar Hero III: Legends of Rock*. The popular sequel had shifted 16.39 million units for PS2, PS3, Wii and X360 consoles.

3,722

Notes in DragonForce's "Through the Fire and Flames" on *GH III*. The song lasts for 7 min 24 sec, which works out at 8.38 notes every second!

10 YEARS OF *GAMER'S*

On 23–26 Feb 2012, Patrick Young (USA) achieved the **longest marathon on Guitar Hero** by playing for 72 hr 17 min.

Highest score on *Guitar Hero III* (female)

On 30 Sep 2010, Annie Leung (USA) racked up a score of 789,349 playing DragonForce's classic *Guitar Hero* track "Through the Fire and Flames" at her home in San Francisco, California, USA. Annie honed her gaming skills playing Epic Games' 1999 FPS *Unreal Tournament*, before switching her attention from the gun to the guitar.

Largest funeral for a fictional object

On 23 Nov 2006, a funeral for the air guitar was held in London, UK, to mark the launch of *Guitar Hero II*. More than 80 "mourners" watched as a guitar-shaped coffin was carried in by goth pallbearers, while a church organist and choir performed songs such as Boston's "More Than a Feeling" and Nirvana's "Heart-Shaped Box".

GIANT GAME WORLDS

Developers constantly push the boundaries of game worlds. Handcrafted areas, drawn with detail and character, form the basis of many popular titles. However, the resurgence of procedural generation has meant that some worlds – or universes – have grown to truly astonishing sizes.

Procedural generation is a technique in which terrain is randomly generated by algorithms rather than designed by hand. By employing it, developers can create games in which unique landscapes are created on the fly by the game's code. It sounds futuristic, but procedural generation has been around since the late 1970s and 1980s. In those earlier days the technique was popular because it saved on file size; less space is required to write a set of simple rules for how levels should be assembled rather than describing the exact appearance of each level. The technique fell out of favour in the 1990s with the rise of compact discs and increased storage space.

Today, the vast wealth of processing power and the popularity of open-world titles such as *Minecraft* and *Star Citizen* mean that it's firmly back in fashion – and, as a result, game worlds are now truly super-huge.

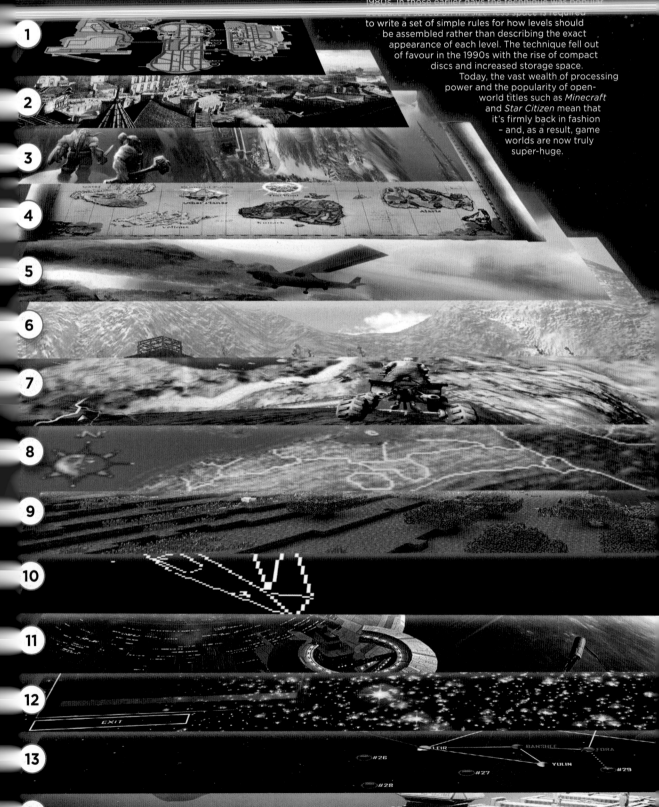

1

2

3

4

5

6

7

8

9

10

11

12

13

14

Here are some of the largest and most iconic game worlds (all sizes approximate)

1. *Grand Theft Auto III*
- Rockstar, 2001
- Size: 9 km² (3.4 sq mi)

A landmark title for the games industry, this crime romp featured an open 3D world of seemingly limitless possibility. However, its size is pretty small by modern standards – at 127 km² (49 sq mi), 2013's *Grand Theft Auto V* is more than 14 times larger.

2. *The Witcher 3: Wild Hunt*
- CD Projekt, 2015
- Size: over 136 km² (52.5 sq mi)

Prior to its release, developers claimed that *The Witcher 3* would be 35 times the size of its predecessor. The epic RPG sequel features the free city of Novigrad, which carries a sizeable population of 30,000, and a group of six islands known as the Skellige.

3. *World of Warcraft*
- Blizzard, 2004
- Size: 200 km² (77 sq mi), pre-*The Burning Crusade*

With five expansions released as of Apr 2016 (and a sixth in the works), *WoW*'s total playable size remains a mystery. However, prior to the release of expansion *The Burning Crusade* (2007), player "Tobold Stoutfoot" calculated it by running in a straight line from the east end of Thousand Needles to the west coast of Feralas.

4. *EverQuest*
- Sony Online Entertainment, 1999
- Size: 906 km² (349.8 sq mi)
- Procedurally generated

Launched soon after *Furcadia* (1996) and *Ultima Online* (1997), *EverQuest* is still an MMORPG pioneer. The game is set in Norrath, a vast, medieval world divided into more than 500 zones.

5. *Just Cause*
- Eidos, 2006
- Size: 1,012 km² (390 sq mi)
- Partially procedurally generated

Released around the birth of seventh-gen consoles, *Just Cause* set a new standard for open worlds. Players were discouraged from walking across its tropical island setting owing to an abundance of cars, bikes, boats, helicopters and aircraft.

6. *Vanguard: Saga of Heroes*
- Sony Online Entertainment, 2007
- Size: 1,068 km² (412 sq mi)
- Partially procedurally generated

This fantasy MMORPG's seamless world, known as Telon, was spread across three sprawling islands. Players could travel between each of them by flying on winged creatures, sailing in player-crafted ships, or riding on the backs of "normal" horses.

7. *Fuel*
- Codemasters, 2009
- Size: 14,400 km² (5,560 sq mi)
- Partially procedurally generated

A post-apocalyptic racer, *Fuel*'s hazardous open world is the **largest playable area in a racing game**. Jim Rossignol of Rock, Paper, Shotgun drove around its circumference shortly after the game's release. It took him just under eight hours in a buggy to complete the circuit.

8. *The Elder Scrolls II: Daggerfall*
- Bethesda, 1996
- Size: 161,600 km² (62,394 sq mi)
- Procedurally generated

Thanks to procedural generation, the first two *Elder Scrolls* games dwarf their modern sequels. Predecessor *Arena* (1994) is technically larger, but it's impossible to move from towns without fast-travelling.

9. *Minecraft*
- Mojang, 2011
- Size: 4,096,000,000 km² (1,581,474,441 sq mi)
- Procedurally generated

Minecraft is notorious for its size. The game's physics function on blocks up to 32 million blocks away from its world's centre, allowing for a maximum area that's roughly eight times the surface area of Earth.

10. *Elite*
- Acornsoft, 1984
- Size: 2,048 star systems

When developer duo David Braben and Ian Bell told Acornsoft that their space-trading sim could have 282 trillion galaxies, the publisher told them to limit the game to eight in case players didn't believe them! *Elite* eventually launched with 2,048 star systems, to huge critical acclaim.

11. *EVE Online*
- CCP Games, 2003
- Size: 7,800 star systems

With the release of the *Rhea* update on 9 Dec 2014, the number of star systems in the space-faring MMORPG increased to a whopping 7,800. Of these, 1,907 are in Empire regions, 3,294 are in Outlaw regions and 2,599 are in the tricky-to-access Wormhole regions.

12. *Elite: Dangerous*
- Frontier Developments, 2014
- Size: 400 billion star systems

David Braben's space sequel features approximately 400 billion star systems to explore – more even than our own Milky Way. Around 160,000 of them are based on real astronomical data, while the rest are procedurally generated.

13. *Star Citizen*
- Cloud Imperium Games, 2016
- Size: 4 quadrillion km³ (1 quadrillion cu mi) per star system

The incoming space sim was due to launch with 100 star systems, each one measuring approximately 4 quadrillion cubic km in volume. Explorers of the game's vast, persistent universe will encounter natural effects such as nebulae and asteroid fields alongside man-made structures such as space stations and derelict ships.

14. *No Man's Sky*
- Hello Games, 2016
- Size: 18,446,744,073,709,551,616 planets

The indie space game features more than 18 quintillion procedurally generated planets to explore, each with its own wildlife, plant life and weather systems. Its size earns it the overall record for **largest videogame universe**. To see each planet for one second would take 585 billion years, so it's impossible to see everything! However, players can upload their planetary findings to a universal database known as The Atlas.

MINECRAFT'S MAMMOTH SIZE MAKES IT THE LARGEST PLAYABLE OPEN WORLD IN A LAND-BASED GAME. THE YOUTUBE VIDEO "HOW BIG IS MINECRAFT?" BY "NULLATRUM" EXPLORES ITS SIZE IN VIVID DETAIL, AND HAD EARNED 2,168,071 VIEWS BY 4 MAY 2016.

STAR WARS

No movie-to-videogame licence has been more prolific than George Lucas' *Star Wars*. Diverse titles have enabled gamers to live out their greatest fantasies, from wielding lightsabers and blowing up Death Stars to turning to the dark side...

Largest collection of videogames

A long time ago, in a galaxy far, far away – or, more specifically, 1980 in Australia – Joel Hopkins was bitten by the gaming bug thanks to the Atari home-console version of *Space Invaders*. Over the next four decades, his games collection swelled to 17,466, as counted in Victoria on 12 Jan 2016. Among them is a rare Japanese Mega Drive version of *Tetris* from 1989, of which fewer than 10 are known to exist today. Enviably for Jedi fans, Joel owns a Death Star-sized haul of 325 *Star Wars* games, which includes region-specific releases, cross-platform ports and special editions. He also collects other Jedi-themed merchandise in the shape of toys and figures, maintaining a special display area in his home that is guarded by a menacing, life-sized Darth Vader!

"THESE AREN'T THE GAMES YOU'RE LOOKING FOR..." – JOEL HOPKINS TAKES THE SECURITY OF HIS *STAR WARS* COLLECTION VERY SERIOUSLY INDEED...

A LONG TIME AGO, IN A GALAXY FAR, FAR AWAY...

Large and lucrative, the *Star Wars* franchise has become. Just as George Lucas's sci-fi dynasty has launched countless toys, cartoons and collectible merchandise, it has also inspired 38 years of game adaptations. The *Star Wars*

based on a film licence, with a staggering 137 official titles (excluding ports and expansions) released as of 8 Apr 2016. And it all started on a home computer a long, long time ago, in a living room not so far away...

1978

Apple Computer's *Starwars* cassette game for the Apple II isn't official, but that doesn't bother fans. Playing from a first-person HUD view, trainee pilots have to gun down ships that look like TIE fighters.

1982

Released for the Atari 2600 and Intellivision, Parker Brothers' *The Empire Strikes Back* is the **first official *Star Wars* game**. It casts gamers as Luke Skywalker during the Battle of Hoth, challenging him to fly a snowspeeder against AT-AT walkers.

2000

Star Wars: Force Commander (LucasArts) is the **first *Star Wars* RTS** game. It casts the player as Brenn Tantor, a promising Imperial officer who defects to the Rebels.

1999

Big Ape's *Star Wars: Episode I – The Phantom Menace* leads to a wave of games based on the *Star Wars* prequel trilogy, such as *Battle for Naboo* (2000) and *Obi-Wan* (2001).

2003

Set after the events of *A New Hope*, *Star Wars Galaxies* (Sony Online) is the **first *Star Wars* MMO**. It features familiar locations and 10 playable species. Servers shut down in 2011.

2003

BioWare's mega-acclaimed RPG *Star Wars: Knights of the Old Republic* transports gamers to 4,000 years before the Galactic Empire's reign, to crush Darth Malak.

2004

The FPS *Star Wars: Battlefront* (EA) recruits players for an all-out war between factions from the original and prequel film trilogies. It enjoys two sequels, in 2005 and 2015.

2016

Due for release by Warner Bros. in 2016, *LEGO Star Wars: The Force Awakens* will see the 2015 movie – *Episode VII* – enjoying a bricky adaptation.

2015

Star Wars: Uprising and *Galaxy of Heroes* (above) lead a growing list of mobile titles that offer players a way to save the galaxy while on the go.

2015

Star Wars: Card Trader (The Topps Company) is a digital card-trading app for mobiles. Couch-bound gamers can collect characters from across the entire franchise.

1983

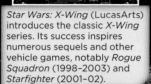

Star Wars: Jedi Arena (Parker Brothers) is the **first game with lightsaber action**. The overhead shooter pits virtual Jedis against one another over four levels of difficulty.

1993

Star Wars: X-Wing (LucasArts) introduces the classic *X-Wing* series. Its success inspires numerous sequels and other vehicle games, notably *Rogue Squadron* (1998–2003) and *Starfighter* (2001–02).

1997

Star Wars: Masters of Teräs Käsi pits the movies' heroes against Arden Lyn and her army in a one-on-one fighter. Leia (above) and Mara Jade both star as playable female Jedis.

1996

Star Wars: Shadows of the Empire (LucasArts) is one of the first N64 games. It introduces fans to Dash Rendar, a Han Solo-like smuggler who aids the Rebel cause.

1995

Star Wars: Dark Forces (LucasArts) brings Rebel fighter Kyle Katarn to *Star Wars*' expanded universe. The game's popularity gives rise to four sequels between 1997 and 2003.

2005

LEGO® Star Wars: The Video Game (LucasArts) is the first of several LEGO-themed action-adventures to emerge from an alliance between the two giant franchises.

2008

One of the first games considered "canon" by George Lucas, *Star Wars: The Force Unleashed* (LucasArts) follows Darth Vader's secret apprentice, Starkiller.

2011

Set thousands of years before the original movies, *Star Wars: The Old Republic* (EA) is a new MMO from BioWare. Players fight for either the Sith or the Galactic Republic.

2015

EA DICE's *Star Wars Battlefront* reboot resurrects the series just in time for the new *Star Wars* movie trilogy. Up to 40 players participate in anarchic skirmishes on iconic planets such as Hoth and Tatooine. The game also features an array of pilotable craft including X-Wings, AT-ATs and speeder bikes (above).

2012

Terminal Reality's *Kinect Star Wars* doesn't shake up the galaxy, but it does add motion-controlled gaming to the mix. It also includes a "Galactic Dance-Off"!

The original *Star Wars* film trilogy coincided with the "Golden Age of Arcade Games" in the late 1970s and early 1980s, which led

arcade titles. Players have racked up astronomical scores playing *Star Wars* pinball games, often on a single credit.

Most points on *Star Wars Trilogy Arcade*

Sega's *Trilogy Arcade* cabinet debuted in 1999 and featured rail-original film trilogy, with bonus missions against Darth Vader or Boba Fett. Ken Towne's (USA) galactic score of 3,612,600 was verified by Twin Galaxies on 28 Mar 2003.

First *Star Wars* arcade machine

Released in 1983, Atari's *Star Wars* had players guide Luke Skywalker's X-Wing on a mission to destroy the Death Star, battling Darth Vader and TIE fighters along the way. The cabinet was available in two versions: upright and sit-down cockpit (pictured above, with *Star Wars* director George Lucas inside).

Highest score on *Star Wars Pinball: Balance of the Force* (Android/iOS)

At the Kiip Mobile Gaming Championship held on 24–26 Jan 2014, Todd Kellen (USA) led a one-man assault on Zen Studios' 2013 pinball title. He racked up 1,960,548,846 points on the game's three *Star Wars*-themed tables, a phenomenal tally considering that the average score was only 4,496,797.

Star Wars: Battle Pod has a "Premium Edition" available in two designs, each weighing 435 kg (959 lb) – the heaviest *Star Wars* arcade machine.

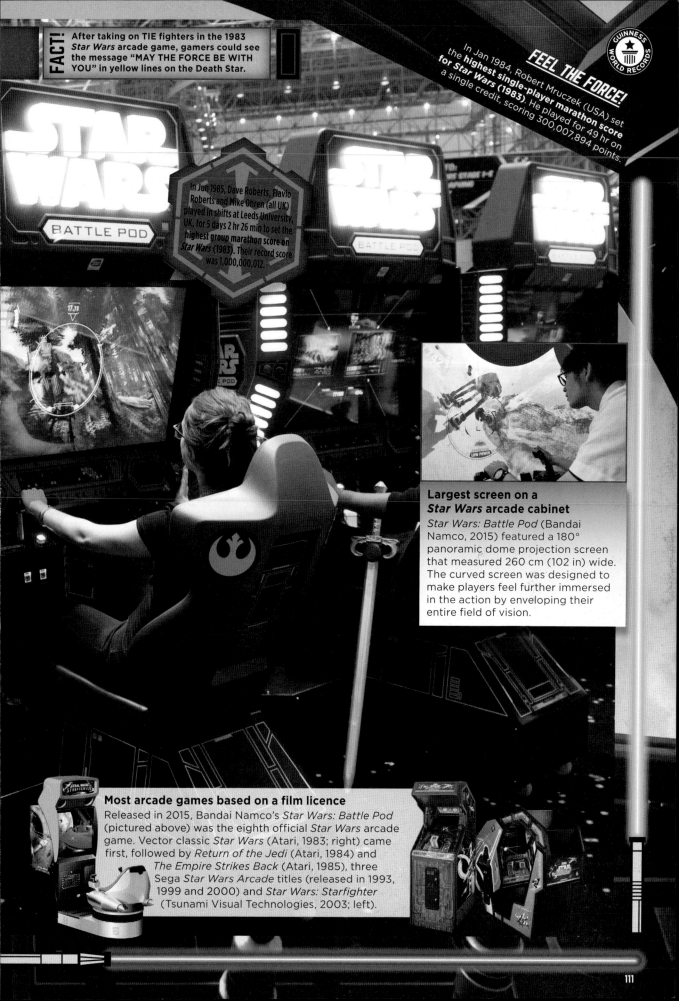

FEEL THE FORCE!

In Jan 1984, Robert Mruczek (USA) set the **highest single-player marathon score for *Star Wars* (1983)**. He played for 49 hr on a single credit, scoring 300,007,894 points.

In Jun 1985, Dave Roberts, Flavio Roberts and Mike Ohren (all UK) played in shifts at Leeds University, UK, for 5 days 2 hr 26 min to set the **highest group marathon score on *Star Wars* (1983)**. Their record score was 1,000,000,012.

Largest screen on a *Star Wars* arcade cabinet

Star Wars: Battle Pod (Bandai Namco, 2015) featured a 180° panoramic dome projection screen that measured 260 cm (102 in) wide. The curved screen was designed to make players feel further immersed in the action by enveloping their entire field of vision.

Most arcade games based on a film licence

Released in 2015, Bandai Namco's *Star Wars: Battle Pod* (pictured above) was the eighth official *Star Wars* arcade game. Vector classic *Star Wars* (Atari, 1983; right) came first, followed by *Return of the Jedi* (Atari, 1984) and *The Empire Strikes Back* (Atari, 1985), three Sega *Star Wars Arcade* titles (released in 1993, 1999 and 2000) and *Star Wars: Starfighter* (Tsunami Visual Technologies, 2003; left).

SHOOTERS

Star Wars boasts a long tradition of action-packed shooters. When EA DICE, the development team behind the successful

was brought on board to reboot the *Star Wars: Battlefront* series, the result was one of the biggest hits of 2015.

Best-selling *Star Wars* game (single platform)

The PS4 version of EA's multiplayer shooter *Star Wars Battlefront* (2015) had sold 7.2 million copies as of 4 Apr 2016, according to VGChartz. The title was a reboot of LucasArts' *Battlefront* series (2004–13). More than 9.5 million gamers played its beta on 8–13 Oct 2015 – the **most popular beta for a shooter**.

Fastest completion of *Star Wars: Republic Commando*

In LucasArts' 2005 FPS, players undertake missions as part of Delta Squad, an elite tactical unit of Clone Army commandos. On 24 Dec 2013, gamer "LazerLong" (USA) battled through the game in just 2 hr 47 min 31 sec, as verified by Speedrun.com.

Fastest completion of *Star Wars Battlefront* survival mode without blasters (team of two)

Playing on the Rebel Depot map on 7 Apr 2016, "Twiinsane", aka twins Liam and Jake Thompson (UK), finished all 15 waves of survival mode in 10 min 24 sec. The Rebel duo were prohibited from using their primary blasters, instead relying on power-up cards.

On 6 Oct 2010, David "RandomEngy" Rickard and Mark "Exploding Cabbage" Amery (both USA) completed the **fastest completion** of *Jedi Knight: Dark Forces II* – 25 min 57 sec, as verified by Speed Demos Archive.

FACT! In the first three weeks following *Battlefront*'s 2015 release, a total of 2.4 million Stormtroopers were hit with rocks thrown by Ewoks.

Released in 1995, Star Wars: Dark Forces was the **first Star Wars FPS**. Players don the guise of Kyle Katarn, a mercenary who uncovers a plot to develop superior Stormtroopers.

Fastest campaign completion of *Star Wars: Battlefront II*

On 23 Feb 2016, gamer "ctc" (USA) finished the 2005 sequel (above) in just 49 min 49 sec.

As of 4 Apr 2016, the **fastest completion of the Clone Wars in *Star Wars: Battlefront* (2004)** was 39 min 8 sec, achieved by "SilenceOfTheLamy", aka Alex Lamy (UK), on 30 Mar 2016.

IT'S FAIR TO SAY THAT EA'S "STAR WARS BATTLEFRONT REVEAL" YOUTUBE VIDEO RECEIVED AN EXCITED REACTION. FOLLOWING PUBLICATION ON 17 APR 2015, THE TRAILER WAS VIEWED 4.5 MILLION TIMES IN 24 HOURS!

Most played special character in *Star Wars Battlefront*

According to figures released by EA, players spent 29.8 million min as ice-cool bounty hunter Boba Fett during the three weeks following the reboot's launch on 17 Nov 2015. Luke Skywalker was the second-most-played special character, with Han Solo coming in third.

STAR WARS TOYS & COLLECTABLES

The fandom surrounding *Star Wars* has not only inspired diehard collectors to haul together all things Jedi, it's also triggered a range of spin-off crossover videogame stars, from *Disney Infinity*'s *Star Wars Rebels* to the mighty *Angry Birds*.

Largest collection of *Star Wars* memorabilia

Steve Sansweet (USA, above) has catalogued 93,260 unique items at Rancho Obi-Wan in California, USA. The haul features arcade machines and videogames, including ultra-rare prototype samples of *Revenge of the Jedi*, before the 1984 game was renamed *Return of the Jedi* to follow suit with the 1983 movie. When the cataloguing of the collection is complete, it may number more than 500,000.

Largest range of toys-to-life figures from a film franchise

Created for use with *Disney Infinity 3.0* (see below), there had been 19 *Star Wars* toys-to-life figurines unleashed as of 5 Apr 2016. Figures include *Star Wars: The Force Awakens* characters Rey, Finn, Poe Dameron and the First Order's Kylo Ren (main picture).

Most viewed *Star Wars* videogame trailer

The "Angry Birds *Star Wars* Cinematic Trailer" had been viewed 52,140,784 times on YouTube as of 3 May 2016. The trailer was published on 7 Nov 2012, and has earned an average of more than 43,000 views a day. Since the release of the *Angry Birds Star Wars* games, its feathery stars have been immortalized in their own range of collectable *Star Wars* toys.

ON 3–4 SEP 2015, LUCASFILM STAGED AN 18-HR LIVESTREAM IN WHICH NEW *STAR WARS: THE FORCE AWAKENS* GAMES, TOYS AND GADGETS WERE UNBOXED BY YOUTUBERS INCLUDING "EVANTUBEHD" AND "ALEXBY11".

FEEL THE FORCE! As of 3 May 2016, the highest score on *Disney Infinity 3.0*'s *Star Wars: Rise Against the Empire*: "Mos Eisley Madness" was 1,130, set by Wii U Jedi "disneyruss24".

GUINNESS WORLD RECORDS

Fastest completion of the *Star Wars: The Force Awakens* Play Set on *Disney Infinity 3.0*

Launched on 28 Aug 2015, *Disney Infinity 3.0* was the third release in Disney's growing toys-to-life series. On 12 Jan 2016, gamer "Zimmycakesrtg" (USA) completed a run-through of *The Force Awakens Play Set* in just 1 hr 2 min 40 sec.

Star Wars: Card Trader is a mobile app that lets fans trade digital cards. The **most valuable card** is the Vintage "Han in the *Millennium Falcon*", of which only 1,500 are available. Copies have sold online for as much as $224.99 (£151.75).

Moviegoers are thrilled by *Star Wars*' deep-space battles and electrifying lightsaber combat. Now games such as *The*

LEGO® series replicate the films' exhilarating action sequences to great success and acclaim.

First *Star Wars* videogame to use mobiles as lightsabers

Google's *Lightsaber Escape* went live in Dec 2015, allowing internet users to turn

sync them to an online *Star Wars* game. By moving their phone, gamers could deflect fire from stormtroopers onscreen.

First *Star Wars* videogame with motion controls

Lightsaber simulations were available to gamers before *Star Wars: The Force Unleashed* (LucasArts, 2008). However, the Nintendo Wii version of the action-adventure was the first to use motion controls to translate Wii Remote movement into lightsaber actions.

The **first game with lightsaber action** was Parker Brothers' *Star Wars: Jedi Arena*, which was released for the Atari 2600 back in 1983.

Fastest completion of *Star Wars: Obi-Wan*

Originally developed for the PC, *Obi-Wan* (2001) was eventually released as an early title for the Xbox. On 19 May 2015, Alex "SilenceOfTheLamy" Lamy (UK) guided the Padawan to victory in just 1 hr 14 min 18 sec, as verified by Speedrun.com.

Rarest *Star Wars* game

Star Wars: Return of the Jedi: Ewok Adventure (Atari, 1983) was a shoot-'em-up designed for the Atari 2600. However, it was shelved after publishers Parker Brothers decided the controls were too difficult. The game's designer, Larry Gelberg, gifted the prototype to a friend's son, who sold it for $1,680 (£980) in 1997.

FEEL THE FORCE!

On 11 Apr 2015, Dan "LifeL1ke" Ciminskie (USA) achieved the **fastest completion of *Star Wars: The Force Unleashed*** in 55 min 29 sec, as verified by Speedrun.com.

Most critically acclaimed game based on a toy

LEGO Star Wars II: The Original Trilogy (LucasArts, 2006) allowed players to take on the guises of more than 50 characters from the *Star Wars* franchise. The PC version had earned a GameRankings rating of 86.83% as of 5 Apr 2016, placing it above *Skylanders: Swap Force*'s 84.68%.

The fastest any% completion of *LEGO Star Wars: The Complete Saga* is 3 hr 44 min 46 sec, by "smkurki" (FIN) on 26 Sep 2015, as verified by Speedrun.com. "I'm done..." said the PC gamer. "Feel free to break all my records."

Best-selling *Star Wars* videogame

First released on 6 Nov 2007, *LEGO Star Wars: The Complete Saga* (LucasArts) featured levels adapted from two previous titles: *LEGO Star Wars: The Video Game* (2005) and *Lego Star Wars II: The Original Trilogy* (2006). As of 4 Apr 2016, the brick-busting release had sold 15.57 million copies across four platforms: Wii, DS, PS3 and Xbox 360.

From the ice planet Hoth to the desert wastes of Tatooine, the *Star Wars* universe offers boundless possibilities for RPGs. Titles such as BioWare's 2003 epic *Star Wars: Knights of the Old Republic* (*KotOR*) have taken full advantage.

First *Star Wars* MMORPG

Twenty-one years after the first licenced *Star Wars* game, *Star Wars Galaxies – An Empire Divided* was published in 2003. By becoming mayors, players had the opportunity to make improvements to civic structures as their cities increased in size and rank – creating the **first player-managed cities in an MMORPG**.

Largest voice-acting project in the entertainment industry

During the making of *Star Wars: The Old Republic* (EA, 2011), 246,250 lines of recorded dialogue were performed by 321 voice actors. More than 4,000 characters were portrayed, speaking 17 alien languages. Played consecutively, this dialogue would have lasted for 11 days.

Highest-scoring gamer in *Star Wars: The Old Republic* – Ranked Warzone Arena

In the 2011 MMORPG, teams aligned to the Sith or the Old Republic can do battle in specially designated zones. As of 4 Apr 2016, the score of 3,302 by Sage Sorcerer "Doublebubbles" in Season 2 remained the highest on the Ranked Warzone Arena Leaderboards.

"Czerka's Crate-O-Matic", a helpful tool in *The Old Republic* that lets the user hide in plain sight, has a drop rate of one in a billion, according to lead combat designer Georg Zoeller. This makes it the rarest item in *Star Wars: The Old Republic*.

FEEL THE FORCE!

The Moraj Memorial flag on Tatooine in *Star Wars Galaxies* (2003) is the **first virtual memorial in a MMORPG**. It paid tribute to beta tester Nathan Larkins, who died in a car accident.

GUINNESS WORLD RECORDS

Most appearances in a *Star Wars* RPG

Perhaps surprisingly, the most prolific RPG character isn't Han Solo or Luke Skywalker but sadistic droid and "meatbag" hunter HK-47. The assassin was a playable ally in both *KotOR* and *KotOR II*, a boss battle in *The Old Republic*, and a preserved artificial intelligence housed in a super computer in *Star Wars Galaxies*.

Most downloaded mod for *Star Wars: Knights of the Old Republic II*

The "Sith Lords Restored Content Modification" fixes a reported 500 bugs and restores cut content from *KotOR II*'s original 2004 release. As of 4 Apr 2016, it had reached 229,479 Steam downloads and 169,568 ModDB.com downloads.

Fastest completion of *Star Wars: Knights of the Old Republic*

On 14 Feb 2014, US gamer "glasnonck" completed *KotOR* in 1 hr 32 min 54 sec (with loads), as verified by Speedrun.com.

"glasnonck" also set the **fastest completion of *KotOR II***, having finished the game in just 1 hr 18 min 15 sec on 13 Dec 2015.

Most critically acclaimed *Star Wars* game

Featuring Jedi Bastila Shan (above), the Xbox version of the RPG *Star Wars: Knights of the Old Republic* (LucasArts, 2003) had a GameRankings rating of 94.21% from 99 reviews as of 4 Apr 2016. It was developed by BioWare, the RPG specialists behind *Mass Effect* and *Dragon Age* who went on to develop the MMO *Star Wars: The Old Republic*.

From AT-ATs to TIE fighters, from X-Wings to the *Millennium Falcon*, the *Star Wars* universe has produced some of the

science fiction. When it comes to piloting them, videogames can make your space fantasies reality...

Most critically acclaimed space-flight game

No game with space flight as its core mechanic has fared better with the critics than *Star Wars Rogue Squadron II: Rogue Leader* (LucasArts, 2001). As of 4 Apr 2016, the dogfighting supremo had scored 90.04% from 75 reviews at GameRankings. Just behind it was *Star Wars: Starfighter* (2001), with 86.01%.

Most kills by a vehicle in *Star Wars Battlefront*

Battlefront (EA, 2015) features a furious blend of FPS warring and vehicular combat. In the three weeks from the game's launch on 17 Nov 2015, the Empire's bipedal AT-STs logged 61 million kills. By comparison, the *Millennium Falcon* (below) had made a "mere" 9 million kills, but given that only one gamer can pilot that ship at any time (and that it's not always available), that's still a lethal return.

How's this for getting the job done? Gamer Jaakko "JichiSenpai" Tammela (FIN) achieved the fastest 100% completion of *Star Wars Episode I: Racer* (LucasArts, 1999) for PC, in 1 hr 46 min 11 sec on 17 Mar 2016.

FEEL THE FORCE!

Released for iOS in Nov 2010, *Star Wars Arcade: Falcon Gunner* was the **first augmented reality Star Wars game**. It featured a 360° view and touch-screen controls.

APPARENTLY A YEAR IN THE MAKING, THE FEB 2016 YOUTUBE ANIMATION "STAR KART – STAR WARS + MARIO KART" BY "DARK PIXEL" FEATURES *MARIO KART* PETROLHEADS RACING IN *STAR WARS* VEHICLES. THE KART AWAKENS!

Fastest completion of *Rogue Squadron III: Rebel Strike*

Playing as the starfighter pilot Wedge Antilles, Michael "Tigger77" Welle finished this 2003 sequel in 27 min 41 sec on 15 Nov 2008, as listed by Speed Demos Archive.

The **fastest completion of Battle of Hoth in *Star Wars Rogue Squadron II: Rogue Leader*** is 3 min 41 sec, achieved by Jon A Palisi (USA) and verified by Twin Galaxies on 22 Sep 2008.

Dagger

Fastest completion of *Star Wars: Starfighter*

On 22 Feb 2015, "oldhog" (USA) flew through this pre-Battle of Naboo space fighter in 1 hr 13 min 6 sec. "It wasn't easy, and it wasn't pretty, but I finally got it," he wrote. The 2001 actioner featured a host of unlockable craft including the *Havoc* and Sith Infiltrator.

A-WING BLUE 4 HAS BEEN DESTROYED.

First *Star Wars* game with Galactic Empire gameplay

Star Wars: TIE Fighter (LucasArts, 1994) was the first licenced *Star Wars* game to let players explore their dark side. After more than a decade of fighting for the good guys, gamers could now represent the Empire by assuming the role of TIE fighter rookie Maarek Stele, who clashes with Rebels.

SCI-FI

Few games stretch our imaginations further than those that cross distant galaxies. From *Star Trek* to *Star Citizen*, from Fox McCloud to Master Chief, our sci-fi chapter celebrates the greatest space games in the universe... and beyond.

Most polygons in a playable spaceship

Star Citizen is renowned for its hi-tech spacecraft, and as of Apr 2016 none come bigger than the *Idris* (main image, hangar shown above). The frigate warship's model is built from a record 3,322,169 polygons and has an in-game length of 239 m (784 ft). To a real-world scale, that's longer than two American football pitches. The ship is being developed for *Star Citizen*'s single-player campaign, *Squadron 42*, set for release in late 2016, shortly ahead of the full MMO.

Star Citizen is an incoming MMO space sim that is being developed by Cloud Imperium. Set in a 30th-century Milky Way, it features a wide variety of advanced spacecraft.

Although the *Idris* is currently *Star Citizen*'s largest ship, its developer is building an even bigger one. The *Bengal* (above) will run at 1,000 m (3,280 ft) in length, and its early models have 7.5 million polygons.

SPACE SIMS

FACT! On 2 Oct 2015, Hello Games' Sean Murray (UK) demoed his game *No Man's Sky* on *The Late Show with Stephen Colbert*. Colbert said: "I thought Morgan Freeman was God. You're the second God I've had on my show now!"

Few gaming genres have generated more publicity than space sims in recent months. Thanks to new technology, gamers can now pilot spaceships through sprawling, procedurally generated universes to thrilling effect.

Largest accurate videogame universe

Elite: Dangerous (2014) simulates a playable solar system that replicates our own Solar System with scientific accuracy. As calculated by developer Frontier Developments, it generates 4,918,906,760,000 cubic light years' worth of area for players to explore.

Longest-running space-simulation series

The *Elite* series was created by David Braben (inset) and Ian Bell (both UK). It debuted on 20 Sep 1984 with *Elite* – the **first open-world game**. Three sequels followed over 30 years 87 days: 1993's *Frontier: Elite II*, 1995's *Frontier: First Encounters* and 2014's *Elite: Dangerous*).

Most crowdfunded videogame

As of 4 Mar 2016, the space-faring MMO *Star Citizen* (Cloud Imperium, 2016) had raised $109,460,348 (£77,637,500) from 1,293,782 backers, many of whom had been buying in-game spaceships. Such support also makes it the **most crowdfunded project overall**.

Q&A: Chris Roberts (*Star Citizen* director)

***Star Citizen* holds the record for most crowdfunded project. Have you been surprised by the response?**
Yes, when I started the campaign I was hoping to raise $4 m (£2.7 m). I thought we'd have to raise money by more traditional methods. So it's been crazy!

Has the financing enabled you to develop a more ambitious game?
Yes, we're now building a game with a level of fidelity that we couldn't have achieved with our original goals. When we've finished, I think it will be up there with anything that the big publishers have made, and also one of the most expensive games in history.

Why are space sims currently popular?
New tech is enabling us to achieve things that we couldn't before. There's a sense of scope and possibility that you don't get with traditional, level-bound shooters, or old school space sims. You're no longer exploring 10-km² areas, you're exploring a whole universe.

84.36%. With a GameRankings score of 84.36%, the ambitious, space-traversing *Freelancer* (Microsoft, 2003) is the **most critically acclaimed space-simulation game.**

GUINNESS WORLD RECORDS

Most explorable planets in a videogame

Space epic *No Man's Sky* (2016) features 18,446,744,073,709,551,616 (that's more than 18 quintillion) planets for players to discover. Its developer, Hello Games (UK), said that even if a planet is found every second, it would still take 585 billion years to see them all, making this the **largest playable game universe**.

SET UP IN 2014 TO COVER THE DEVELOPMENT OF INDIE GAMES, YOUTUBE CHANNEL "COBRA TV" HAS BECOME A POPULAR SOURCE FOR VIDEOS OF *NO MAN'S SKY*, AS WELL AS FOR CRANEBALLS' CROWDFUNDED SCI-FI TITLE *PLANET NOMADS*.

Playing version 0.9 of Squad's *Kerbal Space Program* (2015), Scott Manley (UK) designed a rocket that made the fastest return trip from Kerbin to the Mun, taking 58 min 50 sec.

HALO

Since debuting as a launch title for the Xbox console in 2001, *Halo* has become one of the best-loved FPS franchises in gaming. Originally created by Bungie, but now handled by Microsoft's 343i studio, these militaristic, space-bound epics unfold a deadly struggle between humanity and an ancient alien race known as the Covenant.

Longest *Halo* marathon

Playing in front of the public in a Helsinki shopping mall on 27 Oct 2015, Finnish gamer Paavo "Paavi" Niskala played all five main *Halo* titles for 50 hr 4 min 17 sec. "It was fun to see how things have evolved in the games over the years and which things have not changed," he said. "*Halo 3* was my marathon highlight."

Best-selling sci-fi shooter series

Excluding its non-FPS spin-offs such as the RTS *Halo Wars* (2009), the mighty *Halo* franchise had achieved global sales of 62.8 m as of 17 Feb 2016.

The **best-selling *Halo* game** is *Halo 3* (2007), which has shifted 12.11 m units, according to VGChartz.

Most participants in a first-person shooter relay

Commemorating the *Halo* legacy in style, 54 gamers took turns playing the first four *Halo* games for 47 hr in Madrid, Spain, on 17 April 2015. The event was organized by Xbox Spain as it ramped up the buzz for *Halo 5: Guardians*, which was released six months later.

MASTER CHIEF
HALO SERIES

Alias	John-117
Occupation	Spartan super-soldier
Date of birth	27 Mar 2511
Height (minus armour)	6 ft 10 in
Missions served	200+

As part of 2015's *Halo 5* launch, cosplayer Hsu Chia-Hao (TPE) and designer Jenny Manik Mercian (AUS) created a Master Chief helmet encrusted with 25,000 Swarovski crystals.

In Oct 2010, Katherine "Mystik" Gunn (USA) won $100,000 (£63,192) playing *Halo: Reach*. She is the **highest-earning female gamer**, with winnings of $122,000 (£77,094).

SET UP IN 2007, "FORGE LABS" IS A YOUTUBE CHANNEL SHOWING COMMUNITY-CREATED CONTENT FOR *HALO*. IT FEATURES MAPS BASED ON ANYTHING FROM SKATE PARKS TO *STAR WARS*, PLUS CUSTOM GAMES WITH CRAZY TITLES SUCH AS "DRAWFUL" AND "FLAPJACK FRENZY".

Most watched game launch on YouTube

On 26 Oct 2015, Microsoft complemented the launch of *Halo 5: Guardians* with a six-hour live broadcast on YouTube Gaming. The stream attracted more than 330,000 unique viewers during the evening and amassed 5.5 m total views by the end of the week.

Most critically acclaimed FPS on an Xbox platform

The first *Halo* game, *Halo: Combat Evolved* (2001), remains the most celebrated among critics, having scored 95.54% across 78 reviews on GameRankings. The game is second only to Nintendo/Retro's *Metroid Prime* (2002) as the **most critically acclaimed shooter** overall.

SPACECRAFT SPOTTER'S GUIDE: UNSC SHIPS

YSS-1000 "Sabre"

AV-14 Attack VTOL

Sparrowhawk

SPACE SHOOTERS

FACT! The iconic triangular "Arwing" spacecraft in Nintendo's classic rail-shooter *Star Fox* has made cameos in several gaming franchises, including *Bayonetta*, *The Legend of Zelda*, *Super Smash Bros.* and even *Animal Crossing*.

In space, nobody can hear you scream... but they *can* see you get shot! Nightmarish aliens, towering robots and a blistering array of supersized sci-fi weaponry help to make space shooters one of the most testing and...

FOX MCCLOUD
STAR FOX 64

Spacecraft of choice	**Arwing**
Trademarks	**Red scarf, attitude**
Debut	***Star Fox* (1993)**
Also seen in	***Super Smash Bros.***
Catchphrase	**"Returning to base!"**

ARM CANNON

Power beam

Wave beam

First team to beat the "King's Fall" raid in *Destiny*

Just 13 hr after the unlocking of the fearsome raid mission for *Destiny* expansion *The Taken King* (Activision) on 18 Sep 2015, an intrepid six-player fireteam led by Twitch broadcaster "Gothalion" became the first group to defeat Oryx, the Taken King himself.

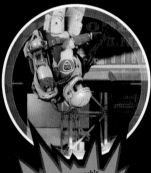

Futuremark's 2009 FPS *Shattered Horizon* was the first videogame to feature "full" zero-gravity gameplay. In the aftermath of a catastrophic lunar explosion, players floated around an open-space landscape.

Longest wall run in *Titanfall*

When outside of their giant mecha exoskeletons, pilots in EA's *Titanfall* (2014) can glide and scramble, parkour-style, along walls. In a video uploaded on 19 Feb 2014, YouTuber "WaRSPiRiTUK" managed to stretch out a balletic wall run for 1 min 4 sec.

Ice beam

Plasma beam

Most disliked videogame trailer

Published on 16 Jun 2015, the E3 trailer for the 3DS game *Metroid Prime: Federation Force* had acquired 84,646 dislikes on YouTube by 2 Mar 2016. The series' loyal fanbase had been unhappy with changes to the *Metroid* world, including the new "3 vs. 3 sci-fi sports game" Blast Ball and the omission of heroine Samus Aran.

Missile launcher

SPACECRAFT SPOTTER'S GUIDE

 Gunship from *Metroid Prime 3: Corruption*

 Arwing from *Star Fox 64 3D*

 Hunter-class gunship from *Metroid Prime*

OUT OF THIS WORLD

Metroid's reveal that Samus Aran was not male but female shocked gamers in 1986, but the **first human female as a playable character** was Toby "Kissy" Masuyo of Namco's Baraduke (1985).

VISOR SYSTEM

Combat visor

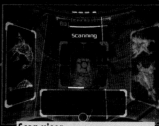

Scan visor

Thermal visor

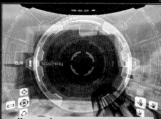

X-ray visor

Morph Ball

Most critically acclaimed FPS

The star of *Metroid Prime* (Nintendo, 2002) is bounty hunter Samus Aran, who dons an exoskeleton known as the Power Suit, which is equipped with an awesome arsenal and the ability to roll up into a small sphere known as a Morph Ball. As of 2 Mar 2016, *Metroid Prime* had a GameRankings score of 96.33% – higher than any other single FPS.

EVE ONLINE

A galactic MMO, CCP's *EVE Online* features epic space battles, rich corporations and exploration through 7,000 star systems. Most notable are its lack of rules, plus its in-game currency of InterStellar Kredits (ISKs), which convert to various real-world currencies.

Largest virtual theft in an MMORPG

A character named Cally set up the *EVE* Intergalactic Bank in 2006, then stole from it an estimated 790 billion ISK (approximately allowed by the game's licence, Cally went unpunished. In 2014, Cynosural Field Theory conned 1.19 trillion ISK from supercapital ship-buyers. However, the ISK-to-dollar exchange rate was lower at the time, so this equated to "only" about $19,200.

Longest-running convention for a single videogame

Since its 2004 debut, the EVE Fanfest in Iceland has attracted fans on an annual basis, missing only 2011. The biggest turn-out was in 2013, when 4,000 gamers celebrated the game's 10th anniversary. At the 2014 event, a team of CCP developers fought MMA fighter Gunnar Nelson (ISL, above right) in submission contests. Unsurprisingly, Nelson won every one of the bouts!

Most Titans lost in a battle in *EVE Online*

A huge battle began in the 49-U6U system, on China's Serenity server, on 25 Mar 2014. The Pan-Intergalactic Business Community and RACOA/FDK coalitions fought for 23 hr until the server went offline for a scheduled update. A total of 5,843 player-controlled characters took part in the battle, which destroyed trillions of ISKs' worth of ships and became known as the Slaughterhouse. Alongside 824 dreadnoughts and 39 supercarriers, a record 84 Titan-class ships were lost, nine more than in the Tranquility server's Bloodbath of B-R5RB (above right) earlier that year.

SPACECRAFT SPOTTER'S GUIDE: *EVE ONLINE* SHIPS

Bowhead

Eagle

Rifter

Protesting in 2011 against the "Incarna" update pack, 5,833 players claimed to have cancelled their *EVE Online* subscriptions. This was the **biggest threatened player walkout in an MMO**.

Most costly videogame battle

The infamous Bloodbath of B-R5RB, on 27–28 Jan 2014, was a 21-hr conflict involving 7,548 player characters. It saw the destruction of 75 Titans, 13 supercarriers, 370 dreadnoughts, 123 carriers and thousands of smaller ships, fighters and drones. The in-game cost of these losses was over 11 trillion ISK, the equivalent of more than $300,000 (£212,260). This was calculated to be an even greater loss than the Slaughterhouse (below left) owing to differences between the main Tranquility server and the Chinese Serenity server.

Most MMO player names on a civic monument

The 5-m-high (16-ft 5-in) Worlds Within a World monument situated in the harbour of Iceland's capital Reykjavik bears the avatar names of every *EVE Online* player active as of 1 Mar 2014. A total of 562,514 are displayed – more than the population of Iceland itself.

WHEN CCP DEVELOPERS FOUGHT GUNNAR NELSON AT EVE FANFEST IN 2014, THE CONTEST WAS IMMORTALIZED ON YOUTUBE. "FANFEST 2014 – EVE OF DESTRUCTION" HAS BEEN VIEWED AROUND 50,000 TIMES.

Rarest supercarrier in *EVE Online*

The Revenant class is a supercarrier for the NPC Sansha faction. As of 1 Mar 2016, only four had been recorded as destroyed on *EVE*'s Tranquility server: on 8 Jul 2013, 5 Sep 2014, 1 Mar 2015 and 8 Jul 2015. The first Revenant destroyed was valued at 309 billion ISK.

SPACE ROUND-UP

The force of space games has awoken, blasting out of sims and shooters into other genres. Veterans such as *Star Trek* have been

Effect – due to get its own ride at the theme park California's Great America in 2017.

Most critically acclaimed RPG

Space adventure *Mass Effect 2* (EA, 2010), on X360, holds 95.77%, from 75 reviews.

However, the series' biggest seller is *Mass Effect 3* (EA, 2012, main picture). Its X360, PS3, PC and Wii U incarnations had shifted a total of 5.71 million units as of 17 Mar 2016 – nearly a million more than its predecessor.

Meanwhile, a survey to find the game's most popular character for romance was topped by the asari scientist Liara T'Soni.

Most videogame releases for a single intellectual property in one year

Seven *Star Trek* games were launched in 2000, including *Voyager – Elite Force*, *Deep Space Nine: The Fallen*, *ConQuest Online* and *Klingon Academy* (above). LEGO® released eight games in 2013, but two of those titles were dual-licences with Marvel.

Most critically acclaimed game based on a sci-fi TV series

As of 17 Mar 2015, *Star Trek: Voyager – Elite Force* (Activision, 2000) had a GameRankings score of 85.65%. Based on the fourth *Trek* series, its gameplay centres on the stranded USS *Voyager* crew's desperate attempts to return to Earth.

The original, box-office-busting *Star Wars* trilogy and a trio of chart-topping *Wing Commander* titles (*III*, *IV* and *Prophecy*) made Mark Hamill the first actor to star in both a movie and videogame franchise with three No.1s.

OUT OF THIS WORLD!

Rapid Reality's sci-fi MMO *Phylon* achieved the dubious honour of being the **shortest-lived commercial MMO**. It was shut down without warning on 10 Jul 2007, after just 20 days.

Most prolific videogame voice actor

From *LEGO® Batman 2* to *Lollipop Chainsaw*, Steve Blum (aka Steven Jay Blum) had contributed to 357 games as of 17 Mar 2016, including an award-winning role in the sci-fi RPG *Mass Effect 3*. That's an average of 16 games voiced per year since the first, 1995's *The Dig*, a LucasArts point-and-clicker.

YOUTUBE CHANNEL "MANY A TRUE NERD" FEATURES "NO GUNS" RUN-THROUGHS OF MASS EFFECT. ITS GAMERS OPT TO THROW ENEMIES OUT OF BOUNDS OR RUN THEM OVER INSTEAD OF USING WEAPONS.

First sci-fi MMORPG

MMOs – once set just in fantasy realms – saw a spacey twist with the release of Sega's *Phantasy Star Online* on 21 Dec 2000. Released for the Dreamcast, it was also the **first console MMORPG**.

In 2001, *PSO* was followed by two other sci-fi MMOs, *Anarchy Online* and *DarkSpace*, both of which were for PC.

SPACECRAFT SPOTTER'S GUIDE: *MASS EFFECT* SHIPS

Normandy	*Turian Cruiser*	*Alliance Fighter*

AWESOME ANNIVERSARIES

A host of much-loved series and consoles are celebrating milestones in 2017. From super-smooth spies to sneaking snakes, here are the numbers behind the record-breakers...

2007
10 YEARS
2007

GameSpot hailed 2007 as the "great" year that defined seventh-gen consoles. It also gave us landmark sequels such as *Resident Evil 4* and *Halo 3*.

PlayStation 3
Japan and the USA got their hands on Sony's seventh-gen console in late 2006, but the rest of the world had to wait until 2007. It has since sold more than 85 million units.

Assassin's Creed (Ubisoft)
This 12th-century thriller was originally conceived as a *Prince of Persia* sequel, but Ubisoft changed tack and a new stealth franchise was born.

1997
20 YEARS
1997

Nintendo 64
The N64 was first launched in 1996, but Europe did not see it until 1997. It initially sold well and was blessed with such classics as *Banjo-Kazooie* and *GoldenEye 007*.

The release of *Final Fantasy VII* in Jan 1997 set a high benchmark for game releases, and the rest of the year didn't disappoint. *Castlevania* had arguably its series stand-out with *Symphony of the Night*, while home computers enjoyed key debuts with *Age of Empires* and *Fallout*.

Final Fantasy VII (Square)
The PS RPG boosted the genre's popularity outside of Japan, owing to a smart battle system, wry plot twists and a host of memorable characters.

1987
30 YEARS
1987

Metal Gear (Konami)
Series sales of 41.38 million, as of 24 Feb 2016, make this the **best-selling stealth series**. Not bad, considering developer Hideo Kojima's (JPN) first attempt to create the game failed.

The golden era of 8-bit and 16-bit gaming, 1987 was also a year when arcade halls were in full flow. Big coin-op hits *After Burner*, *Operation Wolf* and *R-Type* were all released, with each title successfully porting to home platforms in ensuing years.

Sega Master System
Sega's 8-bit originally launched in Japan in 1985 as the Mark III, but was later redesigned and launched in Europe in 1987. Its rivalry with the NES began the first true console war.

Super Mario Galaxy (Nintendo)

The concept of spherical worlds first appeared in the demo *Super Mario 128*, way back in 2000, but it took another seven years of development for *SMG* to emerge.

Guinness World Records Gamer's Edition 2008

Across 10 editions, *Gamer's* has featured hundreds of games and thousands of records, and sold more than 4 million copies globally.

The Orange Box (Valve)

The **most critically acclaimed game compilation**, with 96.36% on GameRankings, this *Half-Life* bundle was the last time that fans saw a new release from the cult FPS series.

GoldenEye 007 (Nintendo)

Perhaps Bond's most celebrated hour, this N64 hit was conceived as an on-rails shooter before being redesigned into an FPS and given an ace multiplayer mode.

Gran Turismo (Sony)

Polyphony's driving sim took five years to develop. It revolutionized car games with unprecedented realism. Scoring 94.95% on GameRankings, it remains the **most critically acclaimed racing game** 20 years later.

Grand Theft Auto (Rockstar)

The original, top-down *GTA* looked and played very differently to later games. But there were still hints of the freedom and zany open-world humour that would define the series.

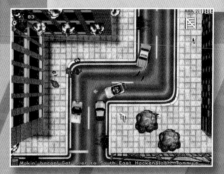

Double Dragon (Technōs)

A landmark moment in co-op brawling, this arcade smash later became the **most ported fighting game**, hitting 23 platforms by 2016.

Final Lap (Namco)

Namco's ground-breaking arcade F1 racer featured an early example of the "rubber-banding" technique that prevents any player from lagging too far behind, which Nintendo later adopted for *Mario Kart*.

Street Fighter (Capcom)

The arcade cabinet for the original game had two pressure-sensitive pads in place of buttons to gauge the strength of blows. It is now the **longest-running fighting game series**.

ROLE-PLAYING GAMES

RPGs invite players to step into alternative realities and lead new lives, whether it's as a musical bard, a grizzled warrior or even a giant frog(!). The only limit now is the imagination...

Fastest completion of *Final Fantasy VII*

"Kynos" (DEU) – seen here toting the Buster Sword as mercenary Cloud Strife – completed a segmented run of Square's 1997 RPG classic *Final Fantasy VII* in just 6 hr 44 min 49 sec, as verified by SpeedDemosArchive.com on 10 Jun 2013. He spent thousands of hours practising his run, using a technique called "step counting" to optimize his time. The secret to his success? Enjoying the game.

RPG ROUND-UP

From the dungeon-dwelling oldies of yesteryear to the massively multiplayer online worlds of *World of Warcraft*, the RPG genre is filled with magic, mysticism and... gnomes.

Most concurrent players for an MMO on Steam

Just two weeks after its release on 5 May 2015, Korean free2play MMO *Tera Online* (En Masse) recorded 18,454 concurrent players on Steam. This figure was more than double that for *Final Fantasy XIV: A Realm Reborn* (7,401) and triple the figure for *The Elder Scrolls Online* (5,067).

CREATED BY BEN SCHULZ, "LEEROY JENKINS" WAS A *WARCRAFT* CHARACTER WHO WENT VIRAL IN 2005 FOR SCUPPERING HIS GUILD'S PLANS. AS OF NOV 2015, THERE WERE 4,607 VIDEOS OF HIM ON YOUTUBE, WITH A TOTAL OF 123,254,604 VIEWS COMBINED!

Most in-game weddings in 24 hours

Love was in the air for players of the MMORPG *Rift* (Trion Worlds, 2011) in 2012. A total of 21,879 in-game marriages were conducted on Valentine's Day, 14 Feb.

First MMO to release an "old school" version

Many games have released updated versions of older games, but not many have released older versions of current games. Yet in 2013, Jagex released *Old School RuneScape*, a standalone title based on the 2007 source code for its MMORPG *RuneScape*. Jagex has been publishing and updating *RuneScape* since 2001.

Highest XP on *Old School RuneScape*

Gamer "Lynx Titan" had scored 2,493,735,243 XP (experience points) as of 28 Jan 2016. This tally was more than 300,000,000 higher than that of nearest rival, "Randalicious", who had racked up 2,141,487,955 XP as of the same date.

FACT! In 1997, "Lord British", the in-game alter ego of *Ultima Online* creator Richard Garriott, was killed by a player casting a fire field spell in the game's beta. Garriott had forgotten to reset his invulnerability following a server crash. MMOCrunch hailed it as the most memorable event in MMORPG history.

100 Number of gamers gathered in *World of Warcraft* in Oct 2005 to remember a Chinese gamer, "Snowly", who had died of fatigue. The event was gatecrashed by a rival clan.

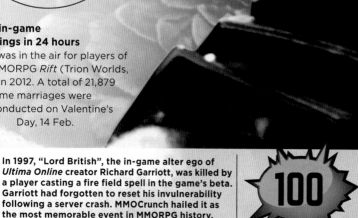

Most played MMO (current)

According to SuperData, *Dungeon Fighter Online* was the most played Massively Multiplayer Online (MMO) game in 2015, achieving an average of 23,777,509 monthly active users. Despite the game's character-driven RPG mechanics, its side-scrolling brawling pays homage to vintage beat-'em-ups such as *Double Dragon* (1987) and *Renegade* (1986). It is published by Neople in South Korea.

First game developer in space

On 12 Oct 2008, "Lord British", aka Richard Allen Garriott (UK/USA), boarded the Soyuz TMA-13 spacecraft and flew off to the *International Space Station*, docking at its destination two days later. Garriott is famous for creating the RPG series *Ultima* for Origin Systems in 1981. He is also credited with coining the term "MMORPG" with the release of *Ultima Online* (EA) in 1997.

Garriott paid some $30 m (£17 m) for the privilege of flying to space. However, space travel runs in the family – he is the son of former NASA astronaut Owen Garriott, who spent 60 days in space in 1973.

First videogame pandemic
In Sep 2005, a deadly virtual plague broke out in *World of Warcraft* (Blizzard, 2001), infecting the avatars of thousands of players. Dubbed the game's first "world event", the "Corrupted Blood" infection meted out by the end boss "Hakkar" in the Zul'Gurub dungeon was only supposed to affect players close to his corpse, but was spread to other areas via a virtual pet.

First live-action movie based on an MMO

Announced at BlizzCon in 2006, *Warcraft* is a live-action film (pictured) based on Blizzard's epic fantasy series. The film was due for global release in Jun 2016.

The **first movie based on an MMO** was the Chinese animated feature *Dragon Nest: Warriors' Dawn*, which hit screens in 2014. The cult film was inspired by the free2play fantasy title *Dragon Nest*, developed by Eyedentity in 2010.

81.77 MILLION
Lines of chat spoken per week between the players of *RuneScape 3*. Its publisher Jagex also reported that there were 4.25 billion lines of chat spoken in total throughout the whole of 2015.

10 YEARS OF *GAMER'S*
In Oct 2008, a 43-year-old Japanese woman was arrested for deleting her online husband's avatar in the MMORPG *MapleStory* (Nexon, 2003) – the **first arrest for the "murder" of a virtual victim**.

Largest virtual gathering of gnomes
"Running of the Gnomes" is a virtual charity run, created in 2010 by *World of Warcraft* players "Dravinna", aka "Magical Warlock Girl", and "Skakavaz". On 24 Oct 2015, at least 2,454 gnomes turned up for its sixth annual run. The group was raising awareness for breast cancer research, so the runners were clad in bright pink tabards.

Longest update support for a game
Since being released in 1992, the sandbox RPG *UnReal World* has been continually updated for 24 years, as of Feb 2016. Among its design changes was swapping a fantasy setting for an Iron Age Finland. Sami Maaranen, one of the game's two developers, said that it was their intention to "keep developing the game, with no end in sight".

ACTION RPGS

Forsaking turn-based combat in favour of real-time brawling, these immersive adventures are designed for gamers who like traditional role-play spiced up with hard-hitting action.

Fastest completion of *Torchlight II*
On 3 Dec 2015, gamer "SomeGuyWithTheBeard" completed Runic Games' 2012 Ember-rich RPG by trekking from the Estherian Steppes to the dwarven ruins of the Grunnheim in just 59 min 33 sec, as verified by Speedrun.com.

The **rarest achievement in *Torchlight II*** is "Trash Magnate", with only 0.3% of players selling the required 50,000 in-game items to unlock it on Steam, as of 21 Mar 2016.

Fastest completion of *Bastion*
By exploiting a glitch enabling him to duplicate Cores, "Vulajin" (USA) completed Supergiant Games' 2011 isometric fantasy RPG in a quickfire 12 min 40 sec on 21 Oct 2014, as verified by Speed Demos Archive.

First expansion pack for an action RPG
Xanadu Scenario II: The Resurrection of Dragon (1986) introduced new enemies and features for fans of Nihon Falcom's 1985 dungeon crawler *Xanadu – Dragon Slayer II*.

Fastest completion of *Axiom Verge*
On 6 Feb 2016, speed-runner "Zecks" (FIN) completed the 2015 Metroidvania sci-fi RPG in 36 min 2 sec, as verified by Speedrun.com.

Fastest completion of *The Witcher 3: Wild Hunt*
On average, *TW 3* takes 100 hr to complete, but on 27 Feb 2016 "Corpseflesh" (DEU) did it in just 2 hr 13 min 15 sec. The **fastest completion of *The Witcher 2: Enhanced Edition*** ("Insane" mode) is 2 hr 50 min 45 sec, by Héctor Ortega Avilés (ESP) on 12 Apr 2015.

FACT! On 23 Mar 2015, gamers in Denmark were offered the opportunity to get their hands on a free copy of Sony's sanguineous RPG *Bloodborne* – provided that they were willing to make a blood donation in return.

The prize awarded to the gamer who could best explain the storyline of *Dark Souls* to new players. The contest was run by Bandai Namco in Feb 2016.

$10,000

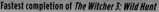

First action RPG
Released for the NEC PC-88, an early home computer sold only in Japan, *Dragon Slayer* (Nihon Falcom, 1984) was the first true action RPG. Including all the hallmarks that helped to define the genre, the game's emphasis was on combat and a limited inventory that forced players to choose what they carried.

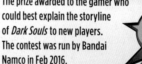

GERALT

THE WITCHER 3

Aka	Gwynbleidd, "White Wolf"
Aka	Butcher of Blaviken
Aka	Sir Geralt of Rivia
Abilities	Alchemy, swordfighting
Likes	Mutagens

Best-selling Western RPG
Featuring dragon shouts, frostbite spiders (below) and a surprising number of adventurers taking arrows to the knee, Bethesda Softworks' *The Elder Scrolls V: Skyrim* proved to be a worldwide smash. Since its release in Nov 2011, the RPG has sold 18.98 million copies according to VGChartz – more than any rival developed in Europe or North America.

Most awards won by a videogame prior to release

Despite not being released until 19 May 2015, sweeping open-world adventure *The Witcher 3: Wild Hunt* (CD Projekt) had amassed 206 awards by 23 Mar 2015, including multiple "Best of E3" gongs and a Golden Joystick for "Most Wanted".

The *Witcher* series is based on a series of cult fantasy novels by Polish writer Andrzej Sapkowski. As of 21 Mar 2016, the PS4 version of *The Witcher 3* boasted a GameRankings score of 92.23% – the **most critically acclaimed videogame based on a book series**.

10 YEARS OF *GAMER'S*

On 16 Jan 2009, Maciej Maselewski (POL) achieved the **fastest completion of an RPG** with a glitched run of *Diablo* (1996) in a jaw-dropping 3 min 12 sec.

First completion of *Bloodborne* without healing, levelling up or using guns

As if FromSoftware's 2015 RPG wasn't notoriously tough enough, Twitcher "Craddoc" (FIN) spent a month trying to defeat its 17 bosses employing only low-damage melee attacks. He eventually slayed the final boss Moon Presence on 30 May 2015.

Most critically acclaimed action RPGs

Game	Publisher	Released	Score %
Mass Effect 2 (X360)	EA	2010	95.77
The Witcher 3: Wild Hunt	CD Projekt	2015	92.23
Mass Effect 3	EA	2012	92.17
Vagrant Story	Square	2000	91.97
Xenoblade Chronicles	Nintendo	2010	91.74
Diablo III: Ultimate Evil Edition	Blizzard/Square	2014	91.25
Bloodborne	SCEA	2015	90.66
Castlevania: Dawn of Sorrow	Konami	2005	90.35
Demon's Souls	SCEA	2009	89.72
Dark Souls II	Bandai Namco	2014	89.68

Source: GameRankings. All figures accurate as of 21 Mar 2016.

DARK SOULS

Both feared and celebrated as one of the most unforgiving series in gaming, the *Souls* games have achieved cult status for their stunning gothic locales and exhilarating swordplay.

Dark Souls was published by Bandai Namco in 2011 as a follow-up to 2009's *Demon's Souls*. Since then, its developer FromSoftware has created two further sequels in the *Souls* series – *Dark Souls II* and *III* in 2014 and 2016, respectively – plus the PS4's *Bloodborne* in 2015. All titles have inspired a generation of quirky challenges, from sharing the same controller in co-op mode to playing the games upside down!

Q&A with "bearzly", aka Benjamin Gwin (CAN)

Why did you start playing *Dark Souls* with unconventional controllers?
I was watching others challenge-run *Dark Souls* in different and exciting ways. It was suggested that someone should try using a guitar controller. So I took the *Rock Band* peripheral that I had lying around at home, started streaming, and the rest is history.

Why *Dark Souls*?
It's my favourite game and I know it very well. It's also notoriously difficult, but I wanted to show to everyone that a game this challenging could still be reduced down to being beaten with a guitar controller... or any other controller!

Was it easy making the controllers compatible with the game?
For the guitar and drums, I used existing tools to make them work. Others, like the bongos, I wrote custom software for because the bongos don't have enough buttons. I have a programming background, which enables me to create runs that nobody else could accomplish.

What has the reaction been like?
I started on Twitch with two viewers and 13 followers. I now have a lot more! The initial reaction was crazy. People are always requesting new things. It's been an amazing experience for me.

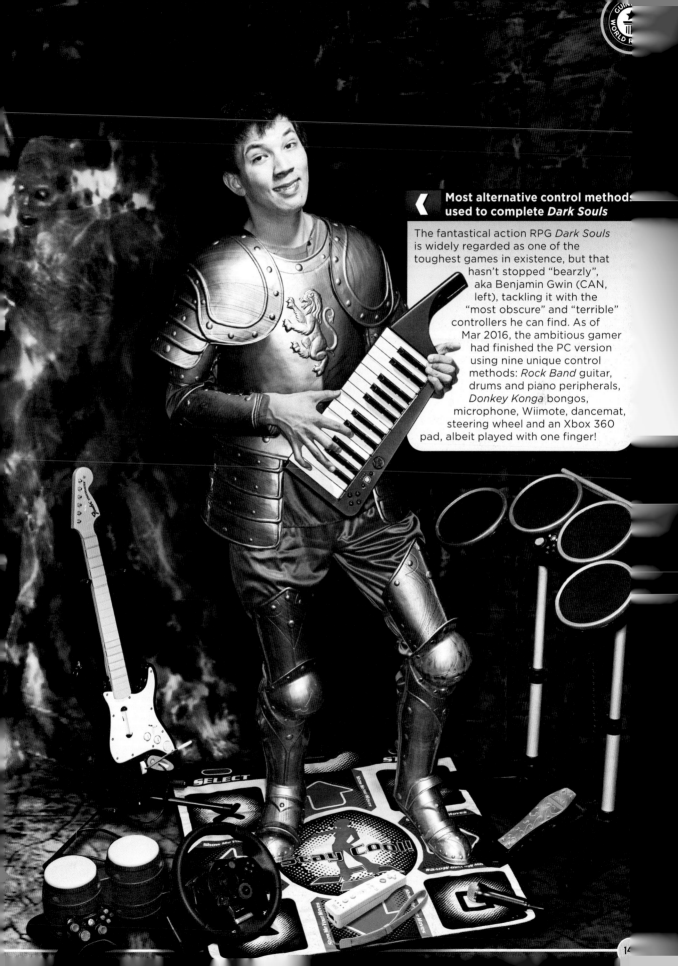

Most alternative control methods used to complete *Dark Souls*

The fantastical action RPG *Dark Souls* is widely regarded as one of the toughest games in existence, but that hasn't stopped "bearzly", aka Benjamin Gwin (CAN, left), tackling it with the "most obscure" and "terrible" controllers he can find. As of Mar 2016, the ambitious gamer had finished the PC version using nine unique control methods: *Rock Band* guitar, drums and piano peripherals, *Donkey Konga* bongos, microphone, Wiimote, dancemat, steering wheel and an Xbox 360 pad, albeit played with one finger!

JRPGS

From mechanical titans and high-school sleuths to Disney stars, Japanese role-playing games have built up huge fan-bases with their exuberant art styles and imaginative worlds.

YU NARUKAMI

Profession	Student
Born	1994
Weapon	Two-handed sword
Renowned for	Not saying much
Critics say	He's suave but odd

Most recruitable party members

The PlayStation game *Suikoden* (Konami, 1995) features 108 recruitable characters, known as the "108 Stars of Destiny". While *Pokémon* has more monsters that you can capture, *Suikoden* is top for "consensual" recruitment.

Most years spanned in a JRPG

Square's *Chrono Trigger* (1995) allows players to venture back in time to 65,000,000 BCE, and as far forward as AD 2300.

Most popular *Persona* character

In a poll conducted by Japan's *Persona* magazine *#ONE MORE* in Sep 2012, Yu from *Persona 4* (see above left) was hailed as the series' most popular star. The high-school hero won 1,451 votes.

Longest JRPG title in English

With a total of 73 characters including spaces, *Shin Megami Tensei: Devil Summoner: Raidou Kuzunoha vs. The Soulless Army* (Atlus, 2006) is the longest JRPG title in the English language. Its 2008 sequel, *Shin Megami Tensei: Devil Summoner 2: Raidou Kuzunoha vs. King Abaddon*, clocks in slightly shorter, at 70 characters.

Most prolific JRPG main series

With 15 main series entries to its name as of Apr 2016, Bandai Namco's *Tales* has released more principal story titles than any other JRPG. Its 16th trip into the fantastical – *Tales of Berseria* – was due out in Japan in Aug 2016, a month before the 15th main *Final Fantasy* game, the much anticipated *FFXV*.

FACT! Konami's *Vandal Hearts* became the **first JRPG to receive an ESRB "M" rating** when it was released in the USA in 1997. The game features an involving political plot set in the fictional "historical" region of Sostegaria.

11 Disney franchises featured in the crossover classic *Kingdom Hearts II* (Square Enix, 2005), including *The Nightmare Before Christmas*, *Pirates of the Caribbean* and Donald Duck.

Longest-running JRPG series

Debuting on the Famicom/NES in 1986, the *Dragon Quest* series was celebrating its 30th anniversary in May 2016 with the spin-off sequel *Dragon Quest Heroes II*. Prior to that, a third version of *Dragon Quest X* (subtitled *Inishie no Ryuu no Denshou Online*) was released in Japan in Apr 2015. The series was created by Yuji Horii and features such monsters as FairyRats, Giant Slugs and its mascot Slime.

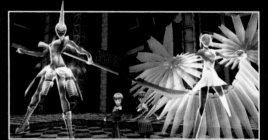

Most critically acclaimed PS Vita game

Atlus' hand-held mystery *Persona 4: Golden* (2014, above) has a GameRankings score of 94.16% – more than any other PS Vita game.

The **most critically acclaimed JRPG on the 3DS** is *Fire Emblem Awakening* (2012), which scores 92.52%. It's the third-highest-rated title on the 3DS overall, behind *Shovel Knight* and *The Legend of Zelda: Ocarina of Time 3D*.

> ## Largest playable area in a JRPG

As estimated by Nintendo World Report in Nov 2015, the playable world in *Xenoblade Chronicles X* (Nintendo, 2015) stretches to around 400 km² (154 sq mi). This makes it potentially three times bigger than the estimated area in the action RPG *The Witcher 3: Wild Hunt*. Players can traverse its vast terrain while riding giant mechs. The sci-fi title is also the **best-selling JRPG for Wii U**. It had sold 780,000 units worldwide by 14 Apr 2016, according to VGChartz.

2,198,350 Likes for the English *Kingdom Hearts* Facebook page, as of 14 Apr 2016. A week earlier, the mobile title *Kingdom Hearts: Unchained X* was released in the USA.

10 YEARS OF *GAMER'S*

A ballet based on *Dragon Quest* was premiered in Tokyo, Japan, in 1996. Choreographed by Minoru Suzuki, it was the **first ballet inspired by a videogame**.

First JRPG based on a book

Atlus' 1987 horror JRPG *Digital Devil Story: Megami Tensei* was based on the 1986 novel *Digital Devil Story: Reincarnation of the Goddess* by Aya Nishitani. The game was released in Japan only and was the first title in the enduringly popular *Megami Tensei* series. It featured a sprawling dungeon maze designed by the demon lord Lucifer, which players explored in order to hunt demons.

Most hit points for a game boss

In the simulation RPG *Trillion: God of Destruction* (Idea Factory, 2015), players star as a demon king trying to save their supernatural realm from destruction. In order to emerge triumphant, players must defeat a main foe named Trillion, who has 1 trillion hit points (HP) to erase. Hit points (effectively "health") are a common denominator in RPGs

POKÉMON

Publisher: Nintendo
Debut: 1996
Games: 50+

Developer: Various
Series sales: 247.84 million
Rivals: *Battle of Beasts*

First videogame series with its own science

The *Pokémon* Research Institute ran at the Miraikan National Museum of Emerging Science and Innovation in Tokyo, Japan, in Jul–Oct 2015. Interactive games that allowed visitors to study and identify different pocket monsters were designed to help students hone skills in observing animals and insects.

Smallest handmade Pokémon sculptures

Clay sculptures by Ruby "Lonelysouthpaw" Huang (USA) measure 2–5 mm (0.078–0.196 in) high. As of 5 Jan 2016, the smallest piece in "Project Pinkymon" was Voltorb (top right), at 2 mm in height, width and depth.

Largest trading-card mosaic
As part of the celebrations for *Pokémon*'s 20th anniversary, artist Quentin Devine (UK, below) created an artwork consisting of 12,987 individual *Pokémon* trading cards. Unveiled in Paris on 21 Mar 2016, the mosaic portrait of Pikachu measured 71.54 m² (770 sq ft), and hung 10.23 m (33 ft 6.7 in) tall and 6.98 m (22 ft 10.8 in) wide.

Most participants in a single-player online videogame

A record-thrashing 1,165,140 Twitchers – dubbed "Twitch Plays Pokémon" – played *Pokémon Red* (1996) from 12 Feb to 1 Mar 2014. Over 16 days 7 hr 45 min 30 sec, concurrent players peaked at a reported 121,000. More than nine million watched, and at least 122 million commands were issued.

FACT! *Pokémon*'s 20th-anniversary hoopla included a commercial aired during the 2016 Super Bowl. Its finer details were noted in UnlistedLeaf's "10 Easter Eggs In The Pokemon Super Bowl Commercial!!", uploaded to YouTube on 27 Jan 2016.

720 Number of Pokémon listed on the official Pokédex, as of 18 Mar 2016. The numerical listing begins with the overgrown, seed-sowing Bulbasaur and continues to number 720, the mischievous magician Hoopa.

First videogame franchise store

Introduced in 1996, *Pokémon* grew in popularity to such an extent that, in 1998, a dedicated store opened in Tokyo, Japan. The Pokémon Center, similar to The Disney Store, sold merchandise including consoles, plush toys, figurines, backpacks, clothing and CDs. More Pokémon Centers have since opened across Japan and the USA.

Largest collection of *Pokémon* memorabilia

After 14 years of collecting, Lisa Courtney (UK) has amassed 14,410 different *Pokémon* items from the UK, USA, France and the game's home country, Japan. On trips to Japan, she has sent home 8–12 boxes full of merchandise. Part of the collection – including her own Guinness World Records certificate – has been displayed at the Hertford Museum in Hertfordshire, UK. Her favourite of all the items is an Absol doll.

‹ Best-selling RPG series

Pokémon games had sold 247.84 million copies as of 18 Mar 2016, according to VGChartz. There have been departures from the RPG format, such as *Hey You, Pikachu!* (below), but most sales come from core titles such as *Pokémon Omega Ruby* and *Alpha Sapphire* – the top-selling games across all platforms in 2014.

100

Weight in grams (3.5 oz) of lightest Pokémon Flabébé, introduced in the first episode of 2013's *XY* TV series.

10 YEARS OF *GAMER'S*

Having triumphed in the 2010, 2011 and 2012 finals, US teenager Ray Rizzo secured the **most wins of the *Pokémon* World Championships**.

First voice-controlled videogame

Hey You, Pikachu! (Nintendo, 1998) bewitched attendees at Tokyo's Space World show on 21–23 Nov 1997. The N64 game, developed by Ambrella, allowed players to ask Pikachu to perform simple tasks such as collecting apples and playing with beachballs. Sales were weak, possibly owing to the expense of buying the game *and* a microphone.

Most film spin-offs from a videogame

The *Pokémon* series had spawned 19 feature-length movies as of 18 Mar 2016, with a 20th scheduled for Jul 2016. *Pokémon: The First Movie* (1998) remains the most successful, with a total gross of $164,644,662 (£101,200,000), making it the **highest-grossing animated movie based on a videogame**.

FINAL FANTASY

Publisher: Square Enix
Debut: 1987
Games: 15 (main series)

Developer: Square Enix
Series sales: 111.55 million
Rivals: *Dragon Quest*

GILGAMESH

FINAL FANTASY XIII-2

Series debut	*Final Fantasy V* (1992)
Weapon of choice	*Naginata* polearm
Trusty companion	Enkidu
Searching for	Excalibur
Says	"Now we fight like men!"

Fastest completion of *Final Fantasy XV: Episode Duscae*

The playable demo of the 15th instalment has attracted its own dedicated following among speed-run fans. On 27 Feb 2016, "zefferss" (USA) uploaded a super-fast any% run-through of *Episode Duscae* version 2.0 to Speedrun.com, clocking a total time of just 23 min 12 sec.

> **Most soundtrack albums to feature music from a videogame series**
> There have been at least 180 commercially released albums containing music from or inspired by the *Final Fantasy* series. They include original soundtracks, compilations, piano collections, classical guitar renditions, 8-bit chip versions and live orchestral performances.

Most ubiquitous *Final Fantasy* character

He may have had to wait to make his debut until 1992's *Final Fantasy V*, but Gilgamesh has made up for lost time. The multiple-armed master swordsman had made a total of 31 series appearances as of 14 Mar 2016, including spin-offs and crossover games. He initially appeared as a boss before eventually becoming an ally of the player party.

Most critically acclaimed *Final Fantasy* game

Final Fantasy IX (2000) for the PlayStation had earned a fantastic GameRankings rating of 92.72% as of 15 Mar 2016.

Yet even the most successful franchises can experience hiccups. Scoring 50.27%, the 2010 MMO *Final Fantasy XIV Online* was the **lowest-rated *Final Fantasy* game**. GamesRadar described it as a "swampy muck of bugs [and] quirks".

FACT! *Final Fantasy*'s iconic side-view battle system took its inspiration from an unlikely source – American football. New to the world of RPGs, designer Hiroyuki Ito (JPN) adapted the turn-based system of pre-planned strategic attack from the sport.

13 Number of years following the release of *Final Fantasy IX* before a gamer unlocked the obscure side quest "The Lost Nero Family" in 2013. It had remained unknown outside of Japan.

Longest videogame reaction video

Following the fevered announcement of the *Final Fantasy VII* remake at E3 2015, YouTuber "JwalkZer0" (USA) spent a day collecting and compiling footage of gamers reacting to the news. As of 15 Mar 2016, "*Final Fantasy 7* Remake Reactions 7-Hour Compilation" had been split into two parts with a total running time of 7 hr 17 min 23 sec! The combined total of views came to 342,351.

Most Facebook likes for a videogame cosplayer

Artist/model Alodia Gosiengfiao (PHL) is the most popular cosplayer on Facebook, with 5,660,594 likes as of 11 Mar 2016. Since 2003, Alodia has cosplayed for such series as *DotA* and *Final Fantasy*, notably dressing as the green-eyed Rikku (right) from *FF X* and *FF X-2*.

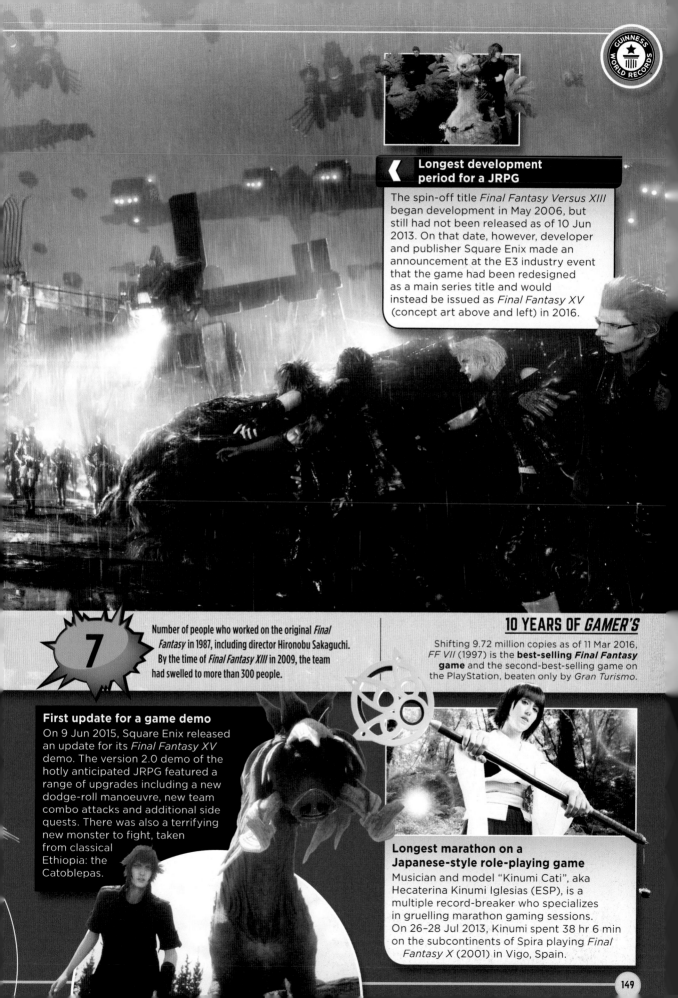

Longest development period for a JRPG

The spin-off title *Final Fantasy Versus XIII* began development in May 2006, but still had not been released as of 10 Jun 2013. On that date, however, developer and publisher Square Enix made an announcement at the E3 industry event that the game had been redesigned as a main series title and would instead be issued as *Final Fantasy XV* (concept art above and left) in 2016.

7 Number of people who worked on the original *Final Fantasy* in 1987, including director Hironobu Sakaguchi. By the time of *Final Fantasy XIII* in 2009, the team had swelled to more than 300 people.

10 YEARS OF GAMER'S

Shifting 9.72 million copies as of 11 Mar 2016, *FF VII* (1997) is the **best-selling Final Fantasy game** and the second-best-selling game on the PlayStation, beaten only by *Gran Turismo*.

First update for a game demo

On 9 Jun 2015, Square Enix released an update for its *Final Fantasy XV* demo. The version 2.0 demo of the hotly anticipated JRPG featured a range of upgrades including a new dodge-roll manoeuvre, new team combo attacks and additional side quests. There was also a terrifying new monster to fight, taken from classical Ethiopia: the Catoblepas.

Longest marathon on a Japanese-style role-playing game

Musician and model "Kinumi Cati", aka Hecaterina Kinumi Iglesias (ESP), is a multiple record-breaker who specializes in gruelling marathon gaming sessions. On 26–28 Jul 2013, Kinumi spent 38 hr 6 min on the subcontinents of Spira playing *Final Fantasy X* (2001) in Vigo, Spain.

GAME JAMS

Stick a bunch of programmers in a room together and magic can happen! Game jams are events in which teams of developers vie to make games from scratch, often while scoffing vast quantities of pizza. Jam participants must design their games around a secret "theme", which isn't revealed until the event starts.

Some games prototyped at jam events have subsequently been made into commercially available titles. Here are four examples that have gone on to do fine things...

Since 2002, jams have been springing up all over the world, with jammers challenged to make their games in strict time limits, typically set at 48–72 hr. Notable regular events include the Nordic Game Jam in Denmark, the long-running Ludum Dare, and the Global Game Jam, whose 2016 event took place across 93 countries.

Here, we serve up a selection of records (below) and highlights from recent game jams (right).

Broforce
Developer: Free Lives (ZAF)
Released commercially for PC in Oct 2015, the side-scrolling action romp *Broforce* was originally conceived as *Rambros* at the Ludum Dare 23 game jam in 2012. The game features fun parodies of big-screen muscle-heads such as Rambo, The Terminator and Conan the Barbarian.

Most participants in a game jam (multiple venues)
Held on 29–31 Jan, the 2016 Global Game Jam saw 36,164 registered participants jamming from 632 locations in 93 countries, including Belarus, Paraguay, Cuba, Guatemala and Nepal. A total of 6,869 games were made, based on the general theme of "Ritual", and 158 of these were virtual-reality titles.

Most participants in a game jam (single location)
Around 1,228 registered jammers gathered in Cairo, Egypt, on 29–31 Jan 2016 to participate in the Global Game Jam, and 135 games were made at the event's official site. Egypt first took part in the annual event in 2013.

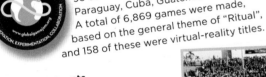

Longest-running organized game jam
The online Ludum Dare game jams had been staged regularly for 14 years 5 days, from 13 Apr 2002 (Ludum Dare 0) to 18 Apr 2016 (Ludum Dare 35). That's a total of 36 main events and 68 mini-LDs, making 104 overall – the **most game jams staged by a single organizer**.

Youngest game jammer
At the Toronto TOJam on 11–13 May 2011, Canada's Cassie Creighton (b. 17 Feb 2006) was just 5 years 83 days old when she joined forces with her programmer father Ryan to develop *Sissy's Magical Ponycorn Adventure*. Cassie drew all of the game's art and developed its story. As of 23 Feb 2016, the online game had raised $3,199.20 (£2,251) in donations towards Cassie's education fund.

Johann Sebastian Joust
Developer: Die Gute Fabrik (DNK)
The winner of the Nordic Game Jam in 2011, *Johann Sebastian Joust* is a "no-graphics" sports title in which players aim to jostle each other's motion-controllers beyond an allotted threshold (shown above). The game picked up the Innovation Award at the Game Developers Choice Awards 2012.

Super Time Force
Developer: Capybara Games (CAN)
The prototype for this time-travelling shooter was conceived at TOJam in May 2011, based on the theme "What just happened". As of Feb 2016, the Xbox One version was the **most critically acclaimed game conceived at a game jam**, with a GameRankings score of 82% from 27 reviews.

Surgeon Simulator 2013
Developer: Bossa Studios (UK)
A blackly comic title about performing surgical operations, *Surgeon Simulator* was conceived at the 2013 Global Game Jam. Its commercial version had sold 3,009,771 copies across all formats as of 17 March 2016, making it the **best-selling game conceived at a game jam**.

Luke Williams (right) was the lead designer on *Surgeon Simulator 2013*, a first-person sim that bore similarities to tabletop classic *Operation*.

Did you have any idea what kind of game you'd make at the 2013 Global Game Jam?
Not at all, which is the way it's intended! You're not given the theme until right before you have to start making a game. That year the theme was simply the sound of a heartbeat, so we took it quite literally and made a game about performing a heart transplant.

When did you realize that your idea could be developed into a commercially releasable title?
It was when we presented it in front of the other teams at the London venue of the event. The whole room was in hysterics and shouting out what tools to use. We all looked at each other and said, "Oh, so it's not just funny to us then?"

Were there many changes between the game prototype and the final version?
None of the core mechanics actually changed. We just polished it all up, refined the controls and added a variety of new transplants!

SHOOTERS

Select a target. Aim. Fire. Repeat. Sounds simple, doesn't it? Think again. Whether you're playing in first- or third-person, shooters require a dead-eye aim and nerves of steel.

When Bethesda released *Fallout 4* on 10 Nov 2015, Twitch star "OMGitsfirefoxx" celebrated by playing the post-apocalyptic shooter for 19 hr. She is shown here cosplaying the game in an abandoned trailer park situated just outside Los Angeles in California, USA. Of her record (see right), she said: "It really makes me feel like I've accomplished something in creating this amazing community that I have on Twitch."

Most followed female on Twitch

"OMGitsfirefoxx", aka Sonja Reid (CAN), has come a long way since her earliest gaming days playing *Wolfenstein 3D* on MS-DOS. The self-proclaimed "full-time dragon slayer, part-time sniper" was the most popular female gamer on Twitch in 2015, boasting 707,540 followers. As of 15 Mar 2016, she was still going strong with 722,912 followers, just ahead of "KittyPlays" with 717,466.

Firefoxx's favourite games to stream include *Minecraft*, *Counter-Strike* and, of course, *Fallout 4*, which was the theme for her *Gamer's* photo shoot.

FIRST-PERSON SHOOTERS

Ever since *Wolfenstein* had gamers romping round 3D corridors, the FPS has spawned hit after hit, from the death matches of *Doom* to the alien scares of *Half-Life*.

Most played multiplayer online shooter (current)

CrossFire, the online FPS, had 45,176,591 monthly active users in 2015, according to SuperData. This put it behind only *League of Legends* as the **most played multiplayer online game** (94,332,069). Launched by Smilegate in 2007, *CrossFire* had 500 million registered players by Apr 2016. By comparison, Activision's FPS blockbuster *Destiny* had 25 million.

Most acclaimed FPS for PC

Valve's legendary FPS *Half-Life 2* (2004) held a GameRankings score of 95.48% as of 26 Apr 2016. The game saw Gordon Freeman (left) fighting to save Earth from an alien empire, using such weapons as the genre-defining gravity gun. DarkZero said of the game: "It is the pure essence of enjoyment from start to finish."

Fastest completion of *Shadow Warrior*

Swedish gamer "elmle" finished Devolver Digital's 2013 reboot of *Shadow Warrior* in 1 hr 13 min 53 sec on 8 Apr 2016.

By contrast, Finland's "Inffi" polished off GT's 1997 original (above) in just 12 min 28 sec. In both games, players star as a ninja who tackles nightmarish creatures using firearms, shuriken stars and a katana sword.

First FPS in which gamers can play the monster

Released some 20 years before 2K's *Evolve* pitted monsters against hunters, *Alien vs Predator* (1994) was the first time that players could choose a monster rather than a hero. The Atari Jaguar title featured three scary scenarios, in which the player is either the Alien, the Predator or a human Marine.

---

10 YEARS OF GAMER'S

Sci-fi FPS *Borderlands 2* (2012) features 300 foes – the **most enemy variants in an FPS**. Among its terrors are sandworms, spiderants and midget skeletons!

14

Schwarzenegger films that spawned games, including Atari's *Terminator 3: Rise of the Machines* FPS from 2003.

Star Trek and *The Force Awakens* director J J Abrams confirmed to IGN in Mar 2016 that movies of *Half-Life* and *Portal* were "in development... we've got writers, and we're working on both those stories".

FACT!

120 MILLION

Dollars awarded in a *Half-Life 3* tournament on e-Sports Earnings on 1 Apr 2016. It was, of course, an April Fool's prank.

Fastest completion of *Wolfenstein: The New Order*

"BloodThunder" (USA) blazed through this alternative-history FPS (Bethesda, 2014) in 1 hr 37 min 10 sec on 13 Jan 2016.

First FPS to feature a sniper rifle

Predating the sniper rifle in *GoldenEye 007* (Rare) by a year, the *Quake Team Fortress* mod introduced gamers to a sniper class when it was released in Aug 1996. A later version added head and body shots.

First multiplayer FPS

Midi Maze (Hybrid Arts, 1987) exploited the Atari ST's then-advanced MIDI ports. This enabled networking that sustained the game's popularity.

> DOOM CO-CREATOR JOHN CARMACK, A FOUNDING FATHER OF FPS GAMES, WAS AWARDED A BAFTA FELLOWSHIP ON 7 APR 2016. THE EVENT WAS STREAMED ON TWITCH. NOW AT OCULUS VR, CARMACK SAID, "I'M JUST GETTING STARTED!"

First World Video Game Hall of Fame inductees

The seminal FPS *Doom* was one of six titles inducted into the first World Video Game Hall of Fame in New York's National Museum of Play, on 5 Jun 2015. It was joined by *PAC-Man*, *Pong*, *Super Mario Bros.*, *Tetris* and *World of Warcraft*.

Smallest FPS

You need 40 million kilobytes to download modern FPS titles such as *Call of Duty: Black Ops III*. At the other end of the scale, *.kkrieger* (.theprodukkt, 2004, beta only) is a fully functioning FPS of just 97 kilobytes, thanks to the developer's procedural content creation and management tool.

‹ Longest-running developer of FPS games

Texas-based id Software is the FPS don. Co-founded by John Carmack (above, far left, in the team's early days), John Romero (centre), Tom Hall and Adrian Carmack, it has unleashed shooters for nearly a quarter of a century. Between the zombie pioneer *Wolfenstein 3D* in 1992 and a reboot of the seminal *Doom*, released in May 2016 (main picture), id's output has included the sci-fi series *Quake* (1996–2007), various *Doom* sequels and expansions, and the post-apocalyptic thriller *Rage* (2011).

First audio-only FPS
In *Shades of Doom* (GMA, 2001), players navigate a mutant-infested military research base, guided only by echoes, footsteps and unsettling noises that occur dynamically. Loosely inspired by *Doom*, whose 2016 reboot is shown above, the game was hailed for its technical innovation.

MILITARY SHOOTERS

Painstaking research and advances in game technology are enabling developers of military shooters to come ever closer to recreating the bloody and harrowing experience of war.

Highest score on *Battlefield 4*

According to the leaderboard at bf4stats.com, "XBuRogers" had scored 614,320,300 points from 6,840 rounds on the PC version of EA DICE's 2013 military shooter, as of 13 Apr 2016. The gamer chalked up 180,989 kills, while dying 29,553 times.

Gamer "sith_darthvader1" has made the **most flag captures on *Battlefield 4***, with 348,980 standards nabbed by the same date. This total was achieved playing 5,393 rounds.

Largest living Easter egg in a game

Battlefield 4: Naval Strike (2014) had a secret lurking beneath the waves of the Nansha Strike map: a mighty Megalodon, measuring 18 m (59 ft) in length.

On 29 Apr 2015, the 100th patch to *Battlefield's* Community Test Environment contained another prehistoric shark, this time on the Paracel Storm map – where, apparently, the DICE developers had intended the Megalodon to first appear.

Most museums consulted for a game

While developing the historical naval MMO *World of Warships* (2015), Lesta Studio and Wargaming consulted 38 museums located around the world, from Chinese Taipei and Australia to Great Britain and Poland. They visited institutions including the Qingdao Naval Museum in China, the National Naval Aviation Museum in Florida and the Naval & Military Park in New York (both USA).

World of Warships Q&A: Markus Schill of Wargaming (far left)

How challenging is it digitally recreating a WWII warship?

The amount of work that goes into them is ridiculous! Many ships from the war were either sunk in battle or never built. So we work with museums and military archives to find the original blueprints to the ships, and these are usually hidden on a dusty shelf somewhere. We've visited many surviving ships, but even a small destroyer takes weeks to measure and scan into 3D.

It must be like researching dinosaurs?

Exactly! They're not as old but they're equally dusty! But by doing this research we've invigorated interest in that part of history. We actually created a web game with the Bovington Tank Museum (UK), where our players are helping the museum to verify 250,000 pictures of tanks that are in their archives.

You work with the War Child charity, too.

Yes, we were looking for a partnership where we could give something back to society. War Child has been instrumental in protecting children from the impact of real war. We've done charity events and sold in-game items where a large portion of the profits went to War Child. Success brings a certain amount of responsibility.

FACT! To ensure that *Tom Clancy's Rainbow Six: Siege* (Ubisoft, 2015) was as realistic as possible, former counter-terrorism and police officers were brought in for the motion-capture sequences. They performed alongside established actors such as Angela Bassett, who played agent "Six".

19,564,204 Views of "Battlefield 1 Official Reveal Trailer", as of 8 May 2016 – just 48 hours after the video was uploaded to YouTube. Scheduled for release in autumn 2016, the FPS is set during World War I.

Most prolific tactical shooter series

Tom Clancy's Rainbow Six (Ubisoft) follows the fortunes of RAINBOW, an elite, UK-based, black-ops counter-terrorism unit. As of 14 Apr 2016, there had been 18 instalments in the series. US author Clancy's name also adorns numerous other military or espionage-themed franchises, most of which are published by Ubisoft. This includes the *Tom Clancy's Splinter Cell* stealth series (2002–13), combat flight sims *H.A.W.X* (2009–10), tactical wargame *EndWar* (2008), TPS *The Division* (2016), and 13 titles in the tactical-shooter franchise *Ghost Recon*. As of 13 Apr 2016, some 46 titles bear Clancy's name – the **most games headlined by a real person**.

Best-selling mod franchise
Starting out as a humble *Half-Life* mod, *Counter-Strike* proved so popular that Valve began releasing games in its own right. As of 13 Apr 2016, sales of the five *Counter-Strike* titles had hit 63.81 million, according to figures compiled by SteamSpy.

Most digital sales of a PC videogame (current)
Valve's FPS *Counter-Strike: Global Offensive* (2012) achieved astonishing digital sales of 4,905,030 in 2015, according to figures from digital-data gatherer SuperData. This was higher than the combined digital sales for Activision's military-shooter *Call of Duty: Black Ops III* (2015) on both the Xbox One and PS4 – the biggest digital sellers on both of those formats.

3,003
Number of hours it took to make the German battleship *Tirpitz* for *World of Warships*, according to the designers. The process required 17 artists working on it for more than seven months.

10 YEARS OF *GAMER'S*
Designed to present the US military in a positive light, *America's Army* (US Army, 2002) was the **first tax-funded videogame**. It was created by Epic Games and was free to play.

Most prolific World War II shooter series
Boasting an initial story by film director Steven Spielberg, the first 12 titles of the *Medal of Honor* series focused on the exploits of US forces during World War II. The 2010 reboot *Medal of Honor* relocated the action to modern Afghanistan. However the sequel, 2012's *Warfighter*, was poorly received and so the series was placed on hold. Sales of the WWII *MoH* games stood at 28.93 million as of 13 Apr 2016 – the **best-selling WWII game series**.

First FPS to recreate a World War I battle
Although *Darkest of Days* (2009) features a level loosely based on the Battle of Tannenberg during the "Great War", *Verdun* (M2H/Blackmill, 2015, above) strives to historically recreate the Battle of Verdun, fought between German and French forces on 21 Feb–18 Dec 1916. Realistic bullet physics, skill-based weapon handling, massive artillery barrages and a claustrophobic gas-mask experience ensure that the PC game is terrifying and educational in equal measure.

CALL OF DUTY

Publisher: Activision
Debut: 2003
Games: 23

Developers: Various
Series sales: 244.2 million
Rivals: *Battlefield, MoH*

$15 BN

Most tournament wins in a single *Call of Duty* game

Call of Duty: Advanced Warfare was released in Nov 2014 to kick-start a new season of pro *Call of Duty* gaming. The US eSports team OpTic marched on to win nine tournaments – a ... title. The clan's final victory, prior to the season's end, came at MLG's World Finals in New Orleans, USA, in Oct 2015.

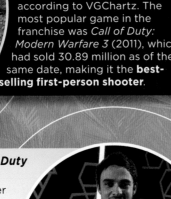

Best-selling first-person shooter (FPS) series

The all-conquering *Call of Duty* series had racked up sales of 244.2 million units across all formats as of 4 Feb 2016, according to VGChartz. The most popular game in the franchise was *Call of Duty: Modern Warfare 3* (2011), which had sold 30.89 million as of the same date, making it the **best-selling first-person shooter**.

Lifetime revenue achieved by the *Call of Duty* series by Feb 2016, according to publisher Activision Blizzard. It began with developer Infinity Ward's *Call of Duty* game in 2003.

10 YEARS OF *GAMER'S*

On 13–19 Nov 2012, Okan Kaya (AUS) played *Call of Duty: Black Ops II* (2012) for 135 hr 15 min 10 sec – the **longest marathon on a shooter**.

Most subscribed *Call of Duty* YouTube channel

As of 2 Feb 2016, YouTuber "Ali-A", aka Alastair Aiken (UK), had attracted 7,549,838 subscribers to his dedicated *Call of Duty* channel. As of the same date, "Ali-A" also had the **most popular *Call of Duty* channel by views**, having accrued 1,750,681,985 video views since launching on 13 Sep 2006.

Most subscribed YouTube channel by an eSports team

The eponymous YouTube channel of FaZe Clan, a successful pro *Call of Duty* team based in the USA, boasted 3,632,567 subscribers as of 4 Feb 2016. The team included Dillon "Attach" Price (USA), the **highest-earning player in *Call of Duty: Advanced Warfare***; the virtual sharp-shooter earned $145,954.50 (£101,384) from competing in 41 tournaments.

Most critically acclaimed *Call of Duty* game

The Xbox 360 version of *Call of Duty 4: Modern Warfare* (2007) scored 94.16% at GameRankings, based on 80 reviews. After the World War II exploits of its predecessors, the game became the first in the series to enjoy a present-day setting.

Call of Duty: Black Ops III beat *FIFA 16* to top YouTube's list of the most popular games of 2015 – based on video views (and length of time watched) for the year.

FACT!

Fastest time to capture the flag in *Call of Duty: Advanced Warfare* (shared controller, team of two)

Playing on the Biolab map of the 2014 FPS, the UK's "TWiiNSANE" (aka twins Liam Thompson and Jake Thompson) took 26.31 sec to capture the flag while battling enemy bots. Their speedy run was achieved on 20 Jun 2015.

923,455

Digital sales achieved by *Call of Duty: Black Ops III* on Xbox One in 2015, according to SuperData.

Most digital sales of a PS4 videogame (current)
It may not have been released until Nov 2015, but, according to SuperData, *Call of Duty: Black Ops III* still achieved more digital sales than any other PS4 title in 2015. The near-futuristic FPS was downloaded 1,648,026 times for the console by the end of the year.

Most watched videogame launch broadcast

On 5 Nov 2015, a total of 442,620 unique viewers tuned in to watch the UK *Call of Duty: Black Ops III* launch event live from Mayfair One in London, UK. The party was streamed via the Twitch channel of internet sensation Syndicate, aka Tom Cassell (UK, above left), and featured YouTubers, pro gamers and soccer stars Héctor Bellerín and Patrick Bamford competing in Activision's latest FPS.

THIRD-PERSON SHOOTERS

Take cover! Unlike their FPS blood brothers, third-person shooters (TPS) let gamers see the character they control. The use of surroundings as tactical cover is critical to success.

Best-selling third-person shooter on the Wii U

Mario rules Nintendo's top-sellers for the Wii U, but the 4.25 million copies of *Splatoon* sold by Nintendo as of 24 Mar 2016 made it the best-selling TPS for the console. Unleashed on 28 May 2015, the shape-shifting, squid-packed gem proved a super-speedy seller in the UK and Japan.

Best-selling TPS

Ka-boom! That's the sound of *Gears of Wars 2* (Microsoft, 2008) decimating its rivals with 6.75 million sales as of 24 Mar 2016, according to VGChartz. The franchise – also comprising *Gears of War* (2006), *Gears of War 3* (2011) and *Gears of War: Judgment* (2013) – has shifted a total of 22.86 million units, making it the **best-selling TPS series**. *Gears of War 4* was due in 2016 as an Xbox One exclusive.

Most followed videogame cosplayer on Twitter

As of 24 Mar 2016, Jessica Nigri (USA) had earned 515,000 Twitter fans through her portrayal of characters such as *Gears of War 3*'s Anya Stroud (left). Jessica has also cosplayed Pikachu, *Lollipop Chainsaw*'s Juliet Starling, and even *Assassin's Creed IV*'s Edward Kenway.

Most popular zombie class in *Plants vs. Zombies: Garden Warfare*

According to data released in Nov 2015, the most used zombie class in PopCap's zany shooter *Plants vs. Zombies: Garden Warfare* (2014) is the Foot Soldier. From 1.4 billion multiplayer games, the undead infantryman had been spawned 545 million times, roughly twice as many as the zombie All-Star, which had 278 million spawns. On the other side of the garden fence, the **most popular plant class** is the Peashooter, with 534 spawns.

Gears of War 2 (Microsoft, 2008) was the **first game with "horde mode"** – an influential TPS concept that pits the player against increasing waves of enemies.

999

Number of limited-edition *Panzer Dragoon Orta* Special Edition Xbox consoles released in Japan on 19 Dec 2002.

Gears of War's Marcus Fenix is named after the Phoenix, the mythical bird that rose from its own ashes. This was revealed on Twitter by designer Cliff Bleszinski, who said that he created Fenix during a turbulent period in his own life.

FACT!

79

Length in years of Sera's bloody Pendulum Wars, before the Locust invasion that kick-starts the *Gears of War* action.

Most critically acclaimed rail shooter

A dragon-filled fantasy shooter released for the Xbox, *Panzer Dragoon Orta* (Sega, 2002) boasted a GameRankings rating of 90.36% as of 29 Mar 2016. This placed it ahead of *Rez HD* (Microsoft, 2008) with 88.62% and *Sin & Punishment: Star Successor* (Nintendo, 2009) with 85.86%.

Fastest completion of *Splatoon* (all scrolls)

Sunken scrolls are items that are collected on every stage of *Splatoon*'s single-player mode, known as "Octo Valley", with further scrolls earned by defeating bosses. On 4 Mar 2016, "TonesBalones" (USA) gathered up every scroll while polishing off the entire game in just 1 hr 10 min 6 sec, as verified by Speedrun.com.

★ YOUTUBER "MOOMOOMILK" IS ONE OF THE MOST PROLIFIC MAKERS OF *GEARS OF WAR* VIDEOS. SINCE LAUNCHING IN 2009, HE HAS PUBLISHED MORE THAN 400 VIDEOS, INCLUDING WEEKLY VLOGS, FUNNIES AND MONTAGES FROM THE SERIES.

First TPS with a cover system

It might be a common feature of today's games, but *Operation: WinBack* (Koei, 1999) – also known simply as *WinBack* – was the first TPS to include a system allowing players to pop out from behind crates and corners and take aim at enemy forces. Its laser sight mechanic would also become a staple of the genre.

First "second-person" shooter

Developed by Japanese indie game studio Himo, 2011's *Second Person Shooter Zato* did exactly what it said on the tin. The player character is blind, and the action is seen from the viewpoint of the enemies as they approach him. The title of the game was inspired by Zatoichi, a blind and brilliant swordsman from Japanese fiction.

Largest gathering of people wearing false moustaches in a game
Warframe is a free2play online TPS charting the battles of a race of ancient warriors known as the Tenno. As part of the charity fundraising month "Movember", in 2014 developers Digital Extremes offered players the chance to earn in-game facial hair by making donations. By 14 Nov, a razor-refusing 10,899 online characters sported virtual moustaches.

Most popular cross-platform game beta for a new IP

Ubisoft's online TPS *Tom Clancy's The Division* had a reported 6.4 million gamers for its beta testing in Feb 2016, smashing the previous record of 4.6 million set by Activision's *Destiny* in Jul 2014. These numbers are even more impressive for the fact that the beta took place across just five days, with PS4, Xbox One and PC players all participating. When *The Division* was released shortly after in Mar 2016, Ubisoft claimed it had the best first-week sales of any new franchise, generating an estimated $330 m (£229.8 m) globally in its first five days.

RPG SHOOTERS

Not content with simply launching you headfirst into battle, these gaming experiences combine twisty plots and open-world freedom with weighty RPG character development.

CLAPTRAP

Race	**Robot**
Skill	**Analysing situations**
Purpose	**Delivering Action Packages**
Key trait	**Talking drivel**
Unlikeliest cameo	*Poker Night 2*

Fastest completion of *Fallout 3*

France's "Rydou" smashed through the 15-min barrier in *Fallout 3*, completing the game in 14 min 54 sec on 29 Dec 2015, according to Speedrun.com.

Most downloaded *Borderlands* fan art

As of 8 Mar 2016, JohnSu's (USA) "Borderlands YEAH" had been downloaded 11,737 times by the DeviantArt community. The lauded piece of art depicted the playable characters Brick, Mordecai, Lilith and Roland.

Fastest completion of *Deus Ex: Invisible War*

Deus Ex franchise fan and Twitcher "jelmeree" (NLD) completed the PC version of *Deus Ex: Invisible War* (Eidos, 2003) in 22 min 41 sec on 21 Feb 2016. "The start was a bit sloppy, very good from Trier until the end," he wrote.

Most concurrent players on Steam for a non-Valve game
As of 8 Mar 2016, the peak for gamers playing *Fallout 4* at the same time on Valve's digital distribution service was 471,955. This put it third overall in the popularity rankings, behind *Dota 2* (with 1,262,612) and *Counter-Strike: Global Offensive* (with 819,902) – two Valve titles that are only available through Steam.

First completion of *Fallout 3* as a baby

On 5 Aug 2015, YouTuber "Bryan Pierre" uploaded five videos of himself playing through *Fallout 3* as a baby. A glitch in Bethesda's 2008 classic meant that it was possible to escape the tutorial as a baby, although Bryan still had to use a mod to give his ankle-biter sufficient skills to finish the story. Inevitably, the run took numerous hours – primarily because the baby could only crawl!

THE 2015 RELEASE OF *FALLOUT 4* SAW A BIG TREND FOR FAMOUS FACES BEING RECREATED IN THE GAME'S CHARACTER-CREATION SUITE. AMUSING ONLINE GALLERIES FEATURED SUCH MUGSHOTS AS DAVID BECKHAM, WALUIGI AND SHREK.

FACT!
In Jun 2015, a *Fallout* fan pre-ordered *Fallout 4* by speculatively posting Bethesda 2,240 bottle caps, the shooter's in-game currency. Amazingly, the publisher accepted the payment – but only as a one-off. It tweeted: "We're rewarding the first guy. Bank is closed :)".

25
The age of *Fallout 4*'s Vault Boy, according to a spoof lonely heart profile that was published on the dating app Tinder ahead of the game's release.

Fastest completion of *Deus Ex: The Fall*

Dutch gamer "jelmeree" sped through the PC version of *Deus Ex: The Fall* (Square Enix, 2013) in 18 min 23 sec (20 min 57 sec including load times) on 6 Mar 2016. The cyberpunk RPG was developed by N-Fusion and was first released for iOS in Jul 2013 before being ported to home computers via Steam in Mar 2014. It's one of the very few games to have been ported from mobiles to PC.

First marriage proposal via a game character

In Apr 2011, *Borderlands* developer Gearbox made a video for a superfan, Ben, who wished to propose marriage to his girlfriend Tora. The NSFW video saw the game's loveable robot, Claptrap, relaying Ben's message in a comedic, uncouth manner. It was aired at a party. Thankfully, a besotted Tora said "Yes"!

Fastest completion of *Fallout 4* (without loads)

On 1 Mar 2016, "JshaKhajiit" (UK) defied *Fallout 4*'s sprawling size by completing Bethesda's post-apocalyptic shooter in 56 min 4 sec. Curiously, when loads were included in the time, the run became slower than several rival runs. This was a likely consequence of gamers triggering different loads depending on their route. The run was listed at Speedrun.com and prohibited the use of the Pip-Boy mobile app, which enables players to operate the game's main gadget on their phone.

10 YEARS OF *GAMER'S*

In 2000, Eidos' *Deus Ex* was the first shooter you could complete without despatching any enemies – the **lowest minimum kill requirement in a shooter**.

Most pop culture references in a game

Eagle-eyed entertainment fiends can uncover 411 references to books, films, TV, popular figures, memes, music and rival games lurking in *Borderlands 2* (Gearbox, 2012). Wryly name-checked throughout are *Minecraft* (above), Shakespeare, *Star Wars*, James Bond, *My Little Pony*, *The Muppets*, and even the United States Postal Service!

Largest 4K screen at a videogame competition

On 9 Sep 2014, gamers Tom Lounsbury and Justin Munoz (both USA) faced off in a *Borderlands: The Pre-Sequel!* (2K Games) competition, battling it out on a giant 4K screen measuring 1,414.36 m² (15,224 sq ft). The 27.7-m-high (91-ft) screen was powered by nVIDIA and was set up at Churchill Downs in Louisville, Kentucky, USA.

VIDEOGAME CONCERTS

Gaming these days is no longer *just* about playing games. It can be about cosplaying as Snake, broadcasting on Twitch, or even enjoying live music. Videogame concerts are now hugely popular. Fervent crowds cram into venues to hear iconic and cult soundtracks being performed by some of the world's finest orchestras.

Producer Thomas Böcker (DEU, right) founded the Symphonic Game Music Concerts, and in 2003 staged the first videogame music concert outside Japan.

What gave you the idea for staging concerts?
I've been interested in games music ever since I was given a C64 when I was seven  or eight years old. Years later, I read about live orchestra performances in Japan and I felt there would be a global audience for this. But I came to the conclusion that if I wanted to hear my favourite game music performed live by an orchestra, then I would have to produce it myself!

Did you have a previous background in music?
I worked on my own projects, including *Merregnon*, where I invited famous game composers such as Yuzo Koshiro [*Streets of Rage*] to compose music for a fantasy story that I'd created.

How many concerts have you worked on?
I've produced or consulted on at least 50 orchestra concerts. I want the music to sound as good as possible, so I always choose classical venues over arenas. The capacities are around 2,000, but when we did the *Final Symphony II* tour of *Final Fantasy* music in Japan in 2015, 7,000 fans attended our three concerts in a week.

What have been some of your most memorable shows?
Without question the *Final Symphony II* shows we did with the London Symphony Orchestra (LSO) in Japan last September were a highlight. The LSO became the **first foreign orchestra to perform videogame music in Japan**. During our second performance, I was standing backstage with *Final Fantasy* composer Nobuo Uematsu and we sneaked out before the encore to watch the audience. The Japanese audience were enthusiastic in a way I've never seen before. They were cheering wildly and giving standing ovations. Uematsu was so moved he hugged me.

Do you have a favourite piece of game music?
I love the piece "Words Drowned by Fireworks" from *Final Fantasy VII*. It is such a beautiful, romantic piece, which is in stark contrast to the dark, somehow depressing, game world.

Most performed composer at videogame concerts

Japanese composer Nobuo Uematsu has composed scores for 13 of the 15 main games in Square Enix's *Final Fantasy* series. As of 27 Feb 2016, Uematsu's music had been performed in at least 535 concerts worldwide, including Distant Worlds (111 dates since 2007), Video Games Live (at least 334 shows) and *Final Symphony I & II* (13 shows to date).

Tommy Tallarico (USA, left) is a game-music composer and creator of the Video Games Live (VGL) concerts. On 20 Mar 2016, VGL staged its 357th show, reaffirming it as the **most performed gaming concert**.

How did VGL come about?
I've been a game composer for over 25 years so I wanted to prove to the world how culturally significant and artistic games have become.

Why is game music so popular?
When you play a game *you* become that character and the soundtrack of the game becomes the soundtrack of *your* life! It's a very different experience than anything else.

What have been your finest shows?
We played to over 60,000 people in Chinese Taipei in 2009. In China we

perform to over 25,000 people in big stadiums. We did a show in Beijing last year which was streamed live and had over a million people watching! But the most special performances are the ones we do in Chile and Brazil. The fans cheer so loud that my ears hurt!

How do you make music come alive?
We use synchronized video, stage show production, interactive elements, rock 'n' roll lighting, special effects and humorous videos – just as an example!

What's your favourite soundtrack?
Uematsu-san's *Final Fantasy VIII*. "Liberi Fatali" is my favourite song.

World of Warcraft (2004)
Position: 53
Composers: Various
Blizzard's MMORPG is almost as famous for its sweeping music as it is for its fantastical denizens. Its composers include Russell Brower (USA).

Kingdom Hearts (2002)
Position: 30
Composer: Yoko Shimomura (JPN)
Composer and pianist Shimomura worked for Square for nine years, and is best celebrated for her work on this Disney-licenced RPG.

Banjo-Kazooie (1998)
Position: 13
Composer: Grant Kirkhope (UK)
Scotland's Kirkhope worked on a number of N64 titles including *GoldenEye 007* (1997). His work on Rare's *Banjo-Kazooie* was hailed as a true classic.

The Elder Scrolls series (2002–present)
Position: 11
Composer: Jeremy Soule (USA)
Soule has been widely heralded as the "John Williams of videogame music". His scores for the *Elder Scrolls* RPGs are often haunting and always utterly epic.

Final Fantasy series (1987–present)
Position: 9
Composer: Nobuo Uematsu (JPN)
No game composer is more celebrated than Uematsu. His magical *Final Fantasy* music has also been released across numerous soundtrack albums.

TOP 5
GAME SOUNDTRACKS IN THE 2015 CLASSIC FM HALL OF FAME
Classic FM is a leading classical music radio station

SIMS & STRATEGY

Whether you're conducting large naval battles, raising a virtual pet or driving a spluttering tractor, these genres often have three key traits: realism, diversity and quirkiness.

> **Most digital revenue generated by a videogame (current)**

Revered for its fast-paced strategic gameplay, Riot Games' MOBA *League of Legends* (2009) managed to generate a staggering $1,627,643,818 (£1,097,840,000) in digital sales revenue in 2015 – despite being a free2play game. The revenue was generated by microtransactions, which allow players to buy virtual items or features within the game.

Most played online multiplayer game (current)
With an average of 94,332,069 monthly active users (MAU) throughout 2015, *League of Legends* is streets ahead of the MMO competition. According to figures compiled by SuperData, its MAU count is more than twice that of online FPS *CrossFire* (Smilegate, 2007), in second place with 45,176,591.

SIMULATION GAMES

Interact with other humans in their everyday lives. Take a trip on a hyper-realistic train or truck. Or just bash things with a goat. With sim games, reality has never been so much fun!

In 2006, Nintendo's *im Nintendogs* was given a PETA *"Pr* *gie"* award for Best Animal-Friendly V *eo Game – the* first videogame to wi *a PETA award.*

Most expensive DLC for a game (combined)

Released in Sep 2015, the mega-detailed *Train Simulator 2016: Steam Edition* (Dovetail Games) offered 247 DLC releases available for purchase through the Steam store as of 7 Jan 2016. On that date, snapping up every one would set back the virtual rail enthusiast £3,348 ($4,904).

Fastest 100% completion of *Animal Crossing* (solo)

On 11 Mar 2015, "Orcastraw" (USA) submitted a video to Speedrun.com of a total completion of community sim *Animal Crossing* (Nintendo, 2001) in 61 hr 31 min 54 sec. It entailed collecting all fish, insects, golden tools, player statues and upgrades to Tom Nook's store, paying off debts and completing the museum's catalogue.

Fastest time to make 10 deliveries in *Euro Truck Simulator 2*

Playing version 1.18B of SCS Software's 2013 "delivery" sim, Norwegian gamer "walland" completed 10 deliveries in his trusty four-wheeler in 6 min 28.85 sec on 9 Nov 2015, before uploading his effort to Speedrun.com.

77

Most critically acclaimed virtual pet

Nintendo's pet sim *Nintendogs: Lab & Friends* was released in 2005 for the DS. Lapped up by gamers, it amassed a top-dog score of 85.05% from 76 reviews on GameRankings.

Most liked game video on YouTube

"FUNNY MONTAGE.. #2" by social media star "PewDiePie" (SWE, inset top left) had been given the thumbs-up 1,017,942 times as of 23 Mar 2015. The video features comic scenes, many modded, from games such as *Farming Simulator 2013* (Focus, above) and *Goat Simulator* (Coffee Stain Studios, 2014).

Different cities featured in runaway sim smash *Euro Truck Simulator 2.*

WITH 43,248,969 SUBSCRIBERS AS OF 11 APR 2016, "PEWDIEPIE" (SWE) HAS THE MOST SUBSCRIBERS ON YOUTUBE. CHECK OUT HIS AMUSING IN-PLAY GAME COMMENTARIES, ESPECIALLY HIS FAVOURITE SIM GAMES.

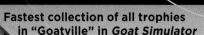

Fastest collection of all trophies in "Goatville" in *Goat Simulator*

Without the aid of "mutators" – crafty mods to make your goat more powerful – "DerToSt" (DEU) collected all 30 trophies in 4 min 20 sec on 21 Jan 2016. The **fastest collection of all trophies in "Goat City Bay" in *Goat Simulator*** is 6 min 28 sec, by "Riekelt" (NLD) on 10 Feb 2016.

You can see a surprising guest star in *The Sims* – the Loch Ness monster appears in the lake on the neighbourhood screen and also in Downtown and Vacation Island. There is also a pre-made Sim named "Nessie Lochlan" in the *Sims 3* Store.

FACT!

GOAT

GOAT SIMULATOR

Special moves	Butting, licking
Likes	Mayhem
Dislikes	Getting hit by cars
Alter ego	Demon Goat
Favourite mod	Jetpack

Most expansion packs for a videogame series
The Sims is renowned for its all-encompassing perspective on contemporary life, and the expansion packs provide a further wealth of new settings, themes, pets, fashion styles, objects, places to go and character traits. By Feb 2016, there had been 54 expansions released across five games.

First god simulation
Peter Molyneux (UK) is an icon in the sim genre. In 1989, his game *Populous* created a new sub-genre of sims by inviting gamers to play as powerful deities.

In 2012, Molyneux made further headlines with his experimental smartphone game *Curiosity – What's Inside the Cube?* This online title offered one gamer the chance to buy a virtual diamond chisel for around $75,000 (£47,000) in real money – the **most expensive in-game purchase**.

Smallest development team to win a simulation BAFTA
Developed by a team of one – Lucas Pope (USA) – *Papers, Please* follows an immigration officer at a border checkpoint in the fictional country of Arstotzka. It won the BAFTA in the "Strategy and Simulation" category in 2014.

Best-selling PC game series
Since the release of life-sim sandbox *The Sims* (Maxis) in 2000, the series has grown into a global phenomenon. Previous estimates of PC series sales have topped 50 million copies, but as of 22 Feb 2016 VGChartz placed total sales at 36.72 million.

The Sims 2 (2004) is the **most critically acclaimed life-sim game**, with a 90.76% GameRankings score as of the same date.

MANAGEMENT SIMS

Build your own sprawling city from the ground up. Guide a species through evolution, or just make a really, *really* slow roller-coaster. Management sims place you firmly in control.

Longest roller-coaster built in *RollerCoaster Tycoon*

Chris Sawyer's 1999 theme-park management sim invites gamers to build the rides of their dreams, but the anonymous creator of "Kairos – The Slow" produced a nightmare instead. Footage first appearing on imageboard 8chan showed a train crawling around an epic track on a journey calculated to last 210 real-life days. That equates to over 3,000 in-game years.

Most viewed fan film based on a city-building game

Uploaded to YouTube on 29 Oct 2012 by "joueurdugrenier", "Papy Grenier - SIM CITY" had amassed 5,180,969 views on YouTube as of 21 Mar 2016. A French-language satire based around Maxis's classic management game *SimCity*, it starred Dorian Chandelier and Yann Chauvière.

DEMOCRACY 3

Best-selling political sim

The leader in an under-represented gaming genre, government sim *Democracy 3* (Positech Games, 2013) had sold 473,539 copies as of 18 Apr 2016, with the vast bulk of its sales being recorded through Steam. The game challenges players to boldly fill the boots of a country's president or prime minister.

One of sim guru Will Wright's more unusual titles, *SimAnt* (Maxis, 1991) had players fighting caterpillars, dodging human footsteps and swapping regurgitated food as they tried to build a dominant ant colony.

FACT!

Smallest functioning prison in *Prison Architect*

On 2 Dec 2015, Joshua Roberts uploaded a design of a prison in Introversion Software's 2015 penal-management game that measured just 6 m x 6 m (19 ft 8 in x 19 ft 8 in). The design worked to rules stipulating that it contain one cell, a kitchen, canteen, shower and yard, with utilities and delivery spaces outside of the grid.

8,146

Residents of the Hamster Tenement, the largest-capacity building in *SimCity 4*.

Most prolific management-sim developer on mobile devices

Management sims were once the preserve of PCs, but an increasing number of titles are now appearing on touchscreen-equipped devices. Japanese company Kairosoft had released 44 management sims on mobiles as of 12 Jan 2016, with titles including *Game Dev Story* and *Dungeon Village*. Thirty had been translated into English.

First city-building videogame

The first construction and management simulation is generally considered to be *Utopia*, released on the Intellivision in 1981. Players are responsible for improving their own island by positioning buildings, feeding citizens and managing the economy.

Most evolutionary periods in a management-sim game

Designed by sim-game legend Will Wright, *Spore* (EA, 2008) challenges players to control the development of a species through four evolutionary stages: microscopic organism, early life form, simple planet-bound tribe and all-conquering intergalactic civilization.

First pop star in a sim game

Best known for 1999 single "Mambo No. 5", Lou Bega (DEU) appears as a dictator persona in island sim *Tropico* (PopTop, 2001).

Largest neural network in a videogame

Democracy 3 uses an artificial neural network (ANN) capable of simulating 4,975 neurons. ANNs are modelled on the brains of animals in order to help machines to learn. In the game, policies, voters and player decisions are all repressed by neurons.

Best-selling city-building videogame series

With sales of over 18 million units as of 21 Mar 2016, Maxis's *SimCity* series has challenged countless gamers to protect their precious metropolises from nuclear meltdowns, earthquakes and the occasional rampaging monster. Its first title appeared on the PC in Feb 1989, and with *SimCity* arriving 24 years later in Mar 2013, it is also the **longest-running management-sim series**.

Largest *SimCity 4* city region
On 27 Aug 2014, YouTube user Peter Ritchie uploaded a monstrous mega-region consisting of 81 large city tiles. Its 26,541 km (16,491 mi) of paved roads, 8,626 km (5,359 mi) of subway lines, 324 hydrogen power plants and over 2,000 schools supported a population of 107,658,254 residents.

STRATEGY GAMES

Whether turn-based or real-time, tactical titles require careful planning, watchful cunning, and plenty of skill and dedication if you are to emerge victorious.

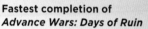

In Jun 2012, "Lycerius", aka James Moore (USA), revealed details of "The Eternal War", an epic game of *Civilization II* (MicroProse, 1996) that he had been playing since 2002. In a Reddit update on 11 Jun 2013, more than 11 years after he had begun playing, Lycerius had reached the in-game year of AD 4200, and a "nightmare world of suffering and devastation".

Fastest completion of *Advance Wars: Days of Ruin*

On 27 Feb 2015, Canada's "Gippy" sped through the "Campaign" mode on the classic Nintendo DS strategy title *Advance Wars: Days of Ruin* (Intelligent Systems, 2008) in just 57 min 2 sec, as verified by Speedrun.com.

Most critically acclaimed turn-based strategy game

A GameRankings score of 93.36% put *Sid Meier's Civilization IV* (2K Games, 2005) ahead of *Galactic Civilizations II: Dark Avatar* (Stardock, 2007), with 92.61%, as of 22 Mar 2016. In third place with 92.52% was *Fire Emblem: Awakening* (Nintendo, 2012) for the 3DS, the **most critically acclaimed hand-held turn-based strategy game**.

Highest-earning *Age of Empires II* player

Despite the demise of its original developer, the historical RTS series still enjoys some popularity on the eSports scene. As of 23 Mar 2016, Kang "iamgrunt" Byung Geon (KOR) had earned $78,666 (£54,296) playing *Age of Empires II: The Age of Kings* (Microsoft, 1999), according to figures by eSportsearnings.com.

FACT! The forces of the undead take on unusual forms in madcap tower defence *Plants vs. Zombies* (PopCap, 2009). The haunted hordes include Snorkel Zombie, Pogo Zombie, Dolphin Rider Zombie and – of course – the Zombie Bobsled Team.

5

Number of iPads *Clash of Clans* legend Jorge Yao, aka George Yao (USA), played simultaneously while he was the world's No. 1. He even wrapped them in plastic bags so that he could play in the shower!

Most watched videogame TV commercial

Featuring a chilling "AngryNeeson52", aka Hollywood actor Liam Neeson, "Clash of Clans: Revenge (Official Super Bowl TV Commercial)" had been viewed 108,095,225 times on YouTube by 22 Mar 2016. The advert was originally shown on 1 Feb 2015 during half-time of Super Bowl XLIX, and reputedly cost $9 m (£5.9 m) to air.

Most revenue by a mobile game (current)

According to SuperData, the strategic war title *Clash of Clans* (Supercell, 2012) generated revenue of $1,345,114,025 (£938,964,835) in 2015, more than any other game for the calendar year. *Clash of Clans* is a freemium title, meaning that it is free2play, but players can purchase virtual in-game items or features by making microtransactions.

Most money raised from a "Humble Bundle"

Humble Bundles are curated collections of PC games sold on a pay-what-you-want basis over a limited time period. The proceeds are split between charities and designers. On 14–28 Aug 2013, EA's "Humble Origin Bundle", containing strategy titles *Populous* (Bullfrog, 1989) and *Command & Conquer: Red Alert 3 – Uprising* (EA LA, 2009), sold 2.1 million copies and raised over $10.5 m (£6.75 m).

◀ Most followed battle in a strategy game

In Aug 2015, Australian Redditor "TPangolin", aka Jett, began simulating a titanic *Civilization V* (2K Games, 2010) clash he dubbed "Battle Royale Mk. II". The game featured a possible maximum of 62 rival civilizations, 61 of which were AI-controlled. TPangolin's "Battle Royale" Subreddit page was still going strong in Mar 2016, by which point it had received a staggering 828,081 views. Monthly unique views peaked at 84,730.

26

"Flavours" used by *Civilization V* to determine the personalities of its AI-controlled leaders and their actions. These flavours range from "expansion" and "defence" to "religion" and "happiness".

10 YEARS OF GAMER'S

Released in 2011, Sega's ultra-detailed *Total War: Shogun 2* featured 80 types of tree – the **most species of tree in a strategy game**.

Largest-scaled LEGO® model based on a videogame map

A LEGO diorama inspired by maps from Blizzard's RTS *StarCraft* games measured 4.267 m x 0.762 m (14 ft x 2 ft 6 in). It was built to a scale of 1:125, meaning a 1:1 map would have measured 51,000 m² (550,000 sq ft) in the game. The diorama was developed over three years by eight LEGO enthusiasts: Bart De Dobbelaer (BEL), Cecilie Fritzvold (NOR), Sean and Steph Mayo (both USA), and Simon Liu, John Moffatt, Chris Perron and Tim Schwalfenberg (all CAN).

Fastest completion of *XCOM: Enemy Unknown*

The transatlantic partnership of "Papers" (USA) and "Twyn" (FRA) successfully headed off the alien invasion depicted in the turn-based campaign of Firaxis Games' *XCOM: Enemy Unknown* (2012) in a segmented run completed on 28 Dec 2014. The super-fast victory took just 29 min 19 sec, as verified by Speed Demos Archive.

HEARTHSTONE

Publisher: Blizzard
Debut: 2014
Games: 1

Developer: Blizzard
Series sales: N/A (free2play)
Rivals: *Elder Scrolls: Legends*

Most pro wins per class in *Hearthstone*

"ThijsNL" (NLD, right) had won 90 pro *Hearthstone: Heroes of Warcraft* matches with the Druid class as of 18 Mar 2016. According to the eSports site GosuGamers, he had also used the Druid class for 152 matches – the **most games played per class** in *Hearthstone*.

Most Twitch followers for a *Hearthstone* player

One of the most recognizable names in *Hearthstone*, pro gamer Jeffrey "Trump" Shih (USA) had 691,465 followers of his "TrumpSC" Twitch channel as of 18 Mar 2016. It was the 30th most followed channel overall. Trump uses his videos to deal out advice for players of all skill levels.

Strongest class in *Hearthstone* ("Arena" mode)

Based on Hearthstats.net data, Rogue is the safest class to wield in *Hearthstone*'s "Arena" mode. As of 21 Mar 2016, it enjoyed a 60.8% win rate. Rogues are championed as stealthy, back-stabbing assassins, skilled in brewing poisons. Pictured left is the Rogue Valeera Sanguinar.

Hearthstone world rankings

Name	Nationality	Win rate	Rating
ThijsNL (Thijs Molendijk)	Netherlands	64%	1,327
Purple (Ryan Murphy-Root)	Canada	64%	1,291
Ostkaka (Sebastian Engwall)	Sweden	53%	1,245
SuperJJ (Jan Janssen)	Germany	61%	1,236
Lifecoach (Adrian Koy)	Germany	57%	1,232
AKAWonder (Esteban Serrano)	Spain	57%	1,222
hoej (Frederik Nielsen)	Denmark	62%	1,212
Dog (David Caero)	USA	56%	1,208
Kolento (Aleksandr Malsh)	Ukraine	58%	1,200
Orange (Jon Westberg)	Sweden	54%	1,191

Source: GosuGamers. All figures accurate as of 3 Apr 2016.

Longest single *Hearthstone* turn

On 25 Mar 2015, Twitcher Florian "Mamytwink" Henn (FRA) took 1 day 21 hr 18 min to complete a single *Hearthstone* turn. The average turn takes around 1 min 30 sec. However, Mamytwink exploited a loophole that enabled him to fire 28,752 arcane missiles instead of the usual three, triggering an epic animation lasting nearly two days!

According to a study in 2015 by *PC Gamer*, a whopping 90% of pro gamers voted for Dr Boom as the most popular Legendary card in *Hearthstone*.

Most *Hearthstone* cards bought at once

In May 2015, Reddit user "MattCauthron" purchased over 2,800 packs of cards in a 48-hr spending spree. He splashed out $3,400 (£2,234) in the process. "I knew I would have to buy a ... amount of packs to ... all the gold cards I wanted," he told *PC Gamer*. He ended up destroying much of his collection – more than 240,000 cards – in return for Arcane Dust, which players use for crafting cards.

Most popular player-made *Hearthstone* deck

"Legend of the Warsong Commander" by "HorLukRos" had 3,480 community endorsements on Hearthpwn.com, as of 18 Mar 2016.

Most money won in a *Hearthstone* tournament

On 17 Dec 2015, "DawN" (KOR) won the World Cyber Arena 2015, taking home CN¥700,000 (£71,975). He beat James "Firebat" Kostesich in the final, utilizing Warlock, Druid, Warrior and Paladin decks.

600

Grams of gold in China's Gold Series trophy, presented to the winners of its *Hearthstone* event in 2015.

THRALL

HEARTHSTONE

Class	**Shaman**
Hero power 1	**Summoning a totem**
Hero power 2	**Lightning Jolt**
Says	**"The elements will destroy you!"**
Originally from	**Warcraft III**

On 4 Jul 2015, "Trump" won his first *Hearthstone* tournament, defeating "nugoory" in the final of HTC Recharged. Trump is widely hailed as *Hearthstone*'s most famous player, yet had never won an event before.

FACT!

Most cards drawn in a *Hearthstone* turn

On 8 Apr 2015, "Mamytwink" (FRA, left) – the "expert of useless *Hearthstone* challenges" – drew 14,745 cards. In the same move, he also took 108,714,885 points of fatigue – the **most fatigue damage in a *Hearthstone* turn**. TouchArcade hailed him as a "mad genius".

Most viewed *Hearthstone* stream
With its simple-yet-intense card battles, *Hearthstone* has become a gripping spectator eSport. This was evidenced in Sep 2015 when a stream of the Archon Team League Championships peaked with 140,730 concurrent viewers – more than any other *Hearthstone* tournament. Cloud9 (USA) emerged victorious.

HAVING DISCOVERED THAT *HEARTHSTONE*'S EFFECTS SOUNDED LIKE PERCUSSION, YOUTUBE DUO "JIMANDNATHANDOTHEGAMES" USED THEM TO MAKE A SONG! AS OF 24 MAR 2016, "RAISE YOUR NATURE – A SONG MADE OF *HEARTHSTONE*" HAD 109,969 VIEWS.

Longest pro win streak in *Hearthstone*

On 13 Nov 2015, Germany's "SuperJJ" beat "ThijsNL" at the SeatStory Cup IV, kickstarting an 18-match win streak in *Hearthstone* tournaments. The run lasted until 27 Nov 2015, when he lost to "Purple" at DreamHack Winter.
 SuperJJ (inset) plays for the eSports team compLexity, and as of 3 Apr 2016 GosuGamers ranked him as the fourth best *Hearthstone* player in the world.

MODS

Over the years, gamers have become more skilled in mastering the tools of digital creation. Meanwhile, game studios willingly allowed access to the engines that power their creations. The result has been a significant trend for game modification – or, as it's more commonly known, "modding". From alterations to existing games, to entire new entities built from the blocks of distinguished releases such as *Doom* and *Warcraft III*, we celebrate some of the most impressive mods created in recent years.

GARRY'S MOD IS AN ENORMOUSLY POPULAR SANDBOX GAME THAT BEGAN LIFE AS A *HALF-LIFE 2* MOD. YOUTUBER "VANOSSGAMING" IS A FAN – HIS *GARRY'S MOD* VIDEOS STARRING *TOY STORY* AND *MATRIX* CHARACTERS HAVE OVER 20 MILLION VIEWS

Black Mesa

Modded from: *Half-Life 2*
Creators: Crowbar Collective
Developed across eight years by some 40 fans and released on Steam in May 2015, *Black Mesa* is a full remake of Valve's seminal FPS *Half-Life*. The mod was created using Valve's Source engine, which was first used to power *Half-Life 2* and *Counter-Strike: Source* in 2004. Despite the remake's superior visuals, its gameplay and story remains faithful to the original 1998 game, evoking identical emotions. Eurogamer Spain hailed it "an excellent work".

Defense of the Ancients

Modded from: *Warcraft III: Reign of Chaos*
Creators: Steve Feak
There might not be any more important mod than *Defense of the Ancients* (DotA). Its initial creation in 2003 spawned the massively online battle arena (MOBA) genre, and without it there would likely be no *Dota 2* or *League of Legends*. *DotA* is primarily a mod of *Warcraft III*, although it actually bases its terrain on the Aeon of Strife map from *StarCraft*. Its success led to its creator, Steve Feak, being hired by Riot Games to help create *League of Legends*.

DayZ

Modded from: *ARMA II*
Creators: Dean "Rocket" Hall
In 2012, New Zealander Dean Hall somehow took a military simulator that prides itself on accuracy and authenticity and turned it into a celebrated zombie survival game. The core appeal of *DayZ* is that nothing in it is certain, with real players vying for limited resources in a world overrun by the living dead. Do you cooperate with others, or do you stab them in the back? The choice is yours...

Brutal Doom

Modded from: *Doom*
Creators: Sergeant_Mark_IV
As its name suggests, *Brutal Doom* (2010) is a mod at the extreme end of the scale. Compatible with *Doom*, *Doom II*, *The Ultimate Doom* and *Final Doom*, it ups the levels of blood in the series and makes the enemies faster and less predictable. As a result, it's not a mod you should install if you're not already a skilled player. John Romero, one of the creators of the original *Doom*, praised the mod for its humour and its dedication to exaggerating everything it possibly could.

Super Mario Generations

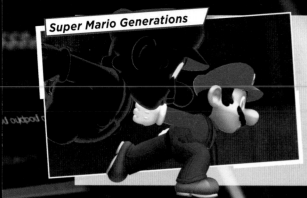

Modded from: *Sonic Generations*
Creators: Daku Neko

The rivalry between Mario and Sonic has been the fiercest in gaming history. So, when modder Daku Neko inserted *Mario* characters into a *Sonic* game in 2015, the world took notice. *Sonic Generation's* (2011) original platforming action remains intact, only this time you're sprinting and rolling through levels at a lightning pace as the Italian plumber rather than the blue hedgehog. Playing as Mario in a *Sonic* framework certainly results in a fun, albeit slightly odd, novelty factor.

The Dark Mod

Modded from: *Doom 3*
Creators: Team Dark Mod

Sometimes fans can't wait for the next iteration of a gaming series – so they make their own sequel instead. That's what happened with *The Dark Mod*, a full game inspired by the stealth-adventure franchise *Thief*. Silence and shadows are your best friends here, with the avoidance of combat the best means to acquiring valuables. *The Dark Mod's* original 2009 release required *Doom 3* to be installed on your PC, but versions since 2013 have removed that condition.

Nehrim: At Fate's Edge

Modded from: *The Elder Scrolls IV: Oblivion*
Creators: SureAI

Created in 2010 by a German team dedicated to making mods for the *Fallout* and *The Elder Scrolls* franchises, *Nehrim: At Fate's Edge* is one of the most exhaustive modding projects ever undertaken. It's been dubbed a "total conversion mod", meaning that much of the original *Oblivion* content has been replaced with new elements. Magic and travel mechanics have been reworked, the game has its own full campaign narrative, and it features entirely new buildings and towns. Pro actors were even hired to voice new characters.

JourneyMap

Modded from: *Minecraft*
Creators: Techbrew

There are many options for modding *Minecraft*, but few of them are as brilliantly useful – and as understated – as *JourneyMap*. Simple in concept, the mod offers a map that updates itself in real time as you explore the gaming world. It stops gamers from getting lost in newly charted regions, while also providing advance warning of nearby players and pets by way of a mini-map. *JourneyMap* can also reveal everything around you – not advisable if you love to explore, but helpful if you're seeking specific terrain types.

SPORTS

Whether you're managing on the sidelines or taking to the field, sports videogames summon the passion and intensity that all true fans understand – whichever sport they follow.

Longest game of *Football Manager*

From early 2013 to Dec 2014, Liverpool FC fan Darren Bland (UK) pursued a single career in *Football Manager 2010* on PC for 154 seasons. He managed just one team throughout – Fiorentina (ITA) – winning 151 league championships and securing "legendary" status. His marathon game was only brought to an end when a liquid spillage damaged his laptop. Incredibly, the in-game year was 2163 and his in-game manager would now have been theoretically more than 180 years old.

SOCCER

Few sports have translated to videogames as beautifully as the "beautiful game" itself. Hit series such as *FIFA*, *PES* and *Kick Off* inspire heated rivalries both on and off the virtual pitch.

Most subscribers for a *FIFA* YouTuber

Olatunji, had 12,001,578 subscribers to his "KSI" YouTube channel, as of 19 Feb 2016. Revered for his *FIFA* game videos, Olatunji also once held the record for the **highest margin of victory against a computer on *FIFA 13***, with 190.

Strongest player in the *FIFA* series

AFC Wimbledon striker Adebayo "The Beast" Akinfenwa (UK) has been the strongest player in four separate *FIFA* games, accruing an average strength rating of 97.6. In *FIFA 16* he earned a mighty 98 – two more than Christopher Samba (COG).

Most regional competitions in a sports videogame tournament

Konami's 2016 PES League eSports competition featured qualifying leagues divided into a globe-spanning 28 regions, including Germany, Israel, India and Peru. Winners of each league would win a place at the world final, to be staged at the San Siro stadium – home to Italian soccer giants AC Milan and Internazionale – on 28 May 2016.

9,132,839

Number of matches played on the mobile soccer-management sim *Top Eleven* (Nordeus) on just one day in 2015.

Q&A: Dino Dini, creator of the *Kick Off* series

Why is the original *Kick Off* still so popular after 25 years?
It's a skill-based game. When you score, you get a real feeling of satisfaction.

How did 2016's *Kick Off Revival* come about?
I gave a talk at the Game Developers Conference in 2013, which moved someone at Sony. They sent me a Vita dev kit, so I started working on a new game.

Do you see many similarities between the gameplay in *Rocket League* and *Kick Off*?
A few years ago I had an idea

of doing a football game with cars, so now I'm kicking myself! But if you're going to play football with cars, there will be a lot of skill involved, and that's the case with *Rocket League*. If you create a game with a lot of depth, you get an intrinsic satisfaction from mastering it. I think we've been losing that in videogaming.

How good are you at *Kick Off*?
Ha, not that good! When I competed at the *Kick Off* World Cup two years ago, I actually came last...

Most successful *PES* League player

Since Konami's official *PES* League became a global competition in 2011, its most decorated gamer is "VietKong90321", aka Ettore "Ettorito" Giannuzzi (ITA). The masterly player was the 2011 world champion and the 2014 UEFA Youth League champion.

Longest-running soccer videogame tournament

Since 2001, an international *Kick Off 2* World Cup has been held in Europe every year, making

for 15 tournaments in total. The most recent event was hosted in Dublin, Ireland, on 7–8 Nov 2015 (below), with more than 40 players signed up to compete.

137

The most playable leagues in a sports videogame can be found in *Football Manager 2016* (Sports Interactive, 2015).

Most *Kick Off 2* World Cup championships

With four tournament victories to his name, Gianni Torchio (ITA) is the king of *Kick Off 2* (Anco, 1990). He also finished runner-up four times (including 2015, when he lost to the UK's Andy G) and third twice – that's 10 medals in all.

Smallest development team to win a sports videogame BAFTA
Winner of the 2013 sports videogame BAFTA, the mobile RPG title *New Star Soccer* was the work of a team of just one – the UK's Simon Read.

Highest-earning *FIFA* videogame player
EA's *FIFA* is one of the most lucrative and eagerly contested series based on traditional sports on the eSports circuit. In 2013, Ivan "BorasLegend" Lapanje (SWE) pocketed $145,378 (£93,735) from winning three tournaments in the *FIFA* series.

MEGAN RAPINOE (BELOW LEFT) AND SYDNEY LEROUX (BELOW RIGHT) WERE AMONG THE USA PLAYERS WHO VISITED EA'S VANCOUVER STUDIO TO PARTICIPATE IN MOTION CAPTURE THAT PUT THE FINISHING TOUCHES TO *FIFA 16*.

First FIFA soccer game to feature female players
Despite the series debuting in 1993, *FIFA 16* (EA, 2015) was the first to feature women's teams – in this case, 12 national sides. International variants of the game also boasted the **first female soccer players on a FIFA cover**: Christine Sinclair (CAN), Alex Morgan (USA) and Steph Catley (AUS).
  The **first soccer game to feature female players** was *Mia Hamm 64 Soccer*, released for the N64 by SouthPeak in Nov 2000.

AMERICAN FOOTBALL

With a tactical mix of running and hard hitting, gridiron has been a smash with gamers. *Madden* may dominate the charts, but other series have thrown some serious weight, too.

Most critically acclaimed

Hailed for its fluid running game, Sega's *NFL 2K1* (2000), released exclusively for the Dreamcast, had scored an end-zone-busting 94.50% at GameRankings as of 5 Apr 2016. Breathing down its neck was *NCAA Football 2004* (EA, 2003), which boasted 93.27%.

Best-selling American sports videogame

Released in 2006, *Madden NFL 07* (EA) featured new rushing controls that allowed players to refine their running game. As of 29 Feb 2016, *Madden NFL 07* had racked up Super Bowl-winning sales of 10.02 million across 10 different platforms.

Longest fumble in a *Madden* videogame

On 13 Sep 2015, the Aimless Adventure Podcast published a video showing a *Madden NFL 16* fumble that lasted 9 min 20 sec. An apparent glitch meant that players from both the Arizona Cardinals and the Carolina Panthers were unable to pick up the ball, which finally rolled harmlessly out of play.

Most votes for a videogame cover

More than 40 million people voted on who should grace the front of *Madden NFL 25* (EA, 2013) – the series' grand 25th anniversary release. A total of 60 players were in the running, but it was former Detroit Lions running back Barry Sanders (USA, left) who came through, pipping 2012 NFL MVP Adrian Peterson of the Minnesota Vikings to the honour.

10 YEARS Patrick Scott Patterson (USA) achieved the **highest margin of victory on *Madden NFL 10*** – a whopping 56 points, as verified by Twin Galaxies on 20 Jan 2010.

First videogame to feature real NFL players and teams

NFL Football, released for the NES in 1989, was intended to represent the 1988/89 NFL formations from the era.

First Super Bowl correctly predicted by the annual EA Super Bowl simulation

Since 2004, EA has tried to predict each year's Super Bowl result by simulating the match through the latest *Madden* videogame. Ahead of Super Bowl XLIX on 1 Feb 2015, *Madden NFL 15* correctly forecasted a 28–24 victory for the New England Patriots against the Seattle Seahawks.

28

Number of titles in the *Madden NFL* series as of 1 Mar 2016 – the most games in an NFL videogame franchise.

Most prolific sports videogame developer

With 68 commercially released sports games developed since 1988, Visual Concepts' credits include work on the *Madden NFL* series and the flagship 2K Sports brand, which includes baseball, basketball and ice hockey titles.

Eagle-eyed gamers will notice unfamiliar faces in the crowd in *Madden NFL 16* – women! It was the first game in the series to feature female fans in the stands.

FACT!

Most viewed American sports videogame video

The *NFL 15* musical promo "Madden NFL 15: Madden Season" is a big-budget production featuring Hollywood actors Kevin Hart and Dave Franco (both above). As of 29 Feb 2016, it had earned 17,126,201 views on YouTube.

5

Number of players on each side in Mattel's 1979 Intellivision classic *NFL Football* – less than half the size of a real team!

Most successful *Madden* player

Three-time winner of the prestigious EA Sports Madden Challenge, Eric "Problem" Wright (USA) earned his nickname for the trouble he caused his opponents. Between 2006 and 2013, Eric won an unprecedented 18 *Madden* gaming titles, with his total earnings amounting to $380,000 (£273,787).

JOHN MADDEN

MADDEN NFL

Special skills	**Commentary**
Catchphrase (I)	**"Boom!"**
Catchphrase (II)	**"Whack!"**
Catchphrase (III)	**"Doink!"**
Favourite tool	**Telestrator**

Most Madden Bowl videogame tournament wins
Held every Super Bowl weekend, the Madden Bowl is a gaming tournament featuring celebrities and athletes. Four US pro footballers have won it twice: Reggie Brooks (1995 and 1996), Jacquez Green (2001 and 2002), Dwight Freeney (2003 and 2004) and Alex Smith (2006 and 2007).

Longest-running sports videogame series

Debuting with *John Madden Football* for PC in 1988, EA's *Madden NFL* series had been going strong for 27 years, as of Aug 2015's *NFL 16*. The series even survived the departure of Madden himself – the **longest-serving videogame commentator** retired in 2008 after 13 years of providing commentary to the games.

BASKETBALL

From the tip-off to the final buzzer, basketball videogames provide non-stop high-octane action, featuring some of the biggest names – and shoe sizes – in global sport.

First basketball videogame

The simply titled *Basketball!* was built for the Magnavox Odyssey and released in 1973, the year after the first-generation console hit stores. Like many Magnavox titles, *Basketball!* used plastic overlays placed over the TV screen to make the basic blocky graphics more visually appealing.

It wasn't until 1980 that the **first videogame with an NBA licence** appeared: *NBA Basketball*, built for Mattel's second-gen Intellivision.

Largest basketball database in a videogame

World Basketball Manager (Icehole, 2014) boasted a roster-busting 12,500 players, 1,400 managers, 194 nationalities, and 972 clubs and national teams.

Longest-running basketball videogame series

The very first game in EA's *NBA Live* series was *NBA Live 95* (1994), predating the first instalment in the *NBA 2K* series – *NBA 2K* (Sega, 1999) – by five years. As of Mar 2016, there had been 19 *NBA Live* titles, with the most recent being 2015's *NBA Live 16*.

1,500

Number of customizable tattoo designs in *NBA 2K16*'s "MyPlayer" basketballer-creation mode.

Most viewed *NBA 2K* video on YouTube

Featuring a soaring slam dunk by Superman and a stadium-shaking alley-oop by the Incredible Hulk, "Avengers Vs Justice League in NBA 2K ! Age of Ultron HD" by "MkElite" (USA) had been viewed 4,485,248 times as of 29 Feb 2016.

Best-selling *NBA 2K* videogame

NBA 2K13 (2K Sports, 2012) summoned an all-star name of its own to act as executive producer: Jay Z. The multi-million-selling rapper not only selected songs for the soundtrack but also appeared in an introduction to the game. As of 29 Feb 2016, *NBA 2K13* had shifted 6.08 million copies across PS3, X360, Wii U, Wii and PC, according to figures compiled by VGChartz.

YouTube video "NBA 2K – 30 Foot Player | Tallest Player Ever!!", posted by "GamingWithOva", shows a giant basketball player causing havoc on court. It had been viewed 3,959,671 times as of 11 Mar 2016.

FACT!

104

Victory margin by Daniel Lee Strickland Perea (USA) on 16 Oct 2015 – the biggest blowout on *NBA Jam for Wii* (single player).

Fastest completion of *Looney Tunes B-Ball*

Sculptured Software's 1995 SNES title was the first videogame to place Bugs Bunny and co. on a basketball court, predating *Space Jam* by a year. Playing as Taz and Marvin the Martian, Alfredo Salaza (CHL) completed the game's tournament mode in 27 min 13 sec on 4 Apr 2015.

Most videogame cover appearances by a basketball player

"His Airness" Michael Jordan (USA) appeared on the cover of seven different titles. These include 1996 movie-tie-in *Space Jam* (Acclaim), the platformer *Michael Jordan: Chaos in the Windy City* (EA, 1994) and three *NBA 2K* games.

First Oscar-nominated film director to direct a sports videogame
The single-player story mode in *NBA 2K16* (2015) entitled "Livin' Da Dream" follows the fictional player Frequency Vibrations. It was directed by the then twice-Oscar-nominated director and diehard New York Knicks fan Spike Lee (USA). Lee later won an Honorary Oscar in Nov 2015.

Best-selling basketball videogame franchise

Since debuting on the Dreamcast in 1999, the sure-footed *NBA 2K* series (Sega/2K Games) has dominated rivals *NBA Live* and *NCAA Basketball* in the charts. As of 17 Jan 2016, the series had sold 52.1 million copies across all iterations according to VGChartz. Pictured left is James Harden of the Houston Rockets, one of three stars to grace the cover of the most recent game, *NBA 2K16*.

EXTREME SPORTS ROUND-UP

From BMX to BASE jumping, snowboarding to surfing, extreme sports mean extreme gaming. One critical and commercial hit dominates the genre: *Tony Hawk's Pro Skater*.

Most critically acclaimed sports videogame

Tony Hawk's Pro Skater 2 (Activision, 2000) on the PlayStation had a GameRankings score of 94.75% as of 24 Feb 2016. Ironically, its most recent iteration, *THPS 5* (2015), was the **lowest-rated sports videogame** with 32.96%, amid reviews citing technical issues.

Highest career score in *OlliOlli* (console)

Roll7's skateboarder gained a cult fanbase following its 2014 release. As of 2 Feb 2016, nobody had scored better than "Strayphside", who racked up 6,445,943 points on the Neon City 5 Pro level of the Xbox One version of the game.

Most videogames endorsed by an extreme sports athlete

Name	Sport	Games	As seen in...
Tony Hawk (USA)	Skateboarding	19	*Tony Hawk's Pro Skater 2*
Shaun White (USA)	Snowboarding	5	*Shaun White Snowboarding: Road Trip*
Dave Mirra (USA)	BMX	4	*Dave Mirra Freestyle BMX 2*
Greg Hastings (USA)	Paintballing	3	*Greg Hastings Paintball 2*
Mat Hoffman (USA)	BMX	2	*Mat Hoffman's Pro BMX 2*
Bode Miller (USA)	Skiing	2	*Bode Miller Alpine Skiing*
Shaun Murray (USA)	Wakeboarding	1	*Wakeboarding Unleashed ft. Shaun Murray*
Shaun Palmer (USA)	Snowboarding	1	*Shaun Palmer's Pro Snowboarder*
Kelly Slater (USA)	Surfing	1	*Kelly Slater's Pro Surfer*
Sunny Garcia (USA)	Surfing	1	*Sunny Garcia Surfing*

All figures accurate as of 24 Feb 2016

Longest "word" in the title of a commercially released videogame

The opening "word" in the offbeat futuristic BASE jumping simulation *AaaaaAAaaaAAaaAAAAaAAAAA!!! – A Reckless Disregard for Gravity* (Dejobaan Games, 2009) and its two sequels is 28 characters long, including exclamation marks. No wonder the games' titles are often abbreviated to *AaAaAA!!!*

Fastest single-segment completion of *Mirror's Edge*

On 19 Jul 2013, Filip "Zubmit" Sahlberg (SWE) finished EA's 2008 parkour-based action-adventure game in just 34 min 49 sec, as ratified by Speed Demos Archive. The game's heroine Faith Connors is shown above.

250

Challenges gamers need to complete in Amateur and Pro Careers before they can unlock "Rad" mode on *OlliOlli 2*.

Most ported extreme sports videogame

Over the course of its 29-year history, *California Games* (Epyx, 1987) has appeared on 16 different gaming platforms. The formats are: Apple II, C64, Amstrad CPC, Atari ST, Amiga, Spectrum, Apple IIGS, Atari 2600, MSX, NES, Sega Mega Drive, Sega Master System, DOS, Atari Lynx, mobile and Wii virtual console. Further plans to port for consoles such as the DS, PS2 and PSP were cancelled.

Fastest "gold" completion of *Trials Fusion*

The fifth game in RedLynx's smash-hit platform racing series, *Trials Fusion* (2014) challenged players to navigate a series of obstacles and complete the trials on a motorcycle, with gameplay modelled on actual physics.

"TheBlazeJp" (UK) achieved a gold medal on every track in a time of just 58 min 51 sec. The run was achieved on the PC version and uploaded to Speedrun.com on 11 Jun 2014.

EA's 2012 snowboarding sequel *SSX* featured 28 real-world mountains generated using topographical data from NASA satellites that was manipulated using 3D software.

FACT!

Highest "Spot" score in *OlliOlli* (console)

A single combo score is known as a Spot on Roll7's 2014 skateboarder. As of 23 Feb 2016, "shine3p" had recorded a leaderboard-topping Spot score of 7,692,221, achieved on the Neon City Spot 1 Pro level of the PS4 version.

The **highest "Spot" score in *OlliOlli 2* (console)** is 4,352,211, pulled off by the aptly named "RaymondTerrific" on the Curse of the Aztec Amateur 4 level.

50

Songs on the soundtrack to snowboarder *SSX*, featuring a diverse range of artists from DJ Shadow to The Hives.

Best-selling extreme sports game series
With worldwide sales of 33.8 million as of 24 Feb 2016, according to VGChartz, *Tony Hawk's Pro Skater* is streets ahead of the competition. To put it into perspective, EA's highly successful *SSX* snowboarding series could muster sales of only 10.14 million by the same date.

Most videogames endorsed by a professional sports athlete

As of 24 Feb 2016, skateboarder Tony Hawk (USA, photo shown inset) had endorsed a total of 19 games for his *Pro Skater* series, published by Activision. The figure included spin-offs, remakes and reimagined ports. This narrowly beat golfer Tiger Woods (USA), who had endorsed 18 *PGA Tour* titles for EA. Although NFL commentator John Madden endorsed more titles, he never played a professional game of American football.

OFFICER DICK

TONY HAWK'S PRO SKATER

Name	Richard Envee
Special trick (I)	Assume the Position
Special trick (II)	Neckbreak Grind
Special trick (III)	Yeehaw Front Flip
Notable cameo	*MTX Mototrax*

SPORTS ROUND-UP

Whether you're smashing balls across a tennis court, blitzing a puny elf catcher, or taking to the soccer field inside a car, there is plenty to play for in the world of sports videogames.

Best-selling ice hockey videogame

Ice hockey has been a huge hit with gamers. As of 22 Apr 2016, Nintendo's 28-year-old NES game *Ice Hockey* (1988) boasted sales of 2.42 million – more than any licenced *NHL* game.

First videogame

Developed by the US physicist William Higinbotham, *Tennis for Two* is often regarded as the first videogame. It simulated a game of tennis or ping pong on an oscilloscope, and was unveiled at the Brookhaven National Laboratory in New York City, USA, on 18 Oct 1958. Inevitably, it was also the **first tennis videogame**, predating the Magnavox Odyssey's *Tennis* by 14 years.

First 3D sports videogame

A launch title for Nintendo's Virtual Boy console on 21 Jul 1995, the 3D game *Mario's Tennis* was the first time that the famous plumber and his pals took to a tennis court. Although the 3D was considered convincing, it was the fun gameplay that led to sequels on later consoles.

Most critically acclaimed tennis videogame

Virtua Tennis (Sega, 2000) on the Dreamcast has a GameRankings score of 91.37%, based on 33 reviews.

FACT! The "Ice cream! Ice cream!" shout in *Speedball 2* is one of gaming's best-loved sound effects. According to Eurogamer, when one of the developers first heard it, he cried: "Wow, that's incredible. That's going to make it fly!"

22 Versions of Nintendo's horse-racing videogame series *Derby Stallion* released between 1991 and 2014.

Best-selling game for a fictitious sport

Based on Games Workshop's tabletop game, Cyanide's *Blood Bowl* (2009) had sold 240,000 physical copies as of 21 Apr 2016, according to VGChartz. The turn-based game features skaven and lizardmen (among other odd races) trying to score touchdowns while causing as much injury to opponents as possible. An improved sequel, *Blood Bowl 2* (left), was released in 2015.

Most ported sports videogame

Going neck-and-neck with the extreme sports classic *California Games* (Epyx, 1987), The Bitmap Brothers' *Speedball 2: Brutal Deluxe* has been ported and remade for 16 different platforms since its acclaimed 1990 debut. The futuristic sport combines elements of handball and ice hockey with lashings of cartoon violence. Its most recent variant was *Speedball 2 HD*, programmed by Jon Hare (UK) for the PC in 2013.

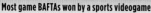

Most game BAFTAs won by a sports videogame
Psyonix's vehicular soccer blast *Rocket League* scooped three awards at the 12th British Academy Games Awards on 7 Apr 2016, in the Multiplayer, Family and Sport categories. It was the night's joint biggest winner, with *Her Story* and *Everybody's Gone to the Rapture* also bagging three gongs.

First motion-sensing multi-sports console

Beating the Wii to the punch, the SSD Company launched the first known motion-sensing home workout in the form of the XaviXPORT. The innovative console was launched in the USA in Aug 2004, with three titles initially available: *XaviX Tennis*, *XaviX Bowling* and *XaviX Baseball*.

TROLLSLAYER

BLOOD BOWL 2

Race	Dwarf
Strengths	Clobbering opponents
Weaknesses	Running
Special skills	Thick Skull, Frenzy
Famous teams	Dwarf Giants

Most goals scored in *Rocket League* (team of three)

Playing in front of a packed-out crowd at the Insomnia festival in Birmingham, UK, on 12 Dec 2015, "DanTDM", James Hayes and Martyn Littlewood (all UK) scored 41 goals against the computer. *Minecraft* YouTuber DanTDM proved to be the team's hotshot, rattling the net around 30 times. A huge indie smash from 2015, Psyonix's *Rocket League* takes the basic rules of soccer, but swaps out human players for futuristic cars.

430,000
Gold coins it costs to hire ogre star player Morg 'n' Thorg in *Blood Bowl 2*. The huge goblin-squasher is one of the sport's toughest players.

10 YEARS OF *GAMER'S*

Wii Sports (2006) is the **best-selling videogame**, with 82.71 million copies sold as of 22 Apr 2016. The five-game sports compendium was typically bundled with the Wii console, which explains the large sales.

First hurling videogame

It took the now-defunct Australian developer IR Gurus Interactive to introduce the Gaelic team sport of hurling to gamers. Released for PS2 in 2007, *Gaelic Games Hurling 2007* features a "season" mode based on Ireland's National Hurling League. Similar in name but completely different in nature, curling has players sliding stones across an icy playing field. The **first dedicated curling videogame** was Nathan Sorenson's *Take-Out Weight Curling*, released in 2002.

First roller derby videogame

Nichibutsu's 1984 arcade title *Roller Jammer* featured a solo skater fighting rivals as they raced around an outdoor track. However, the first game to depict a true team-sport roller derby is Frozen Codebase's *Jam City Rollergirls* (pictured). Released in the wake of the sport's reinvention in the early 2000s, the 2011 Wii exclusive is licensed by the Women's Flat Track Derby Association (WFTDA), with teams including the Dairyland Dolls and Rat City Rollergirls.

MACHINIMA FILMS

Machinima is the art of making animated narrative films from computer graphics, most commonly using the engines found in videogames. Some of the earliest machinima videos were created by editing the gameplay demos in id Software's 1996 FPS *Quake*, but in recent years new tools such as Valve's *Source Filmmaker*, Bungie's *Halo Forge* (first found in *Halo 3*) and *GTA V*'s *Rockstar Editor* have made machinima production more accessible. Usually, the most watched machinima videos come from the most popular games.

MACHINIMA IS ALSO THE NAME OF A POPULAR GAMES WEBSITE, WHICH ENABLES GAMERS TO SHOWCASE THEIR HOME-MADE CONTENT SUCH AS MACHINIMA (NATURALLY). THE SITE HAS A TALENT POOL OF 30,000 PROGRAMMERS

The **first machinima** is *Diary of a Camper*, which is made by United Ranger Films using *Quake*. It is released in Oct 1996 and tells the story of marines fighting a lone sniper, who turns out to be *Quake* co-creator John Romero.

1992

1996

The **first video editor mode in a game** is the "Editing Room" in *Stunt Island* (The Assembly Line). Promoted as "The Stunt Flying and Filming Simulation" game, it features a range of customizable film sets.

With a run time of 130 min, *Devil's Covenant* by Clan Phantasm is the **first feature-length machinima**. It uses the *Quake* engine and its makers are nominated at the *Quake* Movie Oscars for Best Movie Clan.

1998

Edited together from the cutscenes in 1998 platformer *Oddworld: Abe's Exoddus*, *Abe's Exoddus: The Movie* is the **first cutscene movie**. The 14-min 35-sec short is reportedly submitted for consideration at the 1999 Oscars!

First airing on G4 TV in 2002, *Portal* becomes the **first TV series to use machinima**. It is a comedy sketch show in which the host, Cybernaut Dave, aka Dave Meinstein, explores the virtual worlds of MMOs.

2000

2002

The **longest machinima** is *The Seal of Nehahra* (Mindcrime Productions), which runs for 235 min. It is made using a modified version of *Quake* and serves as the backstory to a fan-made game called *Nehahra*.

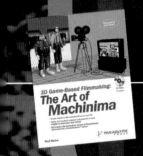

There are many books written on machinima, ranging from academic studies to how-to guides. The **first published book on machinima** is *3D Game-Based Filmmaking: The Art of Machinima* by the director Paul Marino.

2003

2004

The **first machinima music video to air on MTV** is made by Tommy Pallotta (USA) and is created for the song "In the Waiting Line" by UK electro duo Zero 7. It is built using the id Tech 3 engine from *Quake III Arena* (1999).

As of 8 Apr 2016, YouTuber and *GTA V* player "Merfish", aka Comrade Tripp (USA), is the **most prolific maker of *Rockstar Editor* videos**. Of his 123 published videos, many are parodies of TV shows, such as *Teletubbies* (left).

2007

2016

The 2006 *South Park* episode "Make Love, Not Warcraft" features machinima scenes made using *World of Warcraft*. In 2007 it becomes the **first machinima to win an Emmy**, awarded for Outstanding Animated Program. In it, the show's characters exact revenge on a rude *Warcraft* player.

TOP 10 MOST WATCHED MACHINIMA

YouTube is awash with budding film-makers who are using the engines of familiar videogames to make their own pixellated productions. From *GTA* to *Minecraft*, from *Warcraft* to *Five Nights at Freddy's*, machinima videos are among the most watched gaming videos on the web...
(*All data below from YouTube; correct as of 21 Feb 2016.*)

1. *Minecraft*

- "Revenge" - A Minecraft Original Music Video"
- CaptainSparklez, 2011
- 160,312,315 views

2. *Grand Theft Auto*

- "AWESOME GTA 5 STUNTS & FAILS (Funny Moments Compilation)"
- RedKeyMon, 2015
- 62,688,387 views

3. FNAF

- "[SFM/FNAF] Five Funky Night's at Freddy's 2"
- Father ferguson, 2015
- 51,047,885 views

4. The Sims

- "Barbie Girl - Aqua - The Sims 2"
- Amanda Haug, 2007
- 24,668,627 views

5. Counter-Strike

- "Counter-Strike For Kids (Machinima)"
- Machinima, 2008
- 18,069,751 views

6. Team Fortress

- "Team Fabulous 2"
- kitty0706, 2012
- 17,288,292 views

7. WoW

- "That's the World of Warcraft That You Play!"
- Ian Beckman, 2006
- 17,012,342 views

8. Halo

- "Red vs. Blue S8 Tex fights Reds and Blues in awesome action sequence"
- Rooster Teeth, 2010
- 14,048,446 views

9. The Elder Scrolls

- "Gamer Poop - Skyrim (#1)"
- Machinima, 2012
- 8,205,768 views

10. Portal

- "Portal: A Day in the Life of a Turret (Machinima)"
- Machinima, 2008
- 5,909,848 views

TWIN GALAXIES

On 10 Nov 1981, the Twin Galaxies videogame arcade opened its doors in Ottumwa, Iowa, USA. Founder Walter Day sought to turn gaming into an [international sport] by creating contests, enforcing rules, crowning champions – and measuring world records. He collected high scores for games from more than 100 arcades, releasing them as the Twin Galaxies National Scoreboard.

Since then, thousands of videogame scores have been adjudicated and collected, with high scores logged and record holders honoured. Twin Galaxies' state-of-the-art peer-review system adheres to GWR submission guidelines, ensuring that Twin Galaxies remains a gold standard for videogame adjudication. Submit your score at: **www.twingalaxies.com**.

All high scores were correct as of 21 Apr 2016.

Angry Birds Seasons
Rovio Entertainment's 2010 sequel grew out of a spooky spin-off: *Angry Birds Halloween Special Edition*. *Seasons* comprised a series of updates celebrating events from the Chinese New Year to St Patrick's Day. "Arctic Eggspedition" was released in Dec 2013. Lucianna Mee (UK) scored 80,730 playing levels 1–6 on Android, as verified by Twin Galaxies on 7 Oct 2015.

Game	Variation	Player	Score
Android			
Angry Birds	Flock Favorites – 29-2	Andrew Pete Mee (UK)	121,130
Angry Birds Seasons	Arctic Eggspedition – 1–6	Lucianna Mee (UK)	80,730
Angry Birds Star Wars II	1. Naboo Invasion – B1-1	Marc Cohen (USA)	35,890
Beach Buggy Blitz	Points	Max Haraske (USA)	27,573
Crossy Road	Points	Matthew Felix (USA)	399
Hill Climb Racing	Jeep – Cave [Distance]	Camden LeCroy (USA)	1,158
Piano Tiles: Don't Tap the White Tile	Classic – 6 x 6	Chad Liggon (USA)	6.687
Piano Tiles: Don't Tap the White Tile	Relay – 6 x 6	Joshua Arenivaz (USA)	54
Arcade			
Asteroids	Tournament	Brian Nelson (USA)	218,030
Bad Dudes vs. DragonNinja	1-Player – Points	Pete Hahn (USA)	999,999
Blazing Star	Highest Score 1 Player	Richard Evans (UK)	6,659,910
Bubble Bobble	Points [Normal Mode/ 2-Player Team]	Chris Teter & Laura Teter (both USA)	2,809,310
D2K: Jumpman Returns	Points [3 Men To Start]	Roald Podevyn (BEL)	185,900
Death Race	Points [Single Player Only]	Aaron Laberge (CAN)	34
Defender	1-Credit Verified Endurance Marathon	Gary Whittingham (AUS)	3,751,875
Donkey Kong	Most Wall Jumps on a Rivet Board	Alen Staal (AUS)	55
Donkey Kong	Points [Hammer Allowed]	Wes Copeland (USA)	1,195,100
Donkey Kong	Points [No Hammer]	Jeff Wolfe (USA)	735,100
Donkey Kong	Points on "Hard" Romset	Tanner Fokkens (USA)	914,200
Double Dragon [Neo-Geo]	Points [Tournament Mode]	Pete Hahn (USA)	430,500
Elevator Action	Points [Normal – Difficulty 1]	Steve Wagner (USA)	156,550
Mappy	Points	Mike Kasper (USA)	2,313,890
Mario Bros.	Points – No POW Challenge [Single Player Only]	Steven Kleisath (USA)	2,134,120
Metal Slug – Super Vehicle-001	Points [Single Player Only]	Jacob Spring (DNK)	2,761,200
Missile Command	Points [Marathon]	Victor Sandberg (SWE)	103,809,990
Paperboy	Points [Easy Street]	Edward Owen (USA)	168,372
Pole Position II	Test Track – Factory Settings [Points]	Brian Roemer (USA)	89,640
Robot Bowl	Points	Aaron Laberge (CAN)	290
Robotron: 2084	Extreme Endurance Marathon (X-Enduro)	David Gomez (USA)	102,904,275
Robotron: 2084	1-Credit Verified Endurance Marathon	David Gomez (USA)	180,022,000
Atari 2600/VCS			
Berzerk	NTSC – Game 1, Difficulty A or B	Christian Keilback (USA)	1,057,940
Commando	PAL – Game 1, Difficulty B	Peter Nadalin (AUS)	1,030,100
Donkey Kong	NTSC – Game 1, Difficulty B	Steve Germershausen (CAN)	1,472,100
Donkey Kong	PAL – Game 1, Difficulty B	Peter Nadalin (AUS)	1,420,900
Frankenstein's Monster	NTSC – Game 1, Difficulty B	Douglas Korekach (USA)	4,900
Kool-Aid Man	NTSC – Game 1, Difficulty B	Mason Cramer (USA)	214,800
Yars' Revenge	NTSC – Game 2, Difficulty B	Glenn Case (USA)	14,066,997
Atari Jaguar			
Ruiner Pinball	Ruiner [Points]	John M Brissie (USA)	21,561,400
Trevor McFur	Default Settings	Ryan Genno (CAN)	605,280
Commodore 64			
Beach Head	EMU – Game 1	Clay Karczewski (CAN)	161,200
Frogger [Sierra]	EMU – Points	Daniel Desjardins (USA)	64,290
LeMans	NTSC – Points	Brendan O'Dowd (USA)	238,000
Moon Shuttle	Points	Rob Maerz (USA)	33,110
Pipe Dream	EMU – Points	John Eden (AUS)	101,700

Game	Variation	Player	Score
Zaxxon	PAL – Points	Paul Kearns (UK)	17,550
Game Boy/Game Boy Color			
Castlevania Legends	Fastest Completion	Jesse Porter (USA)	36:42.0
Double Dribble: 5 on 5	Biggest Blowout	Rudy Ferretti (USA)	213
Game & Watch Gallery 3/ Game Boy Gallery 4/ Game Boy Gallery 3	Donkey Kong Jr. Classic – Points	Andrew Pete Mee (UK)	652
Mortal Kombat	Points	Patrick Maher (USA)	3,678,000
Oddworld Adventures	Fastest Completion	Mark Cox (USA)	35:11.0
Tetris	Game B – Level 0 High 5 – Points	Ben Mullen (USA)	7,623
Tetris Plus	Classic – Points	Don Atreides (USA)	999,999
Game Boy Advance			
The Legend of Zelda: The Minish Cap	Fastest Completion	Matthew Felix (USA)	02:44:32
Mario Kart Super Circuit	Rainbow Road [Fastest Race]	Ethan Streblow (USA)	01:47.16
Mario Party Advance	See Monkey? [Fastest Completion]	Christian Backes (USA)	17.85
Intellivision			
Burger Time	Burger Time [NTSC/PAL – Points – Fastest Difficulty]	Michael Sroka (USA)	73,500
Donkey Kong	NTSC/PAL – Skill 1	John Pompa (USA)	249,100
Tron: Solar Sailer	NTSC/PAL – Default Settings	Glenn Case (USA)	891,800
iOS			
Angry Birds	Flock Favorites – 29-2	Joe Jackmovich (USA)	118,050
Bejeweled Blitz		Mike Romagnoli (CAN)	247,500
Circle	Points	Terence Wong (AUS)	53
Pinball Arcade	Tales Of The Arabian Nights	Benjamin Sweeney (USA)	60,839,620
Robot Unicorn Attack 2		Jordan Baranowski (USA)	138,045
Multiple Arcade Machine Emulator (MAME)			
Arm Wrestling	Points	George Riley (USA)	605,450
Baluba-Louk No Densetsu	Points	Henning Gundersen (NOR)	3,297,300
Black Widow	Points [Tournament Settings]	David Jury (USA)	313,075
Block Hole	Points	Nick Vis (NLD)	798,940
Burger Time [Data East Set 1]	Points	Jeffrey Lowe Jr (USA)	7,789,300
Crazy Kong [Set 1]	Points [No Hammer Challenge]	Andrew Barrow (NZ)	431,400
Crystal Castles [Version 4]	Points	Ian Purdy (USA)	751,934
Dark Tower	Points [1 Player Only]	Estel Goffinet (USA)	21,235,300
Defend the Terra Attack on the Red UFO	Points	Brian Allen (USA)	45,160
Dimahoo [US 000121]	Points [1 Player Only]	Sebastien Giraud (FRA)	4,112,160
Donkey Kong Junior [US]	Points	Corey Chambers (USA)	1,323,200
Eggs	Points [Marathon Settings]	Jason Vasiloff (USA)	172,780
Galaga [Namco rev.B]	Points [Marathon]	Stephen Krogman (USA)	5,679,450
Golden Tee '99 [v1.00]	Coconut Cove [Least Amount Of Strokes]	J Weaver Jr (USA)	55
Green Beret	Highest Score Completing Stage 1 on 1st Life	Brian Woodward (USA)	52,750
Indian Battle	Points	Michael O'Neill (USA)	23,100
Jr. PAC-Man [Speedup hack]	Points	Jason Vasiloff (USA)	1,394,460
Lethal Enforcers II: Gun Fighters [ver EAA]	Points [Single Player Only]	Travis Warnell (USA)	1,272
Lizard Wizard	Points [Single Player Only]	Chris Teter (USA)	260,600
Lucky & Wild	Points [Single Player Only]	Travis Warnell (USA)	293,700
Ms. PAC-Man [Speedup hack]	Points	Francois Toit (ZAF)	945,260
Ninja Spirit	Points	Graham Hawkins (NZ)	617,300
Super Puzzle Fighter II Turbo	Points [Tournament Settings]	Huy Dinh (VNM)	613,910

Robot Unicorn Attack 2

When Adult Swim created an endless runner in 2010, the cable network ended up spawning a new cult franchise. This 2013 mobile sequel has gamers darting gracefully through rainbow-filled landscapes while battling giants. Jordan Baranowski (USA) scored a magical 138,045 points, as verified on 26 Nov 2015.

Donkey Kong Junior

In Nintendo's 1982 platformer, Mario takes on the role of villain as DK Jr tries to free his father from a cage. In the past, arcade legends such as Billy Mitchell and Steve Wiebe (both USA) have held the overall high-score record. The highest point-scorer on the US version is Corey Chambers (USA), with 1,323,200 on the MAME, as verified on 16 Oct 2015.

Game	Variation	Player	Score
Nintendo 3DS			
Mario Kart 7	GCN Dino Dino Jungle [Fastest Race]	Andrew Carrick (UK)	02:11.158
Mario Kart 7	Rainbow Road [Fastest Race]	Roald Podevyn (BEL)	01:52.17
Tetris: Axis	Single Player – Marathon [Endless] –	John Pompa (USA)	307,536
Nintendo 64			
1080° Snowboarding	NTSC – Trick Attack/ Halfpipe [Points]	Mike Romagnoli (CAN)	59,124
Bust-A-Move '99	NTSC – Challenge [Points]	Shawne Vinson (USA)	61,780,160
Cruis'n World	NTSC – Kenya	Garry Harman (CAN)	37.96
Ken Griffey Jr.'s Slugfest	NTSC – Home Run Derby	Craig Rout Gallant (CAN)	11
Mortal Kombat 4	NTSC – Fastest Completion – Master II	Brendon Meares (USA)	05:14.0
Nagano Winter Olympics '98	NTSC – Luge	Rocky L Rose (USA)	01:05.911
Namco Museum 64	NTSC – Dig Dug [Points, Marathon Settings]	Jeff Stillwagon (USA)	77,330
The New Tetris	NTSC – Sprint – Lines	Don Atreides (USA)	231
Perfect Dark	NTSC – Area 51 – Infiltration – Agent	Wayne Meares (USA)	02:23.0
Perfect Dark	NTSC – Pelagic II – Exploration – Agent	Wayne Meares (USA)	01:59.0
Ready 2 Rumble Boxing	NTSC – Arcade Mode [Most Consecutive Wins]	Joshua Delacruz/ Tom Duncan (both USA)	10
Tetrisphere	NTSC – Rescue	Ryan Genno (CAN)	31,537,900
Nintendo DS			
Arkanoid DS	Clear Mode – High Score	W Michael Dietrich (USA)	239,420
Burnout Legends	Time Attack – Interstate Backward [Fastest Completion]	John M Brissie (USA)	48.89
Elite Beat Agents	NTSC/PAL – Sum 41 – "Makes No Difference" – Breezin' – High Score [Points]	Andrew Pete Mee (UK)	127,208
Mario Party DS	NTSC/PAL – Rail Riders – Longest Distance	Christian Backes (USA)	999.9
New Super Mario Bros.	Mario's Slides	Mitchell Chapman (USA)	34
Nintendo Entertainment System			
10-Yard Fight	NTSC – Biggest Blowout	Andrew Gardikis (USA)	70
Astyanax	NTSC – Points	Jared E Oswald (USA)	2,955,900
Balloon Fight	NTSC – Points [Game B] – 2-Player Co-op	Michelle Ireland & Matthew Miller (both USA)	2,975,250
Battletoads	Extreme – 1 Life Only – High Score	Phillip Ballenger (USA)	313,700
Bee 52	NTSC – Points	Ryan Johnson (CAN)	106,625
Bucky O'Hare	NTSC – Points	Paul Tesi (USA)	195,500
Contra	NTSC – Points [Tournament Settings] – 2-Player Team	Douglas Lida & Vincent Scalpati (both USA)	916,800
Defender II	NTSC – Points	Mason Cramer (USA)	1,524,900
Ice Climber	NTSC – Points	Nicholas Mollica (USA)	2,977,760
Kid Icarus	NTSC-U – Points	Trevor Pawlak (USA)	5,028,200
MiG-29: Soviet Fighter	NTSC – Points	Justin Burchfield (USA)	4,481
Mike Tyson's Punch-Out!!/Punch-Out!!	NTSC – Fastest KO/TKO of Mike Tyson/Mr. Dream	Jason Stanley (USA)	02:15.0

Mario Kart 7

Zooming on to the 3DS in 2011, *Mario Kart 7* was only the third series racer to tear it up on a hand-held. Belgian gamer Roald Podevyn has proved to be one of its fiercest track kings. As of 22 Apr 2016, he held 19 fastest race times on the Twin Galaxies scoreboard. These included 1 min 52.17 sec on the iconic circuit Rainbow Road, as verified on 3 Apr 2016.

Battletoads

Created to cheekily rival a certain mob of reptilian martial artists, Rare's own *Battletoads* were a trio of beat-'em-up warriors who debuted on the NES in 1991 – and boy was their game tough! Credit, then, to Phillip Ballenger (USA), who scored 313,700 points with one life on "Extreme", as verified on 14 Dec 2015.

Game	Variation	Player	Score
Ninja Gaiden	NTSC – Fastest Purist Completion [TGES]	Charles Ziese (USA)	18:01.0
Silver Surfer	NTSC – Points	Tim Raulerson (USA)	803,000
World Class Track Meet/Stadium Events	NTSC – 100M Dash [Fastest Time]	Kevin Holst (USA)	6.31
Nintendo Wii			
The Beatles: Rock Band	Single Player – Bass – "Ticket to Ride" – Points	Marc Cohen (USA)	49,023
The Beatles: Rock Band	Single Player – Bass – "I Am the Walrus" – Points	Marc Cohen (USA)	74,962
Mario Kart Wii	GCN Waluigi Stadium – Time Trial – Fastest Lap	Ethan Evans (UK)	43.427
Mario Kart Wii	Coconut Mall – Time Trial – Fastest Race	Alex Thune (USA)	02:03.916
NBA Jam	Play Now Mode – Biggest Blowout – Single Player Only	Daniel Lee Strickland Perea (USA)	104
No More Heroes 2: Desperate Struggle	Side Job 07 – Getting Trashed	Adam Davis (AUS)	128,910
Super Smash Bros. Brawl	NTSC – Stadium – Target Smash! – Level 4 – Marth	Matthew Felix (USA)	30.61
Wii Fit/Wii Fit Plus	PAL – Strength Training – Side Lunge – 10 Reps [Points]	Daniella Mee (UK)	85
Wii Sports	Training – Boxing – Working the Bag	Tristen Geren (USA)	57
Nintendo Wii U			
Heptrix	Points	John Pompa (USA)	18,074
Mario Kart 8	Time Trials – Retro – Yoshi Valley [Fastest Race]	Andrew Carrick (UK)	02:14.876
Mario Kart 8	Time Trials – Retro – [DLC] Rainbow Road – [Fastest Race]	Leonardo P Bugmann (BRA)	01:34.601
Super Destronaut	Points	Benjamin Sweeney (USA)	898,210
Wii Fit U	Dance – Stamina Steps – Duration [15 min] – Most Points	Pekka Luodeslampi (FIN)	1,087
Wii Party U	Demolition Row [Endless Mode – Points]	Craig Rout Gallant (CAN)	192,800
Zen Pinball 2	South Park: Super Sweet Pinball [Points]	Benjamin Sweeney (USA)	18,790,608

No More Heroes 2: Desperate Struggle

The Wii was hardly blessed with hack-and-slash games, so this stylized action romp proved a real cult smash, challenging players to slice their way to the top of the assassin rankings. Adam Davis (AUS) scored 128,910 points in Side Job 07 – "Getting Trashed", as verified on 24 Feb 2016.

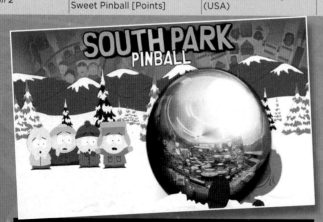

Zen Pinball 2

Zen Studios' 2012 sequel didn't just deliver a mighty fine game of pinball according to the critics – it also offered a number of licenced tables for fans to rack up huge scores on. As verified on 14 Nov 2015, Benjamin Sweeney (USA) mustered a total of 18,790,608 points flipping shiny balls on the "South Park: Super Sweet Pinball" table.

Wii Party U

Wii Party U's huge line-up of party-pleasers ranges from Water Runners, in which you scoop water from a virtual stream using the Wii Remote, to Demolition Row, in which you connect coloured blocks in order to blow them to smithereens. Craig Rout Gallant (CAN) scored 192,800 points in Demolition Row's "Endless Mode", as verified by Twin Galaxies on 27 Sep 2015.

Game	Variation	Player	Score
Nintendo Wii Virtual Console			
Galaga	NES – Points [Tournament]	Andrew Franciscus (USA)	196,030
Ninja Gaiden III: The Ancient Ship of Doom	NES – Points	James Sorge (USA)	1,307,600
Sonic the Hedgehog 2	Sega Genesis/Mega Drive – Fastest Minimalist Completion [Sonic Alone Mode]	Matthew Felix (USA)	38:20.0
Super Street Fighter II: The New Challengers	SNES – Points [Tournament Settings]	Wayne Meares (USA)	7,400
Wario's Woods	NES – Fastest Completion [3 Rounds/Hard Mode]	Matthew Runnels (USA)	02:45.0
Zanac	NES – Points	Jesse Porter (USA)	837,640
PC			
Dig Dug	Default Settings	Dick Moreland (USA)	270,340
Fallout 4	Red Menace – Points	Wes Copeland (USA)	138,000
H1Z1	Battle Royale [Most Kills – Shotgun Only – Regular Server – Solo]	Clement Graham (UK)	28
Mechatron: 2154 (A Robotron Remake)	Enduro (Default Settings)	Travis Warnell (USA)	3,238,025
Risk of Rain	Points – Rainstorm (No Artifacts)	Nick Vis (NLD)	43,509
PlayStation			
Bust-A-Move 4	NTSC – Win Contest Winning Streaks With Chain Reaction	Shawne Vinson (USA)	45
Buster Bros. Collection	NTSC – Buster Buddies – Panic Mode [Points]	Stephen Krogman (USA)	755,200
Crash Bandicoot: Warped	NTSC – Time Trial: 09 – Tomb Time [Fastest Completion]	Kaitlin Degeneffe (USA)	58.06
Crash Bandicoot: Warped	NTSC – Time Trial: 25 – Bug Lite [Fastest Completion]	Kaitlin Degeneffe (USA)	01:12.36
Driver	PAL – Undercover – Maya – Quick, Get Maya [Time Remaining]	Andrew Pete Mee (UK)	21.8
Final Fantasy VII	NTSC – Entire Game [Fastest Minimalist Completion]	Addison Dumke (USA)	13:14:11.0
Gran Turismo	PAL – Quick Arcade – Class A – Deep Forest [Fastest Lap]	Paul Kearns (UK)	01:10.458
Gran Turismo 2	PAL – Arcade Mode – Class B – Apricot Hill Speedway – Forward [Fastest Race]	Paul Kearns (UK)	05:14.531
Madden NFL 98	NTSC – Exhibition [Biggest Blowout]	Matthew Dauer (USA)	100
Mortal Kombat Trilogy	Fastest Completion	Patrick Maher (USA)	15:22.0
Point Blank	PAL – Arcade Mode – Training Mode [Points]	Jacob Spring (DNK)	63,923
Rampage World Tour	Points	Benjamin Sweeney (USA)	96,200
Ridge Racer	PAL – T.T. [Fastest Race]	Jason Newman (UK)	03:12.927
Ridge Racer Turbo/ Hi-Spec Demo	PAL – Mid-Level [Fastest Lap]	Jason Newman (UK)	41.77
Tony Hawk's Pro Skater 3	NTSC – Tokyo – Single Session [Points]	Hector Rodriguez (USA)	1,809,795
Um Jammer Lammy	NTSC – Stage 6 – Teriyaki Yoko – Lammy – Normal Difficulty [Points]	Conner Smith (USA)	32,463
PlayStation 2			
Atari Anthology	NTSC – Dodge 'Em – Game 1, Difficulty B [Points]	W Dietrich/Shaun Michaud (both USA)	1,080
Burnout 2: Point of Impact	NTSC – Time Attack – Ocean Sprint – Forward Track [Fastest Completion]	Don Atreides (USA)	01:59.716
Capcom Classics Collection (Vol. 1)	NTSC – 1943 Kai – Hardcore Difficulty [Points]	Jesse Porter (USA)	203,300

H1Z1

In the post-apocalyptic world of the Daybreak Game Company's survival sandbox MMO, gamers have to contend with the elements, rival scavengers, prowling wolves and angry bears – and zombies. Lots of zombies. Playing the "Battle Royale" scenario on the PC, Clement Graham (UK) achieved 28 shotgun kills roaming the eerily quiet streets, a score verified on 24 Mar 2016.

Risk of Rain

This spacey, rogue-like platformer was developed by two US students, initially for a university project, before being souped-up in 2013 via a Kickstarter campaign. Players are tasked with surviving a hostile planet. As verified on 20 Feb 2016, Nick Vis (NLD) scored 43,509 points on its "Rainstorm" difficulty.

Guitar Hero World Tour

Activision's 2008 *World Tour* was the first *Guitar Hero* game that allowed players to sing or play the drums. Avatars of real-life musicians such as Sting (above) were also available. Playing the guitar on "Medium" setting on 30 Seconds to Mars' 2006 chart hit "The Kill", Matthew Simpson (USA) scored 148,342 points, as verified by Twin Galaxies on 6 Sep 2015.

Samurai Warriors

Set during the "Warring States" period of Japanese history, Koei's 2004 hack-and-slash title had spawned three sequels as of 20 Apr 2016. Under the guidance of Andrew Pete Mee (UK), kabuki dancer Okuni wielded her parasol to deadly effect, scoring 135 KOs during the "Dance of Osaka", as validated on 20 Sep 2015.

Street Fighter II

Capcom's hard-hitting sequel was released in 1991, and was given a makeover in a *Turbo HD Remix* in 2008 (above). *SF II* was notable for the debut of one of the series' most popular characters, Guile. Chris Gleed (USA) scored 425,500 with Guile, playing *Street Fighter II* on its 15th Anniversary Collection for the PS2, as verified on 22 Dec 2015.

Game	Variation	Player	Score
Fatal Fury Battle Archives Volume 1	NTSC – Fatal Fury Special [Tournament Settings]	Monty Meares (USA)	45,800
FlatOut	NTSC – Bonus – Demolition Dash [Fastest Race]	Eddie Hall (CAN)	04:11.36
Gran Turismo 3: A-spec	NTSC – License Test – S-1: Apricot Hill Time Attack [Fastest Completion]	Marc Cohen (USA)	01:42.673
Guitar Hero Encore: Rocks the 80s	NTSC – 1. Opening Licks – "18 and Life" – Hard Difficulty – 1-Player [Points]	Dave Soeiro (CAN)	161,544
Guitar Hero III: Legends of Rock	NTSC – 1. Starting Out Small – "Hit Me With Your Best Shot" – Easy Difficulty – 1-Player [Points]	Jeff Mikuska (USA)	66,121
Guitar Hero World Tour	NTSC – The Eagles – "Hotel California" – Guitar – Easy – 1-Player [Points]	Scott Simpson (USA)	128,668
Guitar Hero World Tour	NTSC – 30 Seconds To Mars – "The Kill" – Guitar – Medium – 1-Player [Points]	Matthew Simpson (USA)	148,342
Midway Arcade Treasures 2	NTSC – Xybots 1-Player [Points]	Stephen Krogman (USA)	179,900
Midway Arcade Treasures 2	NTSC/PAL – Mortal Kombat 3 [Fastest Completion]	Patrick Maher (USA)	11:09.0
Need for Speed: Hot Pursuit 2	NTSC – Championship – 01. National Forest Challenge [Fastest Lap]	Jason Beasley (USA)	01:59.88
Samurai Warriors	PAL – Dance of Osaka – Normal Difficulty [KOs]	Andrew Pete Mee (UK)	135
SNK Arcade Classics Vol. 1	NTSC – Fatal Fury – Insane Difficulty [Points]	Monty Meares (USA)	47,800
Street Fighter II: 15th Anniversary Collection	NTSC – Street Fighter II Mode [Points]	Chris Gleed (USA)	425,500
Taito Legends 2	NTSC – Bust-A-Move Again – Puzzle Mode [Points]	Shawne Vinson (USA)	70,178,910
Tekken 4	NTSC – Time Attack Mode [Fastest Completion]	Pete Hahn (USA)	01:55:38
Tony Hawk's Pro Skater 3	PAL – Rio Ruckus – Single Session [Points]	Andrew Pete Mee (UK)	1,488,703
We Love Katamari	NTSC – Cloud [Number of Clouds – Points]	Joe Jackmovich (USA)	497

Trials Fusion

The physics-based motorbike sim poses a notoriously stiff challenge to would-be speed-runners. Playing on the PS4, Scott Simpson (USA) managed to avoid tears on the Greenhorn's Grove Event "Waterworks" course, completing it in just 35.272 sec – despite his rider crossing the finish line headfirst! His time was verified on 12 Aug 2015.

Crimsonland

The 2014 re-release of 10tons' top-down arena shooter featured the "Nukefism" game mode, in which the hero was left weaponless and having to defeat the growing hordes of spawning enemies using bonuses alone. US gamer Brandon Finton's score of 85,000 on the PS4 was confirmed by Twin Galaxies on 26 Aug 2015.

Game	Variation	Player	Score
PlayStation 3			
Call of Duty: Black Ops	Zombies – Kino Der Toten	Camden LeCroy (USA)	112,030
Final Fantasy XIII-2	Battle Result – Academia 400 AF – Nelapsi x5 – Easy Mode [Score]	Andrew Pete Mee (UK)	19,580
Gran Turismo 6	Special Events – Sierra Time Rally: Challenge 3	Marc Cohen (USA)	844,681
Green Day: Rock Band	Single Player – "When I Come Around" – Guitar	Michael Sroka (USA)	106,969
Just Cause 2	Race Challenge – Crossing Lanes [Stinger Dunebug 84]	Shaun Michaud (USA)	01:13.69
NCAA Football 14	Play Now Exhibition – Biggest Blowout	Matthew Dauer (USA)	92
Pinball Hall of Fame: The Williams Collection	Whirlwind – Points	Marc Cohen (USA)	76,222,110
The Beatles: Rock Band	Single Player – Guitar – "Back in the U.S.S.R." – Points	Michael Sroka (USA)	100,044
UFC Undisputed 2010	Exhibition Mode – Fastest Victory	Matthew Runnels (USA)	25
Ultra Street Fighter IV	Points	Chris Gleed (USA)	752,200
PlayStation 3 PSN			
Geometry Wars 3: Dimensions Evolved	Single Player: Adventure – Level 35	Joe Jackmovich (USA)	224,577,010
Marvel Pinball	Blade – Points	Shaun Michaud (USA)	343,617,400
Need for Speed: Hot Pursuit	Racer – Oakmont Valley – Ultimately Open – Fastest Completion	Scott Simpson (USA)	01:41.8
PAC-Man Championship Edition DX	Dungeon – Score Attack – 5 Minutes	Ethan Daniels (USA)	2,212,100
Zen Pinball	Street Fighter II – Points	Marc Cohen (USA)	436,424,955
PlayStation 4			
Beach Buggy Racing	Easy Street – Race 4	Brandon Finton (USA)	50.28
The Pinball Arcade	Cue Ball Wizard – Points	Marc Cohen (USA)	1,013,823,870
The Pinball Arcade	Monster Bash – Points	Max Haraske (USA)	3,618,437,390
Trials Fusion	Greenhorn's Grove Event – Waterworks	Scott Simpson (USA)	35.272
Ultratron	High Score Challenge!	Joe Jackmovich (USA)	6,485,670
PlayStation 4 PSN			
Crimsonland	Nukefism – Most Points	Brandon Finton (USA)	85,000
Star Wars: Racer Revenge	Tatooine: The Mos Espa Open	Marc Cohen (USA)	02:39.25
Super Meat Boy	The Forest: 1-13 Tommy's Cabin (Fastest Time)	Joe Jackmovich (USA)	3.49
PlayStation Portable			
Atari Classics Evolved	NTSC/PAL – Tempest Evolved [Points]	John M Brissie (USA)	87,191
Burnout Legends	NTSC/PAL – Time Attack – USA – Silver Lake Forward [Fastest Completion]	John M Brissie (USA)	01:39.08
Capcom Classics Collection Remixed	NTSC/PAL – Block Block – Normal Difficulty [Points]	John M Brissie (USA)	9,220
Gods Eater Burst	Difficulty 5 – Nut Cracker – Fastest Time	Brandon Finton (USA)	01:48.0
Sega CD			
Bram Stoker's Dracula	Points	James Barnard (CAN)	23,831
Formula One World Championship: Beyond the Limit	NTSC – Free Practice – Hungaroring [Hungary Budapest] – Fastest Lap	Jared E Oswald (USA)	01:19.28
NHL '94	NTSC – Biggest Blowout	Raphael Frydman (USA)	61
Sega Dreamcast			**(All records NTSC)**
Marvel vs. Capcom: Clash of Super Heroes	Survival Mode [Most Wins]	Victor Delgado (USA)	5
NFL 2K	Biggest Blowout	Timothy Samandari (USA)	189

Game	Variation	Player	Score
The House of the Dead 2	Boss Mode – Hierophant B [Fastest Completion]	Jared E Oswald (USA)	41.11
The King of Fighters: Dream Match 1999	Points [Tournament Settings]	Monty Meares (USA)	108,900
Sega Genesis/Sega Mega Drive			
Ayrton Senna's Super Monaco GP II	PAL – Free Run – Brazil [Best Lap]	Peter Nadalin (AUS)	46.55
Battletoads	NTSC – Fastest Completion	Phillip Ballenger (USA)	52:59.0
Bulls versus Blazers and the NBA Playoffs	NTSC – Biggest Blowout	Timothy Samandari (USA)	53
ClayFighter	NTSC – Points [Tournament Settings]	Enrique Barron (USA)	209,000
Cool Spot	NTSC – Points	Jesse Porter (USA)	358,040
ESWAT: City Under Siege	NTSC – Points	Juan Castellanos (USA)	198,500
Ferrari Grand Prix Challenge	NTSC – American GP – Fastest Lap	Skylar Jones (USA)	01:14.62
Hard Drivin'	NTSC – Points	Marc Cohen (USA)	355,416
NBA Jam	PAL – Biggest Blowout – Single Player Only	Grant Robinson (AUS)	21
NHL '94	PAL – Biggest Blowout	Mikey McBryan (CAN)	18
Ranger X	NTSC – Points	David King (USA)	436,848
RBI Baseball '93	NTSC – Biggest Blowout	Mike Yesenko (USA)	22
Sonic & Knuckles	NTSC – Fastest Full Completion – Knuckles	Charles Ziese (USA)	32:11.0
Sonic the Hedgehog	NTSC – Points	Eric Schafer (USA)	873,520
Sonic the Hedgehog 3	NTSC – Points	Zachary Spencer (USA)	1,000,320
Zoom!	NTSC – Points	Jared E Oswald (USA)	20,400
Sega Master System			
Air Rescue	NTSC – Points	Ryan Genno (CAN)	68,400
Alex Kidd in Miracle World	PAL – Points	Steve Badcock (UK)	81,800
California Games	NTSC – BMX	Clay Karczewski (CAN)	67,200
Sonic the Hedgehog 2	NTSC – Points	Ryan Genno (CAN)	257,700

The House of the Dead 2
Sega's horror-themed rail-shooter was originally released for the arcades in 1998, before being ported to the Dreamcast the following year. Among the vicious bosses gamers encountered along the waterways of Venice, Italy, one of the toughest was the Hierophant, a giant creature wielding a trident. Jared E Oswald (USA) peppered the Hierophant B with gunfire, killing it in 41.11 sec, as approved on 16 Oct 2015.

Sonic the Hedgehog
Eric Schafer (USA) scored 873,520 points playing the original Sonic the Hedgehog on the Sega Genesis/ Mega Drive, as verified on 12 Oct 2015. Released in 1991, the game was the start of a hugely successful franchise that was still going strong on eighth-gen consoles, with 2013's Sonic Lost World (pictured).

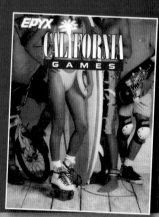

California Games
Back in 1987, before the X Games became a fixture on the US sporting calendar, bikers, skaters and surfers could get their gaming fix tackling Epyx's classic sporting title. Playing on the Sega Master System, Clay Karczewski (CAN) hit a series of front and vertical flips on his way to a huge score of 67,200 points on the "BMX" challenge, as ratified on 16 Oct 2015.

Double Dragon V: The Shadow Falls

Dropping the side-scrolling brawling of its legendary predecessors, 1994 console game *The Shadow Falls* was a one-on-one fighter that shared similarities with *Street Fighter II*. Ryan Genno (CAN) has proved a dab hand at its virtual kung-fu, scoring 836,900 points in "Tournament Mode", as approved on 8 Apr 2016.

Star Fox

The 1993 SNES rail-shooter introduced one of Nintendo's most iconic characters in the form of Fox McCloud, who returned in 2016 with *Star Fox Zero* (above). Matthew Felix (USA) scored 60,000 points on Course 1 of the original, as verified on 16 Oct 2015. This ties the existing record set by Scott Kessler, as verified on 2 Oct 2007.

Game	Variation	Player	Score
Super Nintendo Entertainment System			
American Gladiators	NTSC – Points	Brendan O'Dowd (USA)	45
Chuck Rock	NTSC – Points	Tyler VanderZwaag (USA)	384,275
Cybernator	NTSC – Points	Jonathan Bowen (USA)	343,350
D-Force	NTSC – Points	Benjamin Sweeney (USA)	169,700
Donkey Kong Country Competition Pak	Highest Score	Tim Hanson (USA)	5,316
The Shadow Falls	NTSC – Tournament Mode [Points]	Ryan Genno (CAN)	836,900
Last Action Hero	NTSC – Points	Phillip Ballenger (USA)	466,230
NHL '94	NTSC – Biggest Blowout	Raphael Frydman (USA)	58
Pinball Dreams	PAL – Beat Box [Points]	Andrew Pete Mee (UK)	7,974,500
PowerFest '94	Points	Paul Tesi (USA)	25,163,950
Star Fox	NTSC – Course 1 [Points]	Matthew Felix/Scott Kessler (both USA)	60,000
Super Buster Bros.	NTSC – Panic Mode [Points]	Mason Cramer (USA)	160,420
Super Mario Kart	NTSC – Vanilla Lake 1 [Fastest Race]	Zachary Lynch (USA)	59.89
Super Mario Kart	1-Player – Star Cup – Fastest Completion	Gabriel Deanda (USA)	08:30.04
Timon & Pumbaa's Jungle Games	NTSC – Points [Hippo Hop]	Josh Jones (USA)	34,300
Xbox			
Burnout 2: Point of Impact	NTSC – Time Attack – Interstate Loop – Forward Track [Fastest Completion]	Don Atreides (USA)	01:02.733
Capcom Classics Collection (Vol. 1)	NTSC – Mercs – Normal Difficulty [Points]	Joshua Arenivaz (USA)	169,650
Dynasty Warriors 4	NTSC – Yellow Turban Rebellion – Hard – Fastest Completion	Mark Kakareka (USA)	02:27.0
Juiced	PAL – Arcade/Custom – East Angel Island – Point To Point [Fastest Time]	Andrew Pete Mee (UK)	01:22.85
Mega Man Anniversary Collection	NTSC – Mega Man 1 [Points]	Jesse Porter (USA)	1,322,700
Midway Arcade Treasures	NTSC – Gauntlet [2-Player Team, Points]	Chris Plaza & Michael Sroka (both USA)	43,477
NASCAR Thunder 2002	NTSC – Quick Race – 1-Player – Bristol [Fastest Lap]	Michael Sroka (USA)	15.496
OutRun 2	PAL – OutRun Challenge – OutRun Mission – Stage 1.5 Math Mayhem [Fastest Time]	Andrew Pete Mee (UK)	02:04.916
Taito Legends	NTSC – The New Zealand Story [Points]	Shawne Vinson (USA)	168,800
Taito Legends	NTSC – Zoo Keeper [Points]	Michael Sroka (USA)	412,950
Xbox 360			
Call of Duty 4: Modern Warfare	Mile High Club – Points	Gil Limas (USA)	100,020
Call of Duty: Black Ops	Zombies – Dead Ops Arcade	Joe Jackmovich (USA)	1,126,725
Dance Central	"Funkytown" – Lipps Inc	Andrew Pete Mee (UK)	400,349
Guitar Hero II	NTSC – 2. Amp-Warmers – "Heart-Shaped Box" – Expert Difficulty – 1-Player [Points]	Jenna Matthews (AUS)	225,320
Guitar Hero III: Legends of Rock	NTSC – Bonus Tracks – "In The Belly Of A Shark" – Expert Difficulty – 1-Player [Points]	Joshua Arenivaz (USA)	228,058
Guitar Hero III: Legends of Rock	NTSC – 1. Starting Out Small – Sabotage – Expert Difficulty – 1 Player [Points]	Dave Soeiro (CAN)	285,494
Guitar Hero World Tour	NTSC – Dinosaur Jr. – "Feel The Pain" – Guitar – Easy – 1- Player [Points]	Jared E Oswald (USA)	115,276
Just Dance 4	Just Dance – "Umbrella" – Rihanna featuring Jay-Z – Single Player [Points]	Lucianna Mee (UK)	10,237

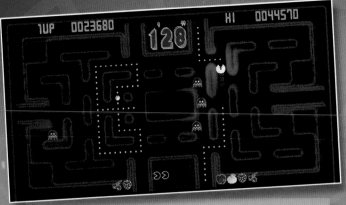

PAC-Man Championship Edition

The dot-gobbling PAC-Man was once voted the **most recognized game character**, with 94% of Americans recognizing his giant yellow head. PAC-Man's 2007 game *Championship Edition* was the final title designed by his creator Toru Iwatani. It featured familiar gameplay but sped up, with mazes split into two halves. As verified on 21 Jul 2015, Michael Ferguson (USA) scored 343,410 points in the game's Championship Mode on the Xbox Live Arcade version.

X-Men

First released in 1992, this Marvel beat-'em-up was ported to the Xbox Live Arcade in 2010. Gamers could select from six characters, including Storm and Cyclops. Dave Soeiro (CAN), however, opted to take on the minion hordes of Magneto using Wolverine and his adamantium claws. He scored 131 points, as ratified on 26 May 2015.

Game	Variation	Player	Score
Midway Arcade Origins	Wizard of Wor	John M Brissie (USA)	37,900
Namco Museum Virtual Arcade	Metro-Cross – Points	Ryan Sullivan (USA)	136,950
Namco Museum Virtual Arcade	Pole Position II – Seaside Track – Points	Michael Ferguson (USA)	20,340
Pinball Hall of Fame: The Williams Collection	Jive Time – Points	Philip Ryder (USA)	95,710
Rock Band	NTSC – Death of the Cool – "Can't Let Go" – Bass – Medium – 1-Player [Points]	Jared E Oswald (USA)	55,757
Rock Band	NTSC – Yeah Yeah Yeahs – "Maps" – Guitar – Easy – 1-Player [Points]	Will Love (USA)	30,394
Sonic's Ultimate Genesis Collection/ Sega's Ultimate Mega Drive Collection	NTSC – Golden Axe I – Arcade Mode [Fastest Completion]	Jesse Porter (USA)	14:22.0
Ultra Street Fighter IV	Points	Chris Gleed (USA)	1,234,800
Xbox 360 Live Arcade			
Aegis Wing	Points – Normal Difficulty	David Kinnick (USA)	169,980
Contra	Points	Pete Hahn (USA)	3,669,800
Galaga	Points	W Dietrich (USA)	327,160
Mr. Driller Online	Quest Driller – China	Jacob Spring (DNK)	448,720
NBA Jam: On Fire Edition	Biggest Blowout – 1-Player Only	Daniel Lee Strickland Perea (USA)	43
PAC-Man Championship Edition	Points [Championship Mode]	Michael Ferguson (USA)	343,410
The Pinball Arcade	Theatre of Magic – Points	Philip Ryder (USA)	1,556,960,960
Robotron: 2084	Points	David Gomez (USA)	434,700
Track & Field	Points	Gil Limas (USA)	3,237,170
Trials HD	Hello World! – Fastest Completion	Scott Simpson (USA)	23.716
X-Men	1-Player – Points	Dave Soeiro (CAN)	131
Xbox One			
The Pinball Arcade	Medieval Madness	Philip Ryder (USA)	126,377,260
The Pinball Arcade	Creature from the Black Lagoon	Jordan Baranowski (USA)	285,290,100
The Pinball Arcade	The Addams Family	Jordan Baranowski (USA)	1,821,222,150

Golden Axe

Sega's 1989 Mega Drive classic gave the beat-'em-up genre a fantasy makeover, with gamers battling as an axe-wielding dwarf, a female warrior and a Conan the Barbarian lookalike. Jesse Porter (USA) finished the game's Arcade Mode in 14 min 22.0 sec. He was playing it through the 2009 compilation *Sonic's Ultimate Genesis Collection*.

YOUR NEW FAVOURITE GAMES

Bored of *Bloodborne*? Fallen out with *Fallout 4*? Has *The Witcher 3* lost its spell? Don't worry: we've got four pages crammed with exciting new titles that will soon be breaking records of their own – from offbeat coming-of-age dramas to gritty sci-fi shooters.

Bloodstained: Ritual of the Night
Platform: Multiple
Upon leaving Konami, *Castlevania* series producer Koji Igarashi set to work on a new castle-based action-adventure. A Kickstarter campaign raised $5.5 million (£3.8 million) towards the game, in which orphan Miriam battles a curse that is turning her body to crystal.

The Legend of Zelda
Platform: NX, Wii U
Action-adventure fans are waiting with baited breath for the 19th instalment in the *Zelda* series. Moving out of the dungeons, Link can now explore a vast open-world gamescape on his horse Epona. Producer Eiji Aonuma has stated that Nintendo's aim is to produce "the ultimate *Zelda* game".

Night in the Woods
Platform: Mac, PC, PS4
In this crowdfunded indie adventure, feline Mae drops out of college and discovers that she possesses paranormal powers. The result is a quirky and intriguing mystery. "The world in peril is boring," noted developer Scott Benson, "but heartbreak is the apocalypse."

The Last Guardian
Platform: PS4
Eleven years after *Shadow of the Colossus* was released in 2005, director Fumito Ueda has finished his long-awaited new game. Part-puzzle, part–adventure, *The Last Guardian* tells the story of a boy held prisoner in the ruins of a vast castle, and a creature named Trico who tries to help him escape.

Persona 5
Platform: PS3, PS4
The latest addition to the cult JRPG series, *Persona 5*'s offbeat premise centres on a group of high-school students who form the heroic outsider group the "Phantom Thieves of Hearts". Director Katsura Hashino has promised "characters that are going to be a little rougher around the edges".

Scalebound
Platform: Xbox One
An epic third-person action RPG, *Scalebound* is slated for a 2017 release. It's being developed by PlatinumGames, the team behind *Bayonetta*. In the game, a modern hero named Drew is transported to the fantasy world of Draconis, where he teams up with fearsome AI dragon Thuban.

Cuphead
Platform: PC, Xbox One
The brainchild of Studio MDHR – brothers Chad and Jared Moldenhauer – *Cuphead* is drawn in the style of classic 1930s cartoons. When Cuphead loses a bet with the Devil, he has to fight a stream of bosses to repay it. Don't be fooled by the cute look: this is one *seriously* tough side-scroller.

Vampyr
Platform: PC, PS4, Xbox One
Set in a flu-gripped London in the aftermath of World War I, Dontnod's action RPG follows the vampire doctor Jonathan E Reid. Painstaking research has helped create an eerie and atmospheric game. Will players stalk the city feasting on victims, or try to remain true to their doctor's oath?

YOUR NEW FAVOURITE GAMES

Planet Coaster
Platform: PC
Described as a "spiritual successor" to *RollerCoaster Tycoon 3*, the construction and management sim challenges players to create the perfect theme park. The game was built using Frontier's in-house COBRA engine. Players will be able to share their attractions in a "global village" of UGC.

Final Fantasy VII
Platform: PS4
Judging by the reactions to its announcement (see p.148), the *Final Fantasy VII* remake may be the most hotly anticipated title in gaming. It will be released in an episodic format with a new real-time battle system. Producer Yoshinori Kitase has told fans to expect some storyline changes.

Shenmue III
Platform: PC, PS4
Originally developed for the Sega Dreamcast, the first two parts of Yu Suzuki's revenge epic *Shenmue* gained a cult following, if not the hoped-for sales. Fans pressed for *Shenmue III* for over a decade, and thanks to a wildly successful Kickstarter campaign they will get their wish in 2017.

Tacoma
Platform: Mac, PC, Xbox One
Fullbright have followed up their 2013 hit *Gone Home* with a sci-fi mystery set in a near-Earth space station. Amy Ferrier arrives at Tacoma only to find it deserted – what has happened to the crew? Augmented reality blogs help to expand the plot and deepen the mystery.

Mass Effect: Andromeda
Platform: PC, PS4, Xbox One
BioWare has been clear that its new action RPG is not a direct sequel to *Mass Effect 3*. The events take place in a different time period and a new location – the Andromeda galaxy. Fans are unlikely to mind. Look out for a new and improved Mako, the ATV last seen in the original *Mass Effect*.

Yooka-Laylee
Platform: Multiple
The colourful 3D platformer is the work of Playtonic Games, including personnel from the *Banjo-Kazooie* team. Chameleon Yooka and his bat pal Laylee explore the worlds contained within magic books. According to the website, "there may or may not be a move involving a giant fart bubble".

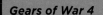

Sea of Thieves
Platform: PC, Xbox One
Legendary UK studio Rare is taking to the high seas with this nautical MMO. The developer has described the adventure as the "most ambitious game" it has ever created, and promises a multiplayer experience enriched with UGC. Naval battles, mutinies and walking the plank are all in the offing.

Crackdown 3
Platform: Xbox One
This futuristic sandbox TPS promises mass destruction on an unprecedented scale. Drawing on the power of the Microsoft Cloud platform, it offers online multiplayers the chance to fight in a persistent, destructible city. Watch bridges burn and buildings crumble in the heat of battle.

Gears of War 4
Platform: Xbox One
Set 25 years after *Gears of War 3*, the latest sci-fi TPS boasts a new hero – JD Fenix, son of Marcus – and a new enemy in the Swarm. Humans have been almost wiped out on Sera, and players will have to contend with violent "windflares" that rage across the planet.

CONTRIBUTORS

These are the experts who contributed to the 10th anniversary *Gamer's Edition*, sourcing and writing the records, facts, figures and trivia that go into the book.

MATT BRADFORD

Matt is a Canadian writer, editor and voice actor who has covered the industry since the 1990s. He can be heard on the *Zombie Cast* and *Video Game Outsiders* podcasts.

Which games did you play most this year?
Far Cry Primal, *Undertale* and *Fallout 4*. I'm still not done exploring the Boston wastes.
What was this year's most exciting event?
Watching the VR revolution take shape.

DAVID CROOKES

David's written for *Retro Gamer*, *games™*, *The Independent*, *i*, the *Evening Standard*, and Xbox, Nintendo and PlayStation magazines. He's also curated two videogame exhibitions.

Which games did you play most this year?
Life is Strange, *Day of the Tentacle* and *Hitman*.
What was this year's most exciting event?
The build-up to *Uncharted 4*'s launch. It's a series that brings out my inner Indiana Jones.

MATTHEW EDWARDS

Matthew wrote for Eurogamer and *games™* and is now a Capcom UK community manager.

Which games did you play most this year?
Street Fighter V, *Monster Hunter Generations* and *Dark Souls III*.
What was this year's most exciting event?
Street Fighter V replacing *Ultra Street Fighter IV* on the Capcom Pro Tour. It's a new era and the competition keeps getting fiercer.

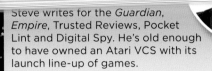

STEVE BOXER

Steve writes for the *Guardian*, *Empire*, Trusted Reviews, Pocket Lint and Digital Spy. He's old enough to have owned an Atari VCS with its launch line-up of games.

Which games did you play most this year?
Dark Souls III, *Hitman* and the hardy *Destiny*.
What was this year's most exciting event?
VR headsets becoming available to the public, and learning what Nintendo's NX is all about.

ROBERT CAVE

Rob is a lifelong videogame enthusiast. He has worked on the *Gamer's Edition* since its launch in 2008 and is proud to see it has reached its 10th edition.

Which games did you play most this year?
Fallout 4. But the one I enjoyed playing the most was *Everybody's Gone to the Rapture*.
What was this year's most exciting event?
VR. I hope it's not just an expensive gimmick.

PAUL DAVIES

Paul wrote for the *Nintendo* magazine, edited *Computer and Video Games* and helped launch its website. He manages his own editorial agency and writes for *Gamereactor* and VG247.

Which games did you play most this year?
Destiny, *The Division*, *Paragon* and *Black Ops III*.
What was this year's most exciting event?
I was engrossed in *Destiny: The Taken King*, but it was fascinating to see VR take shape.

DANIEL GRILIOPOULOS

Dan has written about videogames for IGN, GameSpot, *Edge*, Kotaku and *PC Gamer*. He's a narrative designer on five games, and is writing two books about gaming.

Which games did you play most this year?
The Witcher 3: Wild Hunt.
What was this year's most exciting event?
VR. It will change entertainment completely.

DAVID HAWKSETT

David has been a science consultant and contributor for Guinness World Records for 16 years. He's an advisor on *Gamer's* when not busy with his UK Planetary Forum.

Which games did you play most this year?
ARMA 3 and *Elite: Dangerous*.
What was this year's most exciting event?
The release of *Elite's* major *Horizons* update.

JOHN LEARNED

John has contributed to GamesRadar, USgamer and Twin Galaxies. He often chooses writing and *Street Fighter III* over sleep.

Which games did you play most this year?
Dark Souls III and *Salt and Sanctuary*.
What was this year's most exciting event?
The influence of *Dark Souls* made manifest in *Salt and Sanctuary*, *Eitr* and *Death's Gambit*.

MATT WALES

Matt has written about games for over a decade, from IGN and CVG to Eurogamer and Kotaku.

Which games did you play most this year?
The Witness, Stardew Valley, Subnautica, Hyper Light Drifter, Ark: Survival Evolved, No Man's Sky and my big-budget highlight *Dark Souls III*.
What was this year's most exciting event?
It's hard not to get excited by E3 each year.

STACE HARMAN

Stace is a freelance writer, games consultant, author of the book *Independent By Design: The Art & Stories of Indie Game Creation*, and an admirer of all those who have set the records that have made up 10 years of *Gamer's*.

Which games did you play most this year?
The Banner Saga 2, Hearthstone and *XCOM 2*.
What was this year's most exciting event?
The rise of VR gaming.

TYLER HICKS

Tyler is an analyst for the eSports organization Team Liquid and an avid fan of all things competitive gaming.

Which games did you play most this year?
Halo 5. I helped Team Liquid secure a top-eight finish at the *Halo* World Championship.
What was this year's most exciting event?
The *Final Fantasy XV* "Uncovered" event in which they revealed their plans for its release.

JOHN ROBERTSON

John is a writer and photographer specializing in videogames and their cultural impact on wider society. He tries to avoid playing games on his phone as much as possible.

Which games did you play most this year?
Undertale and *The Witness*.
What was this year's most exciting event?
The launch of VR gaming.

INDEX

PICTURE CREDITS

5 Paul Michael Hughes/ GWR, James Ellerker/GWR, Ranald Mackechnie/GWR; 6 Kevin Scott Ramos/GWR, Ryan Schude/GWR, Ranald Mackechnie/GWR, James Ellerker/GWR; 7 Paul Michael Hughes/GWR, Ryan Dix/ GWR; 8 Paul Michael Hughes/ GWR; 9 Getty; 10 Express & Star; 11 Getty; 16 James Ellerker/GWR; 18 Patrick Strack/ESL; 19 opterown; 20 Paul Michael Hughes/GWR, Jonathan Leibson; 21 Getty, Shutterstock; 22 Patrick Strack/ ESL; 26 Alamy, Kevin Chang; 27 Major League Gaming; 28 Red Bull; 29 fightinggm; 30 Stephanie Wunderl; 31 Helena Kristiansson/ESL; 34 Paul Michael Hughes/GWR; 38 Dara Phan; 44 America Pink; 48 Kamil Krawczak/ GWR; 54 Game Culture, Reuters, Shinsuke Kamioka/ GWR; 56 Alamy; 57 Alamy, 3D Arcade; 58 Alamy; 59 Reuters; 60 Shutterstock; 61 Kevin Scott Ramos/GWR; 62 Paul Michael Hughes/GWR; 66 James Ellerker/GWR; 69 AP/PA, Rex; 70 Kevin Scott Ramos/ GWR; 84 iStock; 87 Ryan Dix/GWR; 88 Alamy; 93 Paul Michael Hughes/GWR; 97 April Massirio; 98 Shinsuke Kamioka/ GWR; 100 Alamy; 101 Alamy; 102 Ryan Schude/GWR; 106 Jeff Crow/*Edge* magazine; 108 Alamy; 110 Alamy; 111 Getty, Arcade Flyer Archive; 114 Ryan Schude/GWR; 133 Alamy; 136 Paul Michael Hughes/GWR; 138 Alamy; 139 Alamy; 142 James Ellerker/GWR; 146 Getty, Paul Michael Hughes/GWR; 147 Alamy; 149 Paul Michael Hughes/GWR; 150 Corbis/ Getty, iStock, Sara Bobo, Shutterstock; 152 Ryan Schude/ GWR; 159 Tristan Fewings; 164 Philippe Ramakers, Getty, Shutterstock; 165 Mark Glaviano; 174 Laurent Henn; 178 Ranald Mackechnie/GWR; 180 Paul Michael Hughes/GWR; 181 Jeff Vinnick; 182 Chris Park; 215 ZAGG Studios

ACKNOWLEDGEMENTS

Guinness World Records would like to thank the following for their help in compiling *Gamer's Edition 2017*:

2K Games (Gemma Woolnough, Aaron Cooper); Activision Blizzard (Sam Bandah, Emily Woolliscroft, Kevin Flynn, Keith Cox, Jonathan Fargher, Rachael Grant); Ali-A; Phillip Aram; Arcade Flyer Archive; Arcade History; Arcade Museum; Jim Bagley; Bandai Namco (James Anderson, Gareth Bagg, Lee Kirton); Sam Barlow; Thomas Bocker; Bossa Studios (Poppy Byron); David Braben OBE; Capcom (Matthew Edwards, Laura Skelly); CCP (Paul Elsy); CD Projekt RED (Robert Malinowski); Sami Cetin; Julian Checkley and Order 66 Creatures and Effects; Cloud Imperium Games (David Swofford, Chris Roberts); Alfie Crook; DanTDM; Walter Day; Dead Good Media (Stu Taylor, Carly Moxey-Kim); Decibel PR (Sam Brace); Disney (Cliff Jin); Double Fine Productions (James Spafford); e-Sportsearnings.com; *Edge* magazine; Electronic Arts (Tristan Rosenfeldt, Bryony Gittins, Shaun White); Endemol Shine UK (Elspeth Rae); ESL (Anna Rozwandowicz); FJT Logistics; Frontier Developments (Michael Gapper); GameRankings; Games Press; Gazillion Entertainment (Chris Baker); Global Game Jam (Gorm Lai, Giselle Rosman); GosuGamers (Victor Martyn, Lars Lien, Glen Ainscow, Boris Mihov, Nick D'Orazio); Benjamin Gwin; Jace Hall; Harmonix (Criss Burki, Daniel Sussman); Ryan Hart; Joel and Mandy Hopkins; Indigo Pearl (Caroline Miller, Ben Le Rougetel, Tom Regan); Isaiah "Triforce" Johnson; Mike Kasprzak (Ludum Dare); Koch Media (David Scarborough); Konami/Voltage PR (Steve Merrett); Anchel Labena (IGDA Denmark); Lick PR (Kat Osman and Lucy Starvis); Arturo Manzarek Dracul; Franny Maufras; Jim McGinley (TOJam); MCV (Alex Calvin); Microsoft (Richard Chen, Rob Semsey); Moby Games; Mojang; OP Talent Limited (Liam Chivers); Paavo Niskala; Stefano Petrullo; Premier PR (Will Beckett, Lauren Dillon, Gareth Williams, Yunus Ibrahim, Daniela Pietrosanu); Sonja "OMGitsfirefoxx" Reid; Revolution Software (Charles Cecil); Riot Games (Becca Roberts); Rockstar Games (Hamish Brown, Patricia Pucci, Craig Gilmore); Roll7 (Simon Bennett); Sega (Sarah Head, Peter Oliver); Sony Computer Entertainment (Sarah Lowers, Hugo Bustillos); Speed Demos Archive; Speedrun.com (Peter Chase); Sports Interactive (Ciaran Brennan, Neil Brock, Alex Sloane); Square Enix (Ian Dickson); Square in the Air (Andrew Pink); SuperData (Sam Barberie, Albert Ngo); Syndicate (Tommy Tallarico; Alex "PangaeaPanga" Tan; Jessica Telef; thatgamecompany (Jennie Kong); TT Games; TWiiNSANE; Twin Galaxies; Twitch (Chase); Ubisoft (Oliver Coe, Stefan McGarry); Vault Communications (Mark Robins); VGChartz; Wargaming (Frazer Nash, Markus Schill); Warner Bros. (Mark Ward); Danielle Woodyatt; YouTube Gaming (George Panayotopoulos); Zebra Partners (Beth Llewelyn)

COUNTRY CODES

Code	Country	Code	Country	Code	Country
ABW	Aruba	GMB	Gambia	PCN	Pitcairn Islands
AFG	Afghanistan	GNB	Guinea-Bissau	PER	Peru
AGO	Angola	GNQ	Equatorial Guinea	PHL	Philippines
AIA	Anguilla			PLW	Palau
ALB	Albania	GRC	Greece	PNG	Papua New Guinea
AND	Andorra	GRD	Grenada		
ANT	Netherlands Antilles	GRL	Greenland	POL	Poland
		GTM	Guatemala	PRI	Puerto Rico
ARG	Argentina	GUF	French Guiana	PRK	Korea, DPRO
ARM	Armenia	GUM	Guam	PRT	Portugal
ASM	American Samoa	GUY	Guyana	PRY	Paraguay
ATA	Antarctica	HKG	Hong Kong	PYF	French Polynesia
ATF	French Southern Territories	HMD	Heard and McDonald Islands	QAT	Qatar
ATG	Antigua and Barbuda	HND	Honduras	REU	Réunion
		HRV	Croatia (Hrvatska)	ROM	Romania
AUS	Australia			RUS	Russian Federation
AUT	Austria	HTI	Haiti		
AZE	Azerbaijan	HUN	Hungary	RWA	Rwanda
BDI	Burundi	IDN	Indonesia	SAU	Saudi Arabia
BEL	Belgium	IND	India	SDN	Sudan
BEN	Benin	IOT	British Indian Ocean Territory	SEN	Senegal
BFA	Burkina Faso			SGP	Singapore
BGD	Bangladesh	IRL	Ireland	SGS	South Georgia and South SS
BGR	Bulgaria	IRN	Iran		
BHR	Bahrain	IRQ	Iraq	SHN	Saint Helena
BHS	The Bahamas	ISL	Iceland	SJM	Svalbard and Jan Mayen Islands
BIH	Bosnia and Herzegovina	ISR	Israel		
		ITA	Italy	SLB	Solomon Islands
BLR	Belarus	JAM	Jamaica	SLE	Sierra Leone
BLZ	Belize	JOR	Jordan	SLV	El Salvador
BMU	Bermuda	JPN	Japan	SMR	San Marino
BOL	Bolivia	KAZ	Kazakhstan	SOM	Somalia
BRA	Brazil	KEN	Kenya	SPM	Saint Pierre and Miquelon
BRB	Barbados	KGZ	Kyrgyzstan		
BRN	Brunei Darussalam	KHM	Cambodia	SRB	Serbia
		KIR	Kiribati	SSD	South Sudan
BTN	Bhutan	KNA	Saint Kitts and Nevis	STP	São Tomé and Príncipe
BVT	Bouvet Island				
BWA	Botswana	KOR	Korea, Republic of	SUR	Suriname
CAF	Central African Republic	KWT	Kuwait	SVK	Slovakia
				SVN	Slovenia
CAN	Canada	LAO	Laos	SWE	Sweden
CCK	Cocos (Keeling) Islands	LBN	Lebanon	SWZ	Swaziland
		LBR	Liberia	SYC	Seychelles
CHE	Switzerland	LBY	Libyan Arab Jamahiriya	SYR	Syrian Arab Republic
CHL	Chile				
CHN	China	LCA	Saint Lucia	TCA	Turks and Caicos Islands
CIV	Côte d'Ivoire	LIE	Liechtenstein		
CMR	Cameroon	LKA	Sri Lanka	TCD	Chad
COD	Congo, DR of the	LSO	Lesotho	TGO	Togo
COG	Congo	LTU	Lithuania	THA	Thailand
COK	Cook Islands	LUX	Luxembourg	TJK	Tajikistan
COL	Colombia	LVA	Latvia	TKL	Tokelau
COM	Comoros	MAC	Macau	TKM	Turkmenistan
CPV	Cape Verde	MAR	Morocco	TMP	East Timor
CRI	Costa Rica	MCO	Monaco	TON	Tonga
CUB	Cuba	MDA	Moldova	TPE	Chinese Taipei
CXR	Christmas Island	MDG	Madagascar	TTO	Trinidad and Tobago
CYM	Cayman Islands	MDV	Maldives		
CYP	Cyprus	MEX	Mexico	TUN	Tunisia
CZE	Czech Republic	MHL	Marshall Islands	TUR	Turkey
DEU	Germany	MKD	Macedonia	TUV	Tuvalu
DJI	Djibouti	MLI	Mali	TZA	Tanzania
DMA	Dominica	MLT	Malta	UAE	United Arab Emirates
DNK	Denmark	MMR	Myanmar (Burma)		
DOM	Dominican Republic			UGA	Uganda
		MNE	Montenegro	UK	United Kingdom
DZA	Algeria	MNG	Mongolia	UKR	Ukraine
ECU	Ecuador	MNP	Northern Mariana Islands	UMI	US Minor Islands
EGY	Egypt				
ERI	Eritrea	MOZ	Mozambique	URY	Uruguay
ESH	Western Sahara	MRT	Mauritania	USA	United States of America
ESP	Spain	MSR	Montserrat		
EST	Estonia	MTQ	Martinique	UZB	Uzbekistan
ETH	Ethiopia	MUS	Mauritius	VAT	Holy See (Vatican City)
FIN	Finland	MWI	Malawi		
FJI	Fiji	MYS	Malaysia	VCT	Saint Vincent and the Grenadines
FLK	Falkland Islands (Malvinas)	MYT	Mayotte		
		NAM	Namibia	VEN	Venezuela
FRA	France	NCL	New Caledonia	VGB	Virgin Islands (British)
FRG	West Germany	NER	Niger		
FRO	Faroe Islands	NFK	Norfolk Island	VIR	Virgin Islands (US)
FSM	Micronesia, Federated States of	NGA	Nigeria		
		NIC	Nicaragua	VNM	Vietnam
		NIU	Niue	VUT	Vanuatu
FXX	France, Metropolitan	NLD	Netherlands	WLF	Wallis and Futuna Islands
		NOR	Norway		
GAB	Gabon	NPL	Nepal	WSM	Samoa
GEO	Georgia	NRU	Nauru	YEM	Yemen
GHA	Ghana	NZ	New Zealand	ZAF	South Africa
GIB	Gibraltar	OMN	Oman	ZMB	Zambia
GIN	Guinea	PAK	Pakistan	ZWE	Zimbabwe
GLP	Guadeloupe	PAN	Panama		

STOP PRESS!

Most people playing a single game of *Pong*

On 7 Jan 2016, a total of 251 people played the classic 2D tennis title *Pong* at an event in Sandusky, Ohio, USA. The game was organized by Zachary, Steven and Kristi Sneed and the CodeMash conference (all USA). Players were split into two teams and given laser pointers, whose movements were run through a computer program to guide the *Pong* paddles.

Highest score on *Donkey Kong*

On 5 May 2016, Wes Copeland (USA) racked up surpassing his own previous records set on 4 Jan 2016 (see p.57) and on 19 Apr 2016. It's speculated that Copeland's latest score includes every known point in the game. However, the gamer claimed that it could still be beaten with "a lot of luck". He told IGN: "It's the equivalent of playing poker and being dealt 10 royal flushes in a row."

Fastest accumulation of 1,000 mass on *Slither.io*

The 2016 browser game challenges players to expand snake avatars by eating dots and colliding with other gamers. "ZerGreenOne" (AUS) achieved a size of 1,000 mass in 7.55 sec on 17 Apr 2016.

Fastest completion of *The Witness*

Gamer "taru" navigated the mazes of 3D puzzler *The Witness* in 18 min 41 sec on 24 Feb 2016.

Most disliked trailer

Uploaded on 2 May 2016, the "Official Call of Duty®: Infinite Warfare Reveal Trailer" earned 1,518,525 dislikes in just eight days from 15,987,374 views. The trailer showcases the 13th main entry to the military FPS series and introduces a space setting for the first time. Journalists speculated that the backlash was a consequence of the series' overwhelming success. Publisher Activision told Polygon that no entertainment franchise can "generate the kind of passion that *Call of Duty* can".

Fastest completion of *Fallout 4*

"BloodThunder" (USA) conquered the RPG shooter in just 49 min 58 sec on 3 May 2016. The gamer took the record by shaving just over a minute off a time achieved by "BubblesDelFuego" in April, which itself beat a March run by "JshaKhajiit" (see p.163).

Most popular cross-platform beta for a new IP

On 12 May 2016, Blizzard revealed that 9.7 million players had tested *Overwatch* during the shooter's public beta. This broke the record set by *The Division* (see p.161). It's also the **most popular beta for a shooter**, pipping *Star Wars Battlefront* (see p.112).

Fastest glitchless completion of *Undertale* (Neutral Route)

Taking the Neutral Route through the indie RPG on 8 Apr 2016, "TGH" (USA) finished in 1 hr 4 min 58 sec.

Fastest completion of *SUPERHOT*

On 10 Mar 2016, "Lt_Disco" (USA) finished the 2016 indie FPS in 20 min 20 sec.

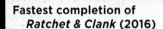

Fastest completion of *Ratchet & Clank* (2016)

Just eight days after *Ratchet & Clank*'s PS4 release in North America, speed-runner "Raikaru" (USA) hurtled through the sci-fi platformer in 1 hr 16 min 45 sec. His run, on 20 Apr 2016, used the Bouncer, a pre-order weapon. The 2016 version of *Ratchet & Clank* is a reimagining of the first title in Sony's series, which debuted on the PS2 in 2002.

Fastest completion of *Super Mario Bros.*

Not content with setting a world-record time of 4 min 57.427 sec on 14 Jan 2016 (see p.55), Twitcher "darbian" (USA) continued to speed-run the seminal platformer on the NES. On 13 Apr 2016, he improved his time to 4 min 57.260 sec. He declared: "I have reached my potential in this category – I'm done! My quest is over."

Fastest completion of *Ninja Gaiden III: The Ancient Ship of Doom*

On 4 May 2016, Chinese gamer "100Ton" finished Tecmo's 1991 martial-arts platformer in 12 min 49 sec.

Most liked game video on YouTube

Uploaded on 6 May 2016, EA's "Battlefield 1 Official Reveal Trailer" had won 1,194,442 likes as of 10 May 2016. It's not only the **most liked game trailer**, but also the most liked game video overall, smashing the record held by PewDiePie's "FUNNY MONTAGE.. #2" (see p.168). The video unveiled the 14th *Battlefield* title and is set during World War I. Some outlets linked its popularity to the backlash suffered by its FPS rival *CoD* (see left).

Most BAFTAs won by a one-man dev team

Sam Barlow (UK) won three awards for his crime mystery *Her Story* at the 12th British Academy Games Awards on 7 Apr 2016. These were for Mobile & Handheld, Debut Game and Game Innovation. Barlow had previously found fame as the lead designer and writer for the *Silent Hill* games *Origins* (2007) and *Shattered Memories* (2009).

Fastest completion of *Star Fox Zero*

Playing in the Arcade mode, US gamer "Rodriguezjr" finished the space shooter in 36 min 29 sec, as verified by Speedrun.com on 2 May 2016.

Fastest completion of *Dark Souls III*

"Distortion2" (USA) sped through FromSoftware's gloomy masterpiece in 1 hr 2 min 49 sec on 28 Apr 2016. They also achieved the **fastest completion (all bosses)**: 1 hr 17 min 1 sec on 3 May.

Distortion2 also holds the same records for *Dark Souls II*: **fastest completion** (16 min 20 sec on 12 Sep 2014) and **fastest completion (all bosses)** (2 hr 24 min 55 sec on 10 Mar 2016).

Most concurrent views for a *Counter-Strike* tournament

Held on 30 Mar–3 Apr in Columbus, Ohio, USA, the 2016 *Counter-Strike: Global Offensive* Major Championship peaked with 1.6 million viewers. This beat a record set at the ESL One Cologne *CS: GO* tournament in Germany on 22–23 Aug 2015 (see p.31). A combined total of 45 million hr was watched by fans.

Highest-earning *Halo 5: Guardians* player

As of 5 May 2016, Bradley "Frosty" Bergstrom (USA) had earned $259,600 (£178,847) playing the sci-fi FPS in tournaments. The bulk of his record haul came from winning the *Halo* World Championship with the Counter Logic Gaming team (see picture above left). Each of the four members netted a cool $250,000 (£172,233).

Fastest completion of *Resident Evil 0 Remaster*

PC gamer "uhTrance" (UK) finished Capcom's HD horror remake in 1 hr 21 min 16 sec on 12 Feb 2016.

Highest matching score on *Fruit Ninja* in one minute (team of two)

Mireille Bills and Megan Weaver (both UK) achieved identical scores of 127 playing Halfbrick's 2010 touch-screen game at Gadget Show Live, NEC Birmingham, UK, on 2 Apr 2016.

Largest prize pool for an FPS eSports tournament

The original $1-m (£690,522) prize pool for 2016's *Halo* World Championship swelled to $2.5 m (£1.72 m) thanks to micro-transactions made by players of *Halo 5: Guardians*. At the tournament – held in Hollywood, USA, on 18–20 Mar 2016 – the Counter Logic Gaming team (above, with coach Wes "Clutch" Price second from left) gunned their way to victory.

Fastest completion of "The Showstopper" in *Hitman*

Set amid the glitz of a Paris fashion show, "The Showstopper" is the main level in the first episode of *Hitman* (Square Enix, 2016). On 29 Mar 2016, gamer "640509040147" (POL) took just 34 sec to eliminate his targets, beginning the level disguised as a member of the stage crew and completing the mission by shooting a balcony heater from long distance.

"640509040147" also set the record for the **fastest completion of "The Showstopper" in *Hitman* (Silent Assassin, Suit Only)** – 1 min 22 sec, without disguises or accruing non-target casualties, as verified by Speedrun.com on 25 Mar 2016. The gamer used a remotely detonated explosive and a proximity mine to assassinate both of his targets with deadly proficiency.

A GALAXY OF NEW RECORDS!

PLUS: EXPLORING SPACE WITH BUZZ ALDRIN & CHRIS HADFIELD!

GUINNESS WORLD RECORDS 2017

OVER 4,000 RECORDS & PHOTOS!

Fastest monowheel motorcycle
Kevin Scott

Most views for a *Minecraft* video channel
Dan the Diamond Minecart

Largest foot rotation
Maxwell Day

Highest jump by a llama
Caspa

WWW.GUINNESSWORLDRECORDS.COM/2017